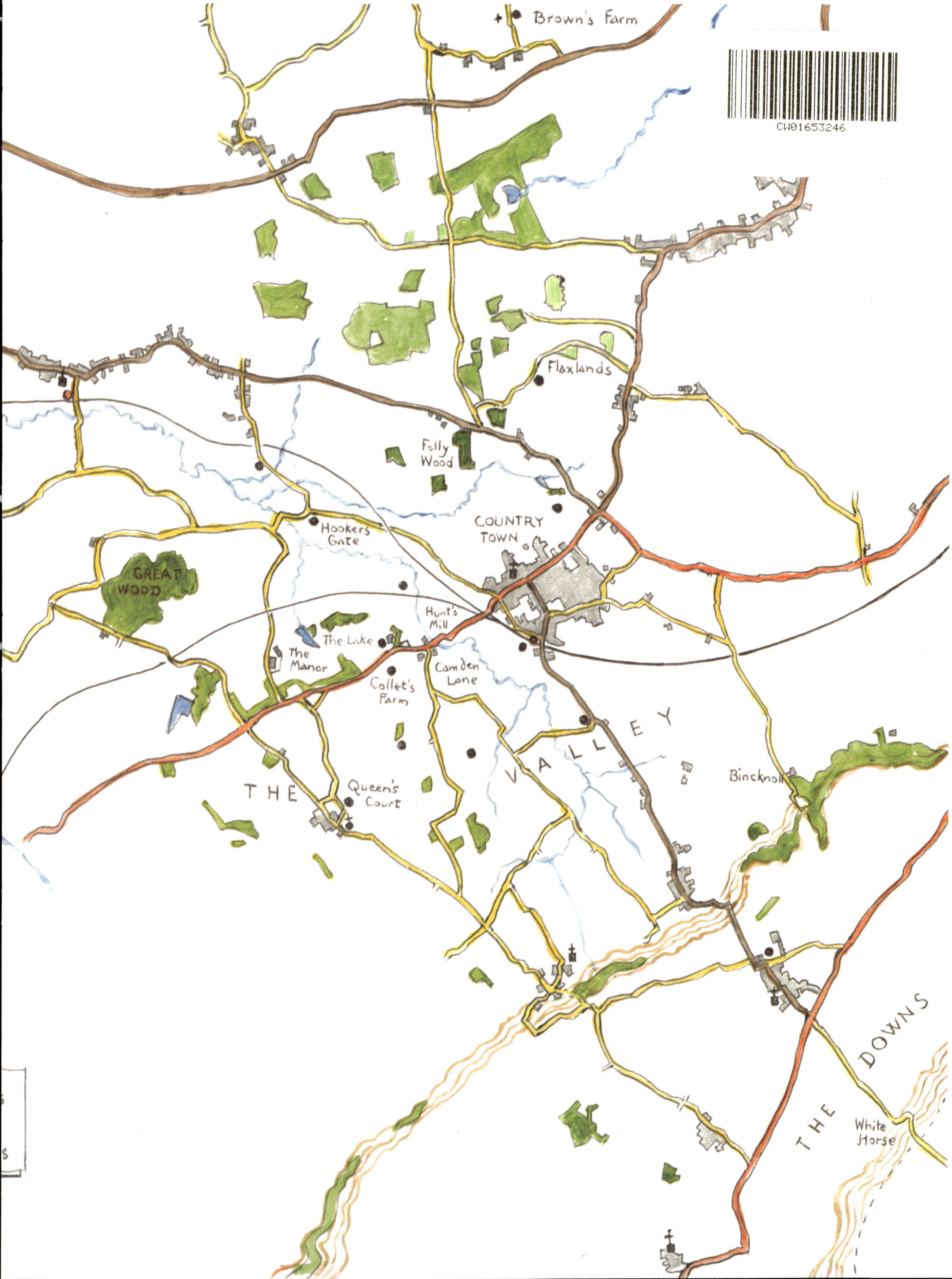
Brown's Farm
Flaxlands
Folly Wood
COUNTRY TOWN
Hookers Gate
GREAT WOOD
Hunt's Mill
The Lake
The Manor
Collet's Farm
Camden Lane
THE VALLEY
Bincknoll
Queen's Court
THE DOWNS
White Horse

A WILTSHIRE CHILDHOOD

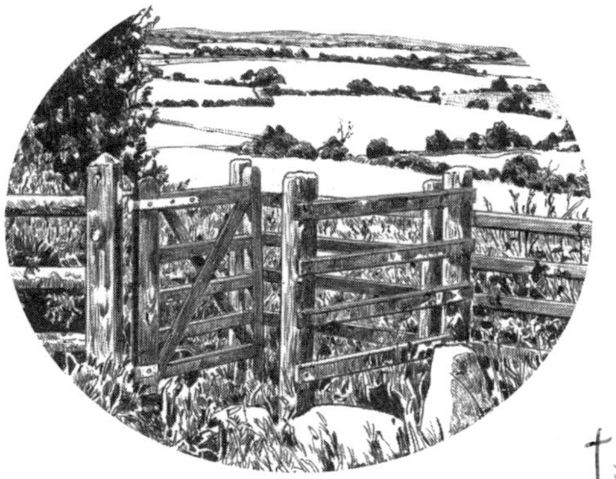

To Clare & Des

Peter Lupton

2021

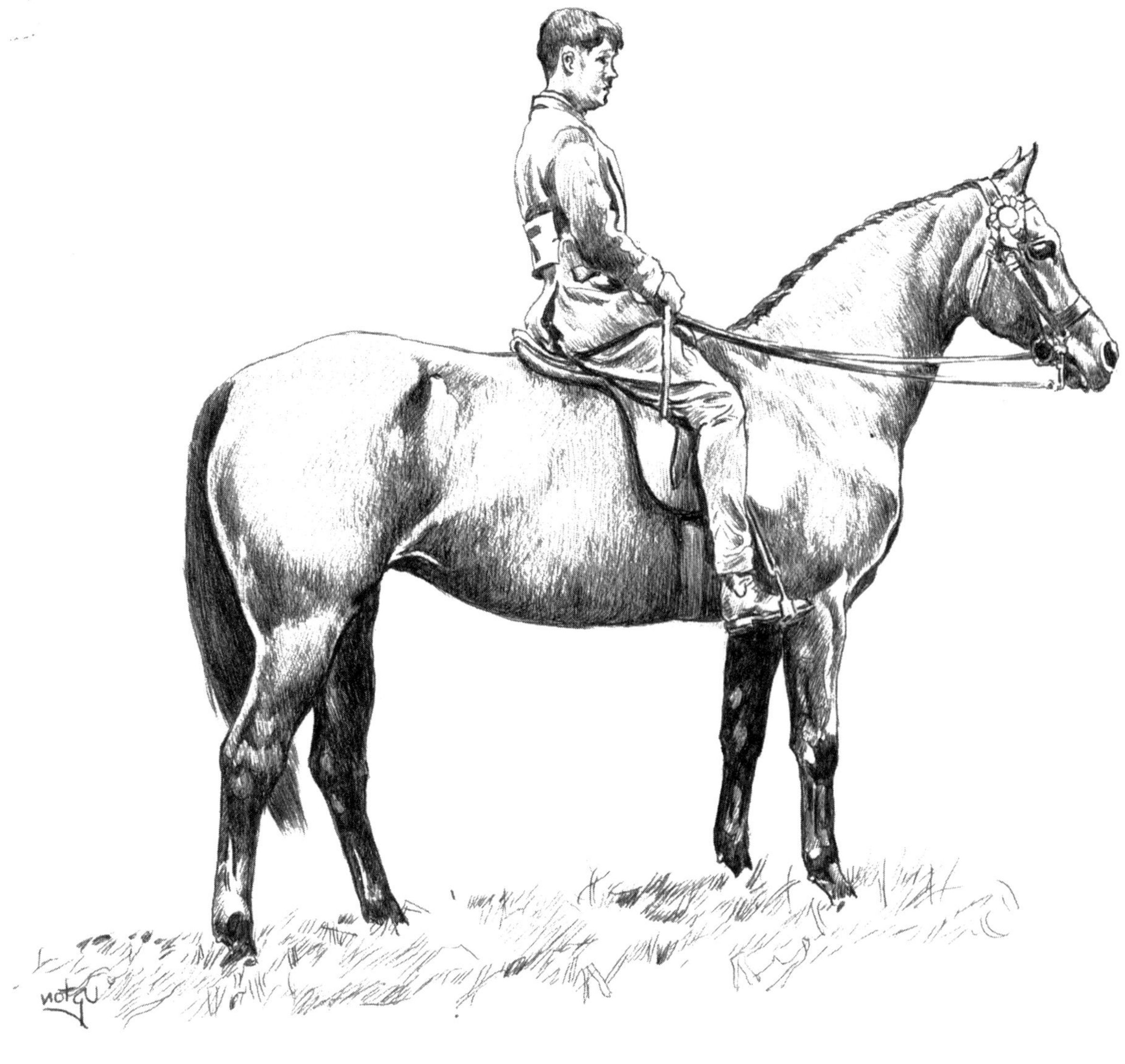

A Wiltshire Childhood

Peter Upton

Queen Elizabeth, "Cecil, were the summers better than they are now, when you were a child?"

Cecil, "Your Grace … Yes, your Grace, I share that common illusion. The summers then were nothing but sunshine. I and the weather have declined together."

(from *Vivat! Vivat Regina!* by Robert Bolt)

Anthony Eyre

MOUNT ORLEANS PRESS

Published 2021 by
Anthony Eyre, Mount Orleans Press
23 High Street, Cricklade, Wiltshire
SN6 6AP
https://anthonyeyre.com

ISBN 978 1 912945 27 6

A CIP catalogue record for this book is available from the British Library

Printed in India

Dedicated to
the Innocence of Youth
and to
my twin brother
who walked the fields
with me.

Contents

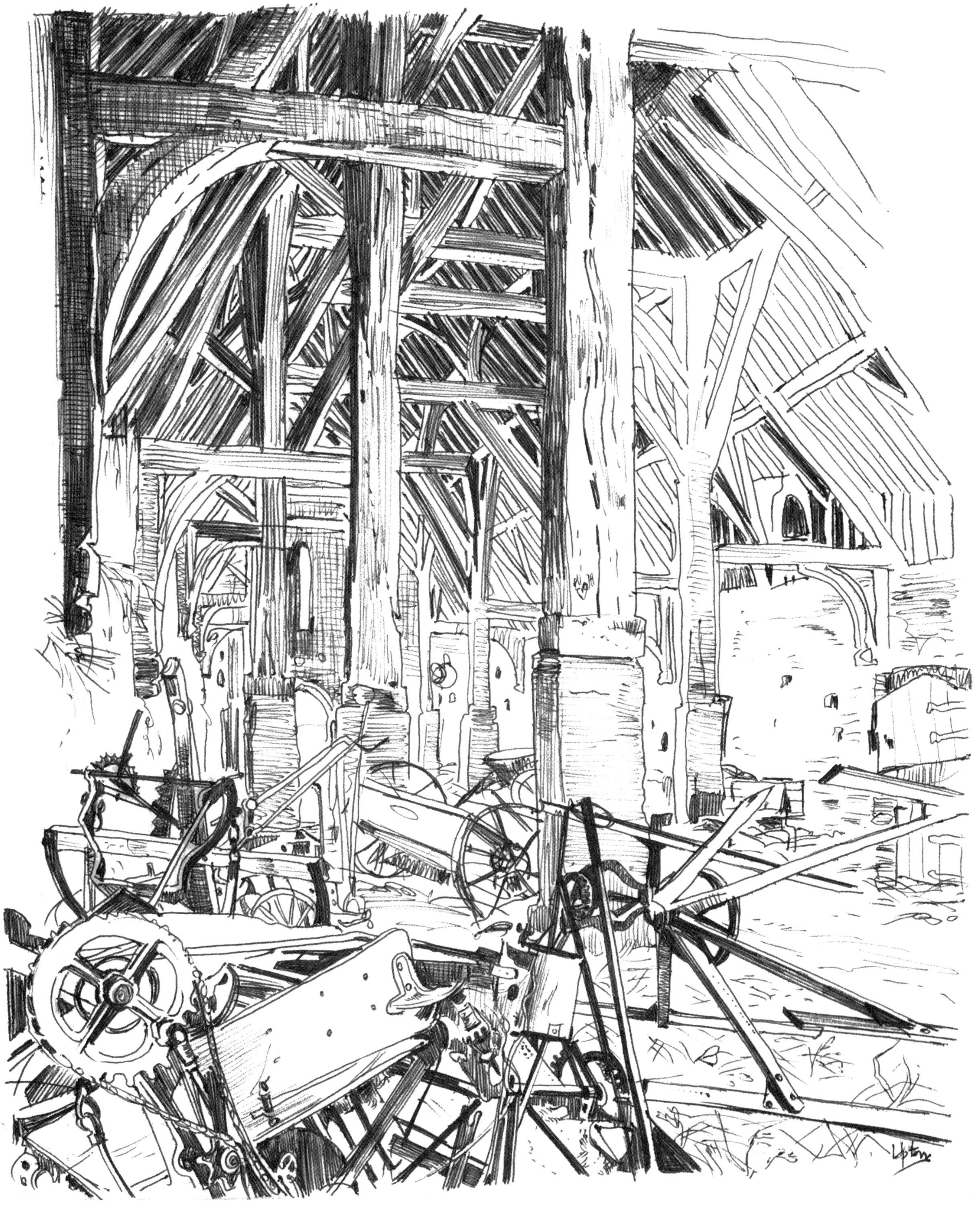

Introduction

THIS COLLECTION OF essays with drawings has been written out of a deep and lasting love for the rural life of my childhood. Only as memories do they remain, for many of the scenes are changed, the people gone, and I fear to return to the fields of my youth.

Beneath the limitless skies of the Downs and in the lush meadows of the valley, we wandered my brother and I, seeking the wild things and learning of beauty and love.

The freedom of the fields and the open air were ours from the sunlit days of June to winter's solitude. We were content, as only children could be, for little marred our vision of the world, and our world was the valley and the downs of rural England.

I believe that in this fast-changing world the past will soon be forgotten, the ways of our youth have already gone. The dignity of rural life spent in sympathy with nature is being engulfed by the artificial and friendless society of urban living. But for the few who open their eyes, the rest seem content to continue blindfold, caught in a web of technology and pollution.

The countryman's way was the seasons' way, he lived by the land and treated it with understanding. He was thankful for the gifts of field and hedgerow. Nothing was wasted for he knew the beginning and end of it. Nothing was won without giving back to the land in order to safeguard the future.

Now, what of the future, has all been discarded and forgotten?

I still have hope that some will remember. Perhaps my own feelings put down in these essays will strike a chord in readers' hearts, if we can but pause for reflection and see once again with the sweet innocence of youth.

Peter Upton
1972

Our Country

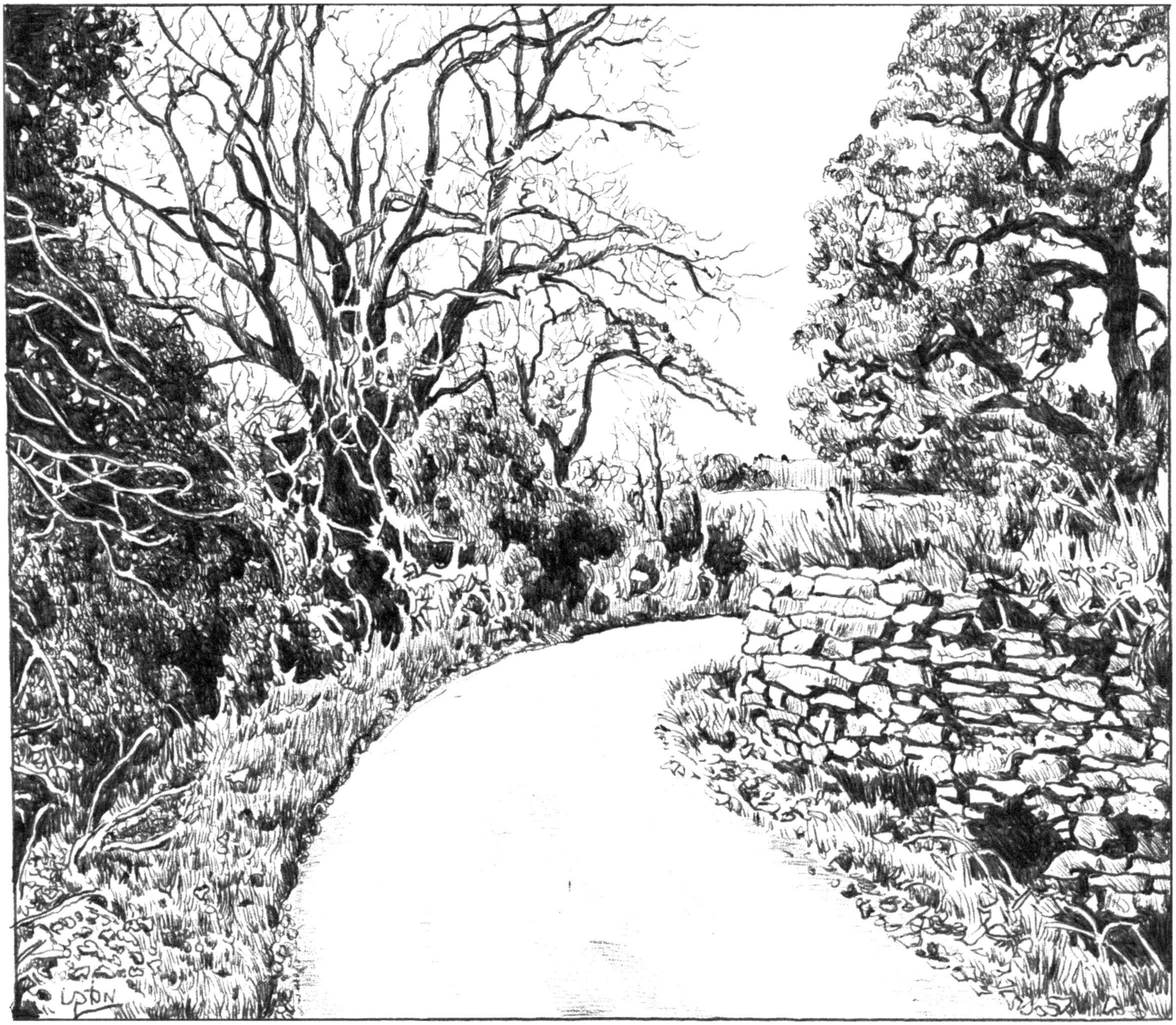

The Lane

The Way to the Village

THE LANE IN summer was hemmed in by heavy crops of wild chervil and cow parsley, swaying in the breeze among seeding grasses. So tall did they grow that the dry-stone walls at the field's edge were almost lost to sight, while beyond, on either side stretched fields of ripening corn.

Butterflies searched aimlessly among the flower heads and lizards sunned themselves on lichened stone.

Quite soon after parting with the highway, by a group of larches, the lane took a bend over a low bridge and thereafter an infant stream kept company with it for a mile or so until another small lane met the first by an ancient mound called The Giant's Cave.

From here on, the lane skirted the edge of a great park where old oak trees and tall elms gave shade to black cattle. Down a wide avenue of limes a limestone house could just be glimpsed as we walked past. Further on at the bottom of the hill a small field pond, overhung by a leaning willow, was fenced off close by the lane and sooty moorhens ran for cover at the sight of us. A stone farm stood on the slope above the roadway where it curved to the right around the edge of some woodland, and there clustered round the green with a backdrop of trees was the edge of the village.

A group of old cottages was gathered round the signpost at the crooked crossroads. Beneath the tall sign was a curving wall, on whose flat top the old men sat and lit their pipes and talked of the weather or dreamed.

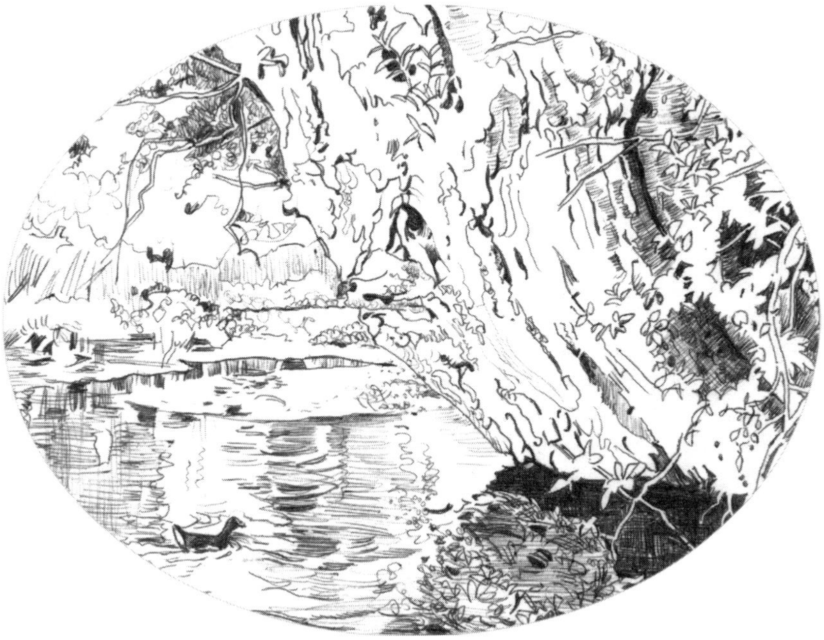

The Pond

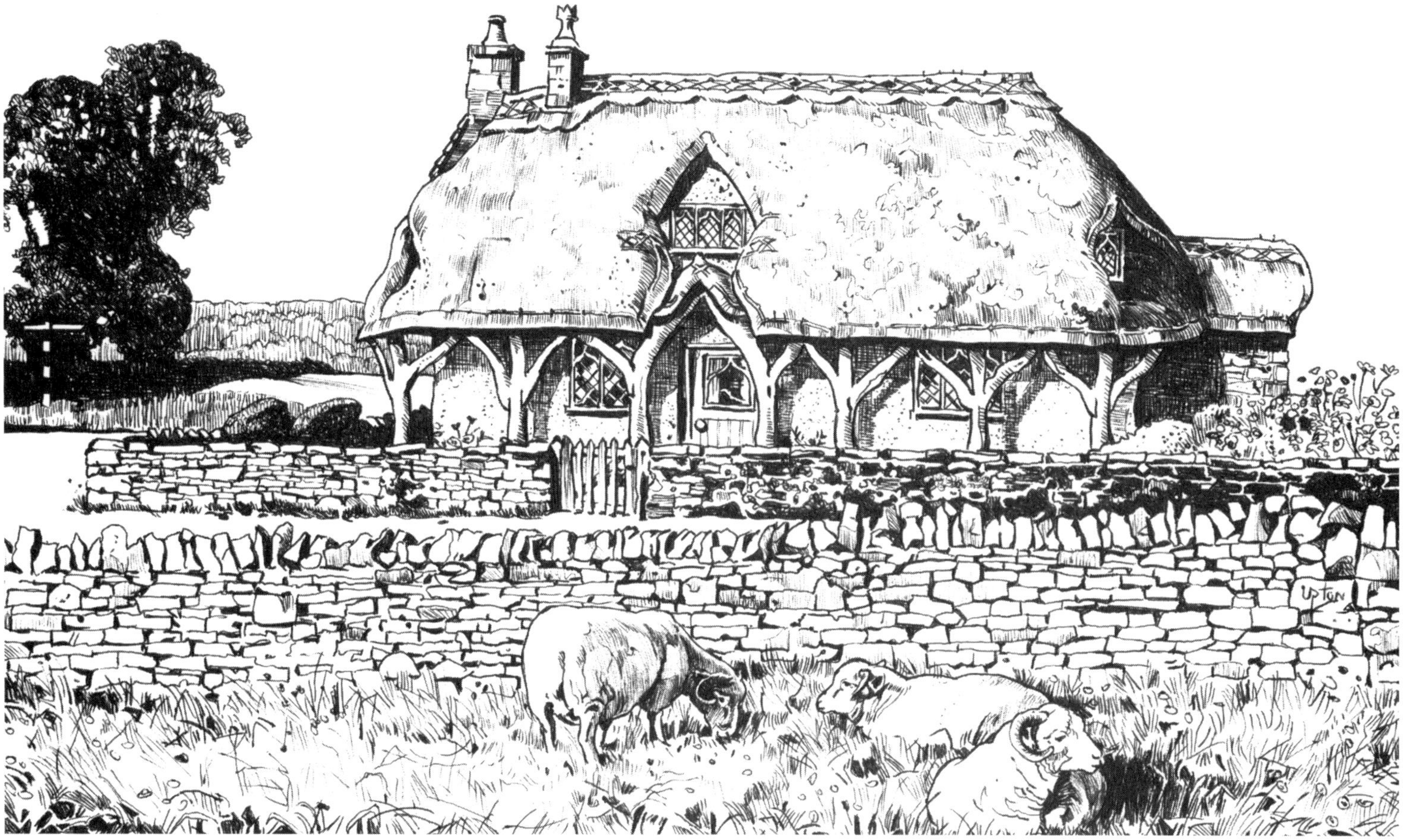

Above: Mrs Witchard's Cottage

One of them, Fred Salt, remembered the first time he had left the village as a young man to fight in the Great War. Not all his friends had come back.

He had been sent to Ireland to join a cavalry regiment. Each month they queued for their pay, but it took three months for the sergeant to reach Salt in the alphabet, and all he got was 1/6d. Still clear to him were the awful charges over the trenches once in France, and the loss of his gallant little mare who was killed in barbed wire. As he looked past old Down Road, he was clearly again back in the days when he was coachman to the big house, with a pair of black Hackneys up front, driving out of the village to catch the train.

Here, where the old men sat, was the parting of the ways: two lanes took you out of the village to 'foreign parts', while the other two wandered quietly through the village past friends' cottages, and around the green to meet again by the Almshouse wall.

The row of sturdy dwellings with dormers in their stone-tiled roofs, and little porches to each doorway, stood opposite the lane to the village farm. Then, right on the corner, was the cottage where Mrs Witchard lived, under a roof of thatch supported on rustic posts. Little Gothic windows, bright with geraniums, nestled deep in the thatch, keeping out the light. Her cottage had stood here, overlooking the crossroads, with its neighbours since the 1680's, but the roadway was much older.

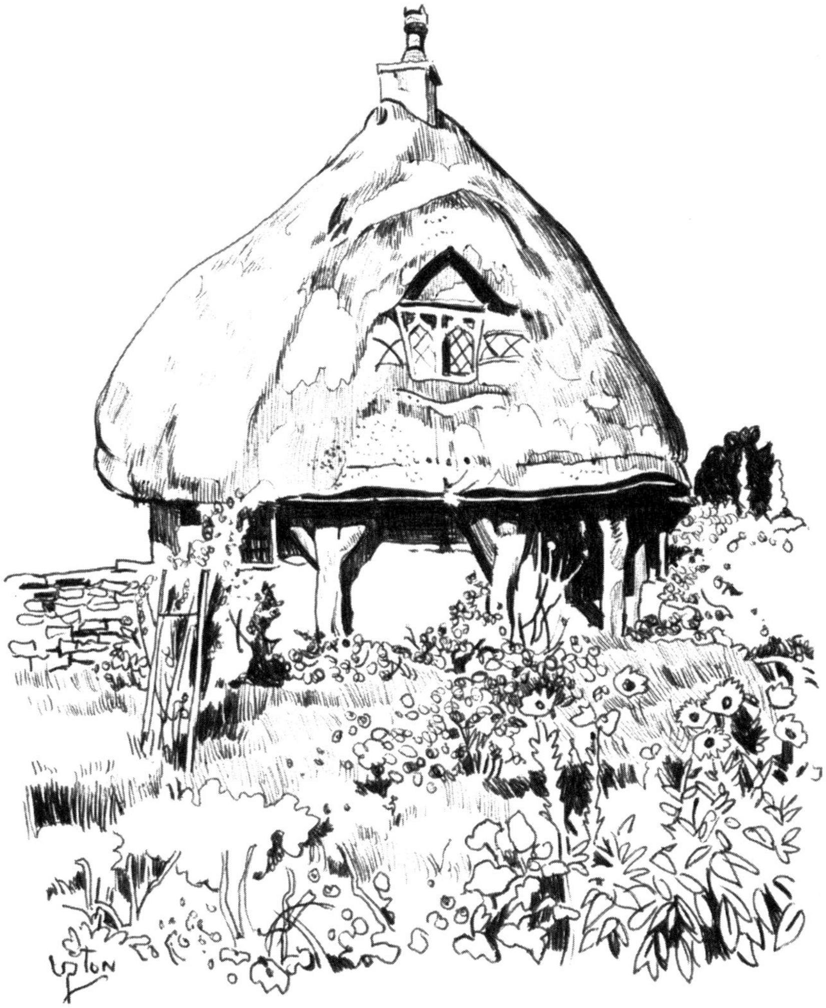

Thatched cottage with capricious Gothic ornaments designed by Thomas Wright between 1748 and 1756.

The Village Street

The main street stretched broad and straight before you, leading to the Estate Office and the drive to the big house. It gave the impression of having gently dreamed its way throughout the centuries into the present one, for little had changed and all was quiet and sleepy in the sunshine.

It's history certainly goes back to the 15th century when the Botelers possessed the estate, though many of the present cottages date from the late 1600's when the woods of Swangrove and Allengrove were enclosed to form a deer park.

Across the road from the Old Vicarage, dark trees shaded the footpath at the end of the main street, opposite a large house with decorated kneelers to the stone gables, the apex crowned by finials. Its windows were tall and surmounted by hood-mouldings which extended to form a string-course, where old wisteria clung to the wall.

Clipped hedges stood each side of the gateway. Beyond were some small cottages with bay windows and next-door Coney's the main shop of the village. It was built in 1875 and the large heavily-framed windows were added later when it opened to sell groceries. The little stone Post Office stood back from the roadway beside a narrow lane, where the old bakehouse, belonging to the Pinnells, and set behind their little shop was now used as a garage and stores. They had given up baking bread some years previously, due to increasing costs and government regulations. Now some speckled and brown hens roosted over the old ovens and scratched for grit in the drangway.

Six more cottages with decorated barge-boards to their gables completed this side of the street. In the end one lived Jim Cross, the village tailor who made hunt clothes. He was a big dark-haired man, with a wonderful bass voice, fond of singing 'Glorious Devon' in the inn, of an evening. Cross's grandfather had been a gamekeeper to the lord's father, and he had been killed by poachers, so the lord of the manor had educated his eldest son and his eldest son's son,who was Jim, the last tailor in the village.

On the other side of the street, beyond the yews, was the agent's house and next to it the old blacksmith's shop, with heaps of iron, broken implements and tools stacked against the walls. Here Elija Russell, well into his late seventies, still worked a little and the rhythmic tap of his hammer echoed in the roadway. Adjoining his sheds was the wheelwright's yard which had lain silent for years, overgrown with nettles and willow-herb. Cole's had been the last wheelwright, but his grandson now ran the garage in the next village.

Beyond the yards were more cottages with steep hipped roofs and enormous stone chimneys. Flagstone paths led between small flower-beds to low doorways, shaded by elegant porches and stout gate pillars were topped by decorations or flat stones.

The farm workers who lived in these cottages were employed on the estate, their wages were not high, for they only paid six shillings a week rent and received free fire-wood, milk and venison at Christmas from the Park.

They had had electricity since 1930, although many did not like the new light at first. One old lady of the village was asked if she found it better for her failing eyesight. She replied that it was very useful, for she could turn it on at dimity to see to light her oil lamps.

The end cottage of this group served as a small butcher's shop, and right next to it were the Almshouses and school. Here the village street came to an end at the Park gates by the lodge.

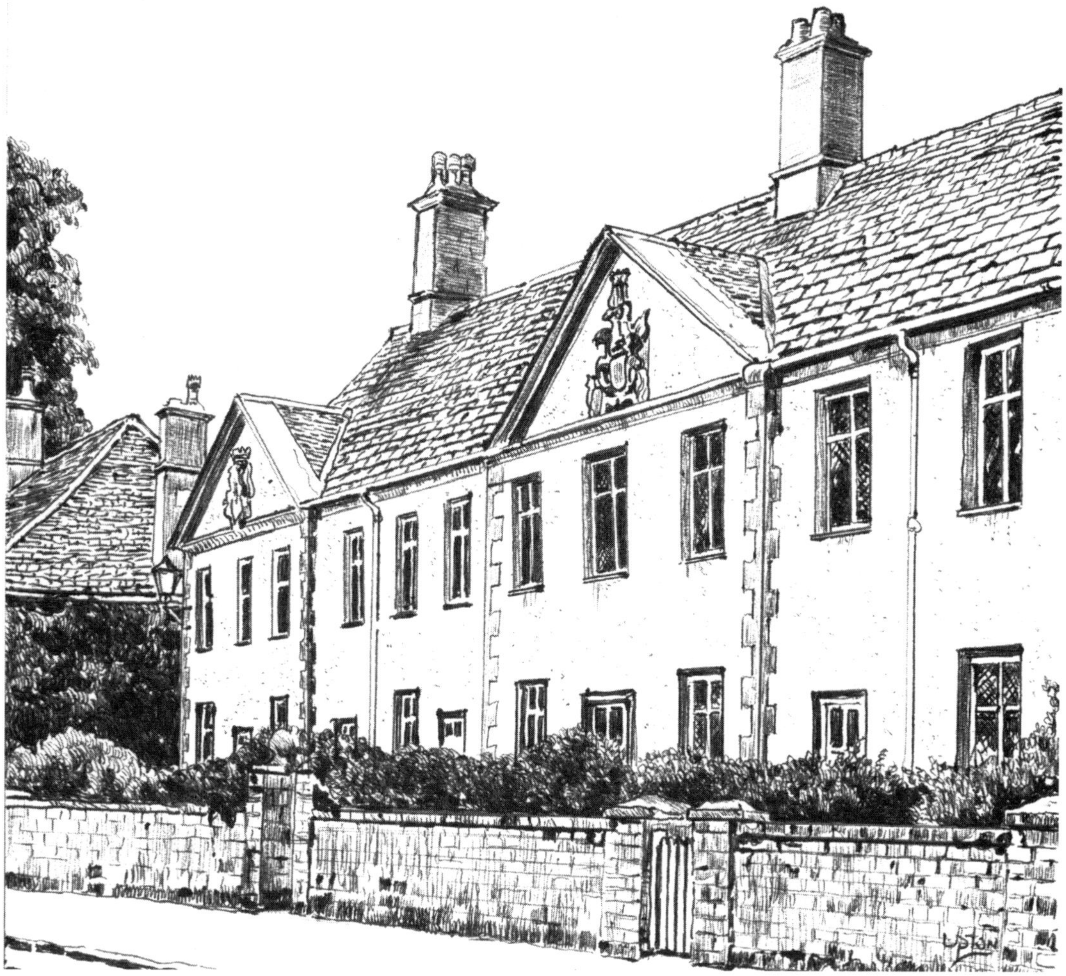

The Almshouses

The Almshouses

The Almshouse stood at the end of the village street, on the corner of a narrow lane called Hayes. The building had a handsome stone front with three gables, each decorated with coats of arms in high relief. Fifteen tall windows gave light to the upper floors, whilst below, more tall windows alternated with the doorways. In front were little gardens and a solid Cotswold stone wall which gave privacy from the street.

Both the young as well as the elderly, sheltered beneath its steep lichened roof, for at one end was the school. Here two teachers instilled the foundations of learning into the minds of tousled-headed children who would far rather have been out in the fields when the sun beckoned.

The Almshouses and school had been built in 1705 and the original deed signed by the Lady of The Manor states that a Free School and Hospital were provided for in the Almshouse building. The headmistress had then received £7 and the children were educated and clothed at the expense of the Lord of the Manor. The endowments were one halfpenny per child each week and by 1872 there were over eighty children attending the school. All the girl pupils going to Sunday School were given red-hooded cloaks. The largest number to attend the school was in 1910

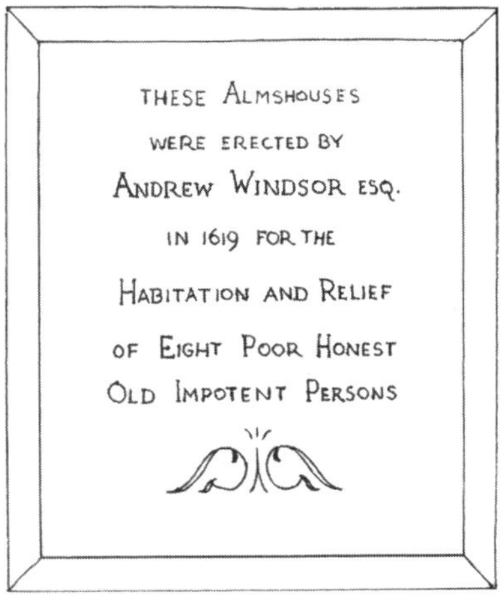

when there were a hundred and thirteen pupils, but now only a little over forty years later the number had dwindled to forty-one.

As for the rest of the building, it provided homes for six very old ladies. How they were chosen, I know not, although another row of mellow brick almshouses in one small town I remember makes it quite clear. Carved above the central door is the following quaint inscription: 'These Almshouses were erected by Andrew Windsor Esq. in 1619 for the Habitation and Relief of eight poor honest Old Impotent Persons.'

The Inn

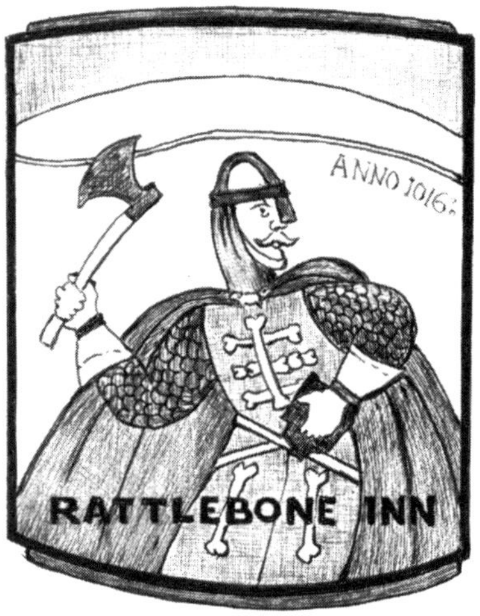

The Inn stood at the corner of the main street, just where the road widened out to provide a long open market place, so it and the church on the other side of the road commanded the entrance to the village.

Above its door was a sign of the great legendary local hero, holding a stone to his wounded side but still wielding his mighty broadsword in battle: its name 'The Rattlebone Inn'[1].

You could climb the worn stone steps to the open door and join the jovial company within. In the long, low tap-room labourers still quenched their thirst with cider, once brewed by the landlord. Tanglilegs they called it. There old men relaxed on oaken settles to play dominoes, or talked of their day's work, one with another.

Some chance remark may stir a memory of the great hiring fairs once held in the street outside, or of the fighting prowess of the village men. There was Butler, a great fighter and son of an earlier landlord of 'The Rattlebones', but he turned to drink, and was eventually transported for horse-stealing. But perhaps the main topic, when the weather turned colder, was always the hunting, for here they lived near the centre of a well-known country. The landlord rode to hounds himself and kept a livery stables in the yard beside the Inn. Bedrooms extended over the loose-boxes, so that visitors staying the night could hear the contented munching of the horses beneath them, as they lay abed.

One of the proudest boasts of our local town was that it once had fifteen inns, and each had its regular champions.

At 'The Cross Keys', the blacksmith took his ale, for his forge was just behind the inn. And approached by an archway beside the building, 'The Angel' was the farmers' inn on market days each Friday. 'The Prince of Wales' could claim an unusual benefit for here Doctor John would twice a week hold his surgery over pints of beer. He understood his older patients, particularly old farm workers, who

1 The Battle of Sherston took place in 1016 where the Saxons were victorious over Canute. It is possible that King Edmund II, known as 'Ironside' being of great strength and stature, was Rattlebones, the warrior and local hero. Edmund's advantage was later lost at their final battle at Ashington, probably due to the defection of one Eadric and his men from Herefordshire and Shropshire. Edmund and Canute were later to meet in Gloucestershire where it was agreed to divide the kingdom, but Edmund was to die a few weeks later, so Canute got the whole realm.

felt uncomfortable in the formal atmosphere of his waiting room, though it was only a large wooden garden shed behind his house. So for them, and for the convivial atmosphere, he practised in the public bar.

Country Town

Behind the broad tree-lined High Street, with its cobbled sidings, was Church Street leading to the old part of the town and beyond was the Butthaye, where possibly in olden days the men of the town practised their archery.

Both Wood Street and Church Street turned downhill and between them was the oldest house in the town. It was said to be part of the thirteenth century Priory Hospital of St. John the Baptist, founded by Philip Bassett. The mellow brickwork and stone-tiled roof showed above the high-walled garden where ivy and wisteria climbed in profusion about the path and small terrace. Within the house, the rooms were small and crowded with antique furniture and works of art. The floor of the study was covered with Indian and Persian rugs, but what really interested us boys was the great tiger skin over the back of the settee—its eyes seemed to regard us! The ancient scholar who lived there had travelled the world in his younger days and loved to tell us stories of his adventures.

From the Priory, Wood Street and Church Street led more steeply downhill between terraced cottages with long flights of steps up to their front doors and

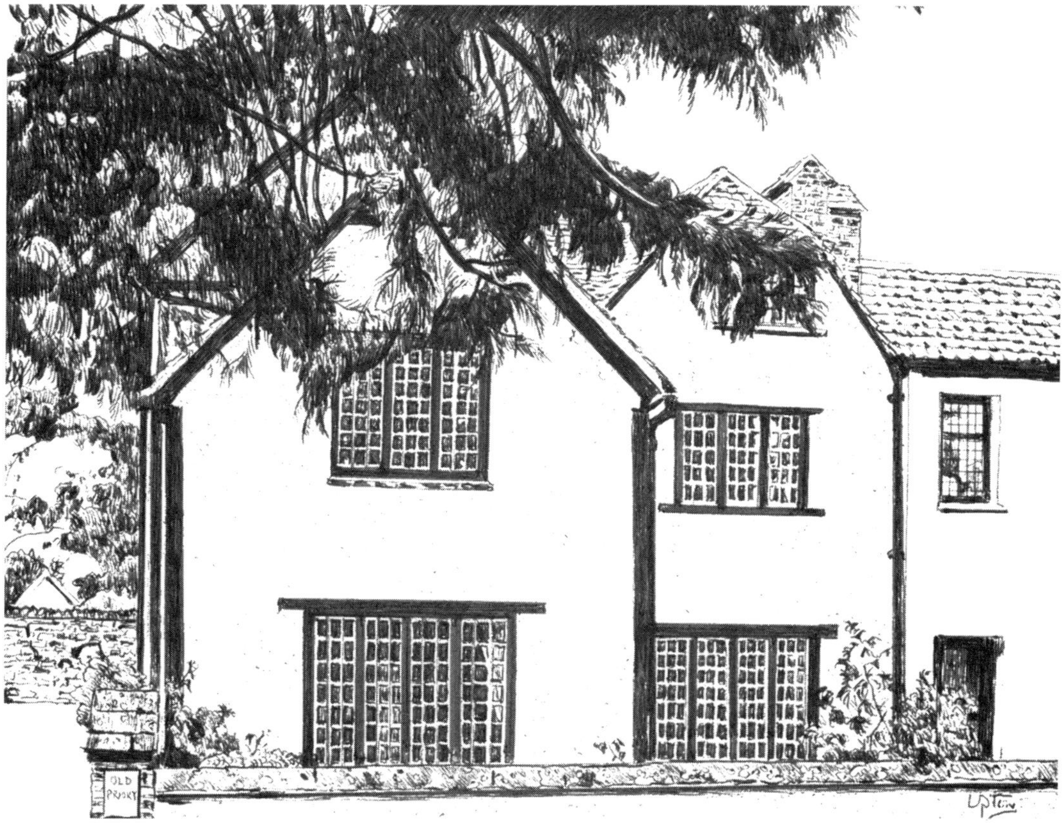

Priory Cottage

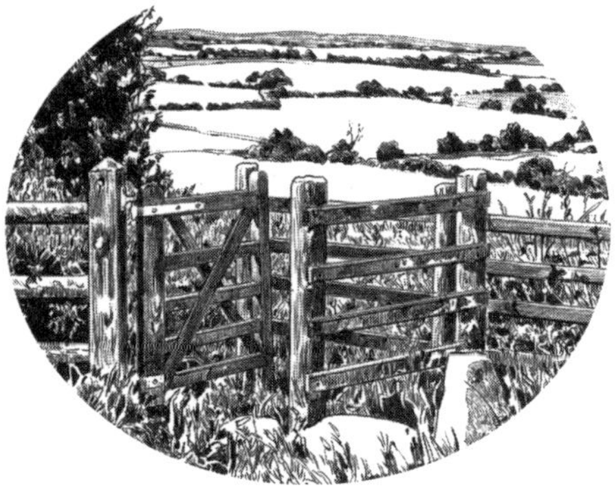

iron railings at the path's edge. Near the bottom of the hill Church Street came to an end at a gate leading into farmer Buckland's fields. Beside this gate a wooden swing-swong stile was built into the fence.

In the middle of the High Street was the half-timbered Town Hall, supported on tall stone pillars,while below was an old fire-engine and the town stocks, a reminder to those who misbehaved.

Farther down the street stood the doctor's elegant Georgian house. Doctor John was a sporting man who loved his hunting. The way to his surgery was through the hall of his house, the front door being open. The surgery, a wooden shed in his garden, included a waiting room in which were hung sporting prints of paintings by Lionel Edwards. We boys loved to look at these, for we were already admirers of his work. Meeting him in the High Street one day, Doctor John asked my twin and I, "Have you got colds or any other illness?" "No", we said. To which he replied, "Be ill on Wednesday, the hounds meet locally at 11 o'clock!"

On the other side of the High Street was the solicitors' stone building in front of which travelling magicians, Punch and Judy shows and small one-man stands with performing goats and dogs would hold us spellbound with their tricks.

Secretly we would vow to live one day the life they led, seeing only the excitement and glamour. Our choice fluctuated with almost every show, not that they were common, and then only when we were not going to be farmers or artists.

Behind Comley's Store there was an open space where Scarrott's Fair used to pitch its side-shows and tents. Best of all was the great steam Galloper, with its

Scarrott's Fair

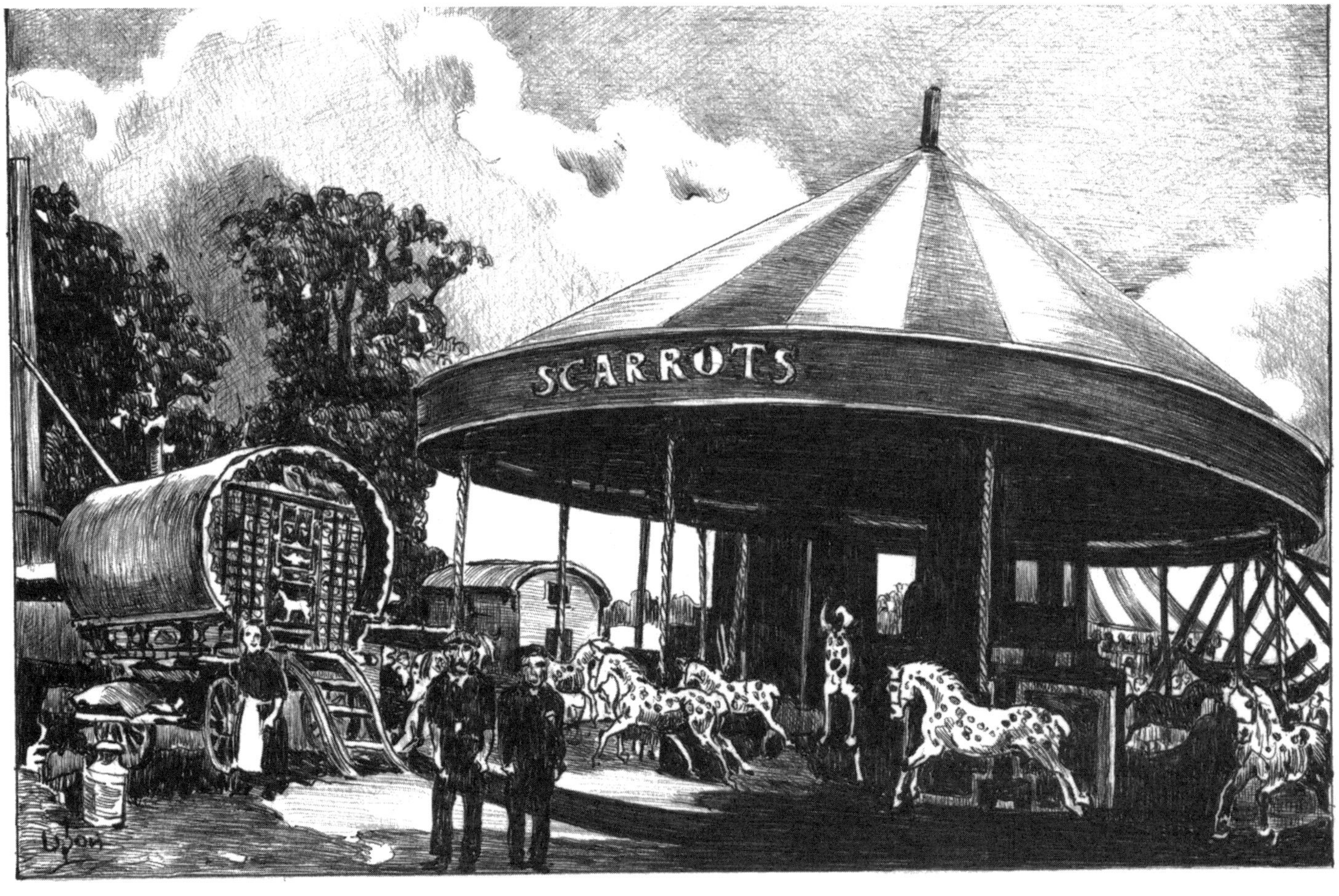

brightly-painted horses rising up and down on spiral poles and moving round and round the painted scenes. We watched in wonder, the music apparently coming from folding cards punched with holes!

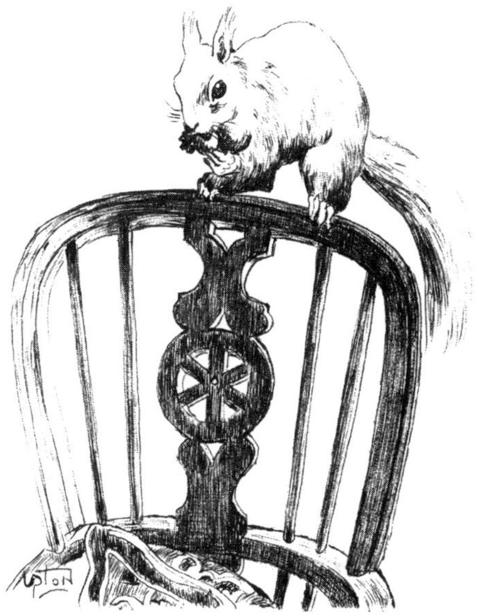

Excited, but a little shy of such noise and the bustling crowds, we danced around eager to see everything. I tried my hand at darts for the first time—and this was during the war when most things were scarce, so only one light bulb illuminated the boards and prizes. The first dart thrown rose high in the air and shattered the bulb, plunging the stand into darkness. I stood poised for flight, but my mother took my hand and made our apologies. From somewhere in the tent a voice was heard, "Soraite, mam, you hadn't pay". We hurried away.

Between Plaister's Meadow and the wide market place, the road narrowed, winding its way out into the country towards the inn at the crossroads. A row of lime trees kept company with the road for a short while and shaded the high wall of the Lime Kiln Garden. A fine many-gabled house stood beyond the wall clung with virginia creeper. Stables and numerous outbuildings added to the pleasing confusion of roof tops about which swallows flew for insects to feed their broods. Opposite was the last cottage on the road and there lived an interesting old lady who kept a pet red squirrel. It would come and sit on your hand or shoulder if given some nuts.

One day we found a young jackdaw and took it home as a pet. His—or should that be her?—ice blue eyes noted everything and, being very inquisitive, was always picking up things or getting himself in trouble. However he was free to roam and eventually became strong on the wing, but came back to us when hungry. His worst habit was to perch on a neighbour's washing-line just when she had put out freshly-washed clothes or sheets. You can imagine the problem and it caused some embarrassment even to us boys. 'Daw' one day, after living with us for some months, did not return. Whether he lived happily ever after, or his life was sadly cut short we never found out. Later, other birds were to follow.

In the other direction, towards the westering sun and leaving the town, one crossed Skew Bridges over the Great Western Railway and shortly afterwards arrived at Hunt's Mill. It was the scene for early industrial action, for here in about 1750, the workers threw the frame of a bolting machine into the mill pond, angry at the use of cloths instead of temzers (sieves) when milling flour.

At the fork in the road by the infant stream, the lane turning uphill and to the left led to Little Park Farm and a narrow way between high hedges was where 'Leggy' Campden used to live in a caravan. Rumour had it that this old one-legged scrap merchant of gypsy origin had thousands of pounds under his bed. But when he died nothing but heaps of old iron was found.

Beyond the Saw Mills, the Manor and Blackdog cottages, a lane led to Queen Court Farm, old and surrounded by a moat. It was so named as it had been for years the property of the Queens of Henry VIII. An early tenant, one Dionisia Parsons, must have often been hard put to keep up with the name of her landlady, but in an agreement with Katherine Parr, she was under an obligation to find, 'Man mate, horse mate and lodging for one night for the Queen's surveyors'. One wonders at the results of such an arrangement, and the likely problems which would ensue.

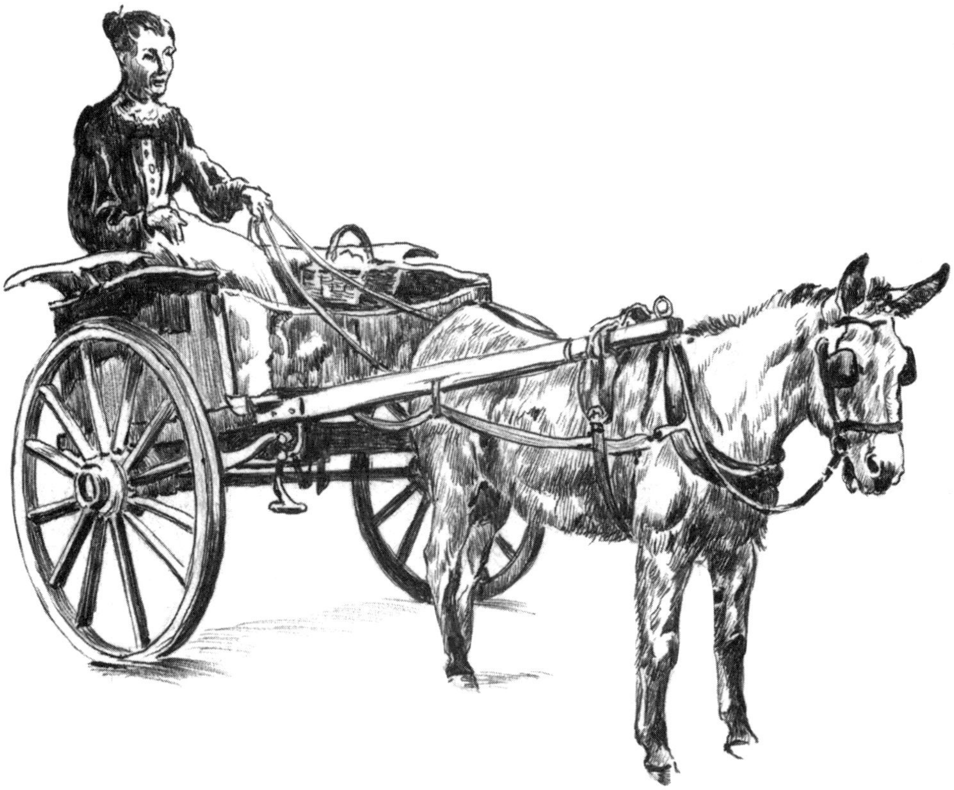

The Lady in Black

About once a month a strange lady would be seen in the village. She was always dressed in an old-fashioned black dress and over it a large white apron. She would go alone save for the little donkey who pulled her cart.

Who she was or where she came from we never found out. Could she be a witch? It was an exciting thought, and when you are young the mind is just full of imaginary notions.

The Milk Round

'Thos. Fry and Sons', these words decorated a curved board over each wheel on the smart outfit of the milk-roundsman. The wooden-wheeled float, shiny green and yellow, was drawn by a good-looking bay pony called Charlie.

Now Charlie was the pride of his owner's heart, and his outfit the smartest in the High Street, but he had one incurable fault. All would go well as he trotted from house to house with scoured churns of fresh milk in the float behind and two cool oval buckets with brass measures, pint and half-pint, hanging on hooks. Cottagers would come to their doors with a jug or metal cannister which Mr Fry would fill according to their needs.

However, should a thoughtless blackbird fly up beneath Charlie's feet, or a

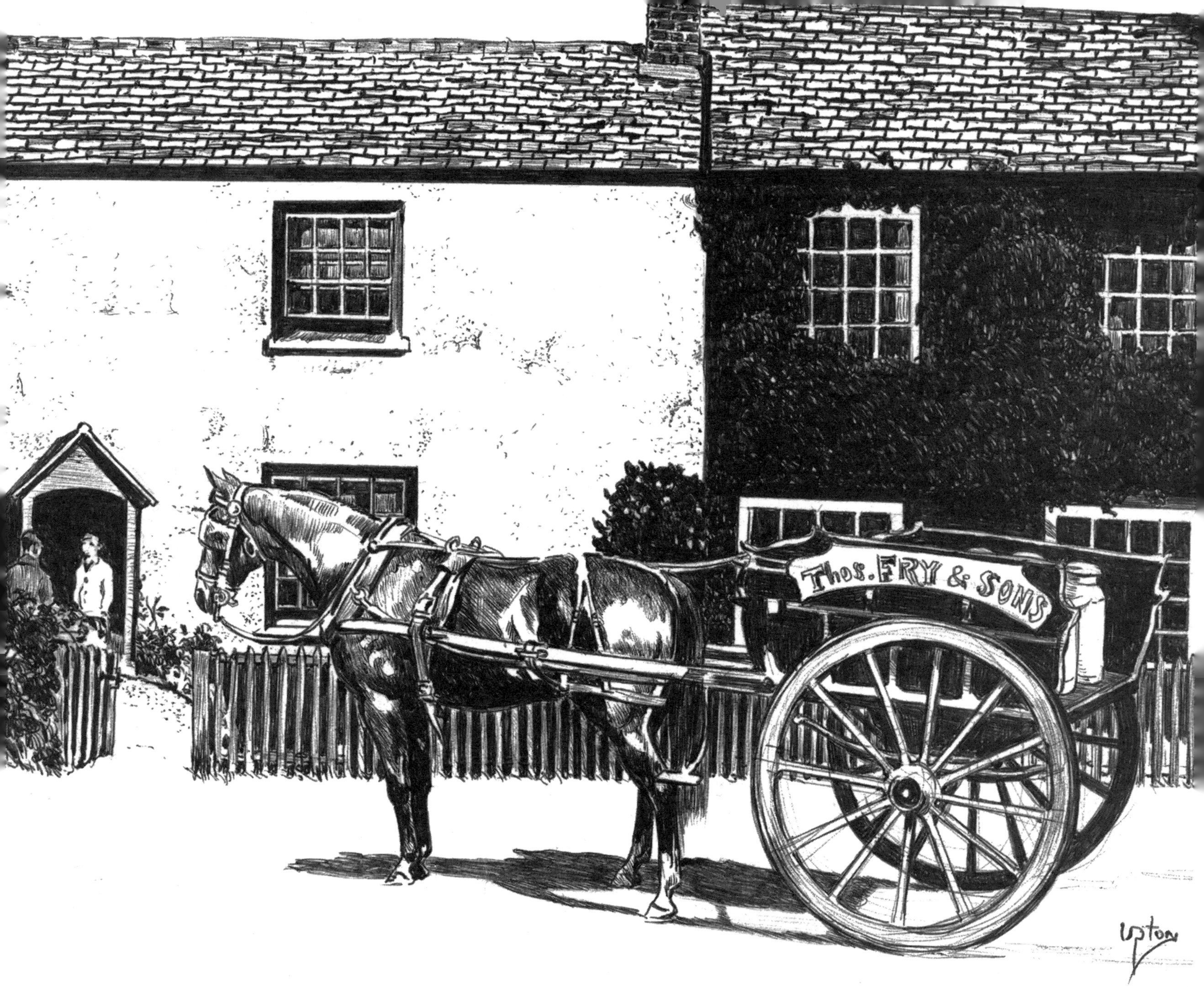

driver of a lorry sound his horn, then off he would fly, smartness and decorum thrown to the winds. It was exciting, the galloping pony and weaving float with a trail of spilt milk marking the course of Charlie's career. The pony would eventually come to a halt, but this behaviour did not improve and was a constant distress to his proud owner, who with much heart-searching eventually exchanged Charlie for a Ford van.

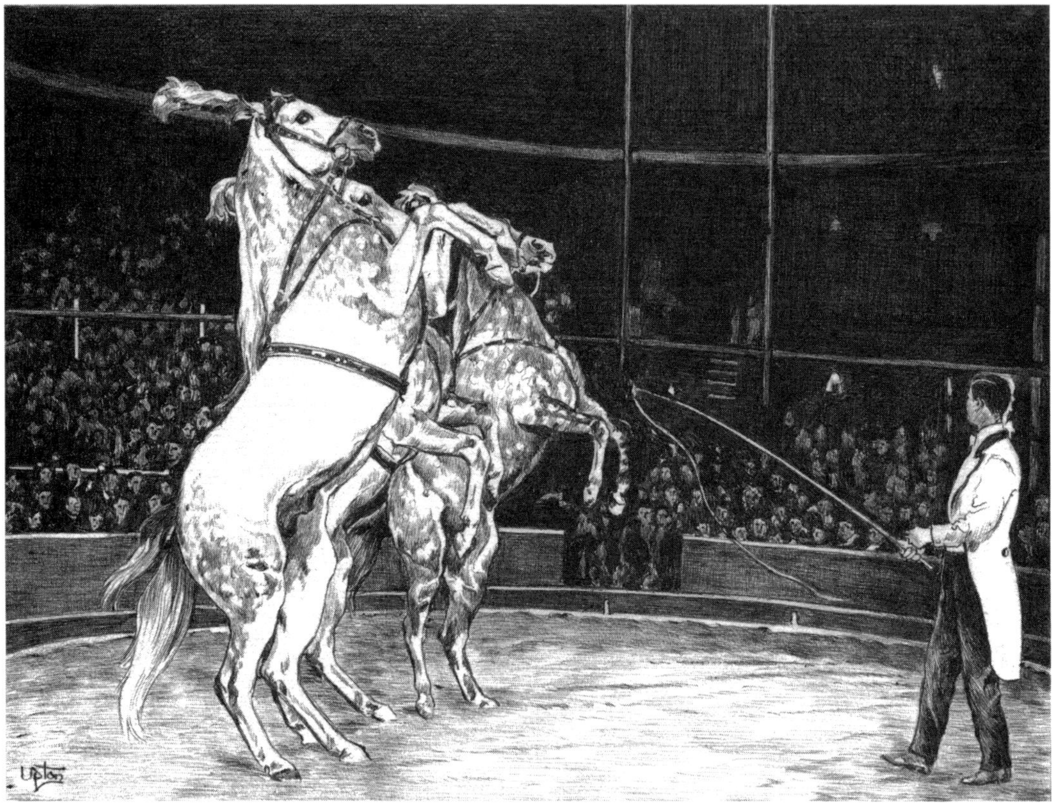

The Circus

Better by far than the fairground were the circuses which came for one night stands to the show ground in Plaister's Meadow. Immediately after seeing the posters proclaiming the arrival of a circus in old Mrs Rowse's shop window, we would hang about the field until the wagons and animals turned in at the gate.

We wanted to be part of the show, so we helped to put up the Big Top. First, the king poles were erected and then the canvas laid out and laced together. Iron stakes were hammered into the grass and then we all hauled together on the ropes to lift the heavy tent slowly to the top of the posts. The side and quarter poles and wall canvas were all fixed in place: the Big Top was up. Then the wooden seating and the ring itself were set up. Next, there were the animals to see to and to feed: the ponies, dogs, elephants and bears.

Once we were invited into the circus boss's ornate Buxton caravan to have tea with some of the performers, the boss being the ringmaster in red tailcoat and back topper. Afterwards we watched the evening performance from the performers' entrance. What an evening of wonder! Six liberty horses moving around the ring, galloping, turning, rearing and bowing at the end of their show. There we also saw a beautiful lady bare-back rider and two dancing bears who worked with the clowns. Then, an amazing Indian acrobat who climbed up a very tall pole, while it swayed to and fro, right to the top of the tent and there performed many tricks, finally lying across the tip of the pole while it swung back and forth.

Later we recognised the beautiful bare-back lady as the boss's wife who had earlier given us tea to thank us for being such a help.

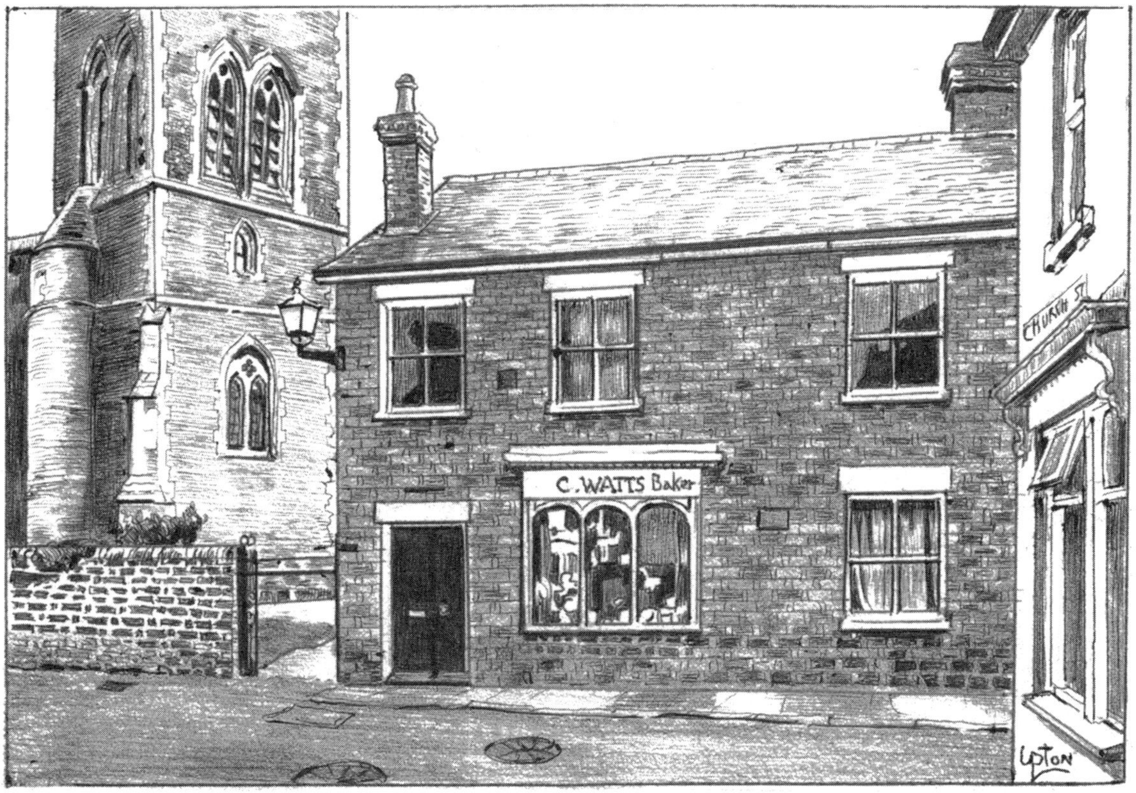

Charlie Watts' Bakery

The Baker

The Butthaye, behind the church in the old part of the town, I will always remember because of the intoxicating smell of newly-baked bread. Charlie Watts, his wife and his sister owned a little faded brown shop, and above the window the signboard read 'Baker and Confectioner'.

Within the shop, the counter was stacked high with loaves, still crusty and warm, and behind its glass-fronted cupboards were full of tall jars of sweets. Despite that, we were more interested in the large room beyond: the bakery. Across the lane, Charlie Watts, the baker, kept his Large White pigs, his pride and joy.

On opening the door to the bakery, Charlie would be found kneading the dough, dressed in a brown overall and flat cap. He would look up in greeting, always with a wide-mouthed smile, ruddy-faced beneath sandy brows and the bluest of eyes. Some people would say that Charlie was not all that bright, but we enjoyed his company. He would bang and fold the dough, on the flour-strewn table, then twist off pieces to fashion into big fat cottage-loaves, or rolled loaves and plaits. He never tired of telling us that the secret in baking was in the wood used for firing the oven—old and fragrant woods like crab and plum. He would wrap the loaves in cabbage leaves before opening the oven door and with a great wooden shovel each loaf would be placed well back on the floor of the oven.

Soon the well-remembered scent would again fill the tall room and drift into the lane outside.

Meanwhile, we would discuss his pigs or go into the little parlour behind the shop for tea. We were always a little in awe of Charlie's sister due to her ginger moustache.

But the parlour was full of interest with its Regency corner-cupboard full of bone-china and a whole collection of little jugs and vases, each carrying the coat-of-arms of an English town or borough, early souvenirs. Although the deep armchairs were liberally filled with prickly horsehair stuffing and their backs draped with crocheted antimacassars, we would perch gingerly on the front edge, careful lest we spill the tea or drop crumbs of scotch shortbread, still awed by that moustache.

Back in the bakery, each singing, warm and fragrant loaf was ladled from the glowing interior of the oven to be stacked in wooden trays. Mouth-watering, crusty, gold-brown bread—food for the gods.

Charlie usually baked once a day, and delivered his many-shaped loaves in an old bull-nosed Morris van. Age and new-fangled orders issued by government caused Charlie to get more and more behind-hand with his baking, until his delivery times became so erratic that the loaves might be placed on our kitchen table at dead of night, ready for next morning's breakfast. So, it all proved too much for him; he gave up the bakery to spend more time with his pigs.

We lost for ever the good wholesome bread baked by Charlie Watts. Only in memory does the fragrance linger on.

All Saints' Church

The 13th century church of St. Bartholomew and All Saints stood well back from the High Street, behind a low wall topped by iron railings. On each side of the gravel path to the south door were many ancient gravestones, some in the shape of Saxon crosses, others as tall slabs, tilting over and partly hidden behind the long grass. Oldest of all appeared to be the low coffin-like tombs, so covered in lichen and ivy that most of the inscriptions were no longer possible to read.

Taking our ponies into the churchyard to graze one day, it seemed to us small boys that the tombs could well serve a more practical purpose. Soon both of us, one on Misty a grey and the other bareback on the roan Tamarisk, were galloping wildly around and around the church jumping over the gravestones.

A loud shout stopped us in mid-flight, as Old MacDonald, the police constable, was seen hurrying through the lych gate. Only then did it suddenly occur to us that perhaps we were doing something wrong. Anyway, not wanting to wait and find out, we fled out at the back gate into Wood Street and crept home. We dared not tell our mother, but kept indoors for a couple of days, expecting a loud knock at the door which would herald a visit from the law. He did not come and soon we were out again and up to more mischief in the valley fields.

Granny or mother would take us to church most Sundays. We would tip-toe to our pews near the back of the church, while a single bell tolled the last minute before Matins. Behind us the ringers would converse in muted tones, except for the one who rhythmically caught and pulled his rope, jacket off and braces showing. Then silence, as the bell was stilled and the insistent sound died away.

The vicar, no longer in his old tweeds, but arrayed in white appeared from the vestry to stand with clasped hands and announce the first hymn. Then, as the organ wheezed out the beginnings of the tune, down the aisle would troop the ringers, hob-nailed boots sound loud on the tiles, between the congregation to the south door on their way to the Bolingbroke Arms for a well-earned pint. This was for us the first of three highlights to our morning service. The second was a view of a bass singer in the choir,with loud Amens. He had the most wonderful waxed moustache, twirled and pointed at the ends, and we felt sure that as the choir processed around the church, he must poke the tenor in the eye.

Fidgeting on our seats as the service proceeded, we sat on our hands through the first lesson read by the sidesman who had the broadest of Wiltshire dialect. We knelt for prayers and then the vicar climbed the steps to the pulpit for the sermon; and we waited in expectation. It was the final act which gave our service its personal touch. Suddenly the silence of the church was broken by a loud, sustained hissing sound which never failed to send us into silent convulsions of mirth.

The cause of this outrage was the Doctor's wife. She was a very religious person indeed, as we knew to our cost, for she would stop us in the street and ask us to recite the ten commandments. It was a habit of hers which made us extremely ill at ease when she approached. But to return to the church: she always left at the end of the vicar's sermon and, due to the hard oak pews took a blown-up air cushion to sit upon. The sound was that of the air being released from the cushion, before she slipped out, quite unaware of the effect on fellow members of the congregation.

Soon, the return of the ringers heralded the end of the service, and then we were free to race out into the open air of our beloved fields.

The Church Fête

Each year the vicar, kind soul, would open the vicarage gardens to the village for the church Fête. This was one of the special treats we looked forward to, along with the Harvest Festival and Supper.

And each year the vicar would stand on the terrace beside the Amaryllis lilies, looking just a little more frail, in his linen jacket and straw hat, smiling benignly on his flock, as the youngsters trampled his flower beds underfoot or scaled the great cedar tree at the bottom of the lawn.

So on this day the peace and calm of his garden was rudely shattered, though I still remember the big impression made on me by the large regency house with stable block, the lawn tennis court and spacious grounds.

Usually the sun shone on such occasions, or so it seemed to me as a child, and the long afternoon was one of delight for the villagers decked out in their Sunday best. We boys in uncomfortable stiff collars and ties—how we wished to discard them and be free. Our big floppy flat caps were doffed to everyone we met, until we got the giggles at our own impertinence.

Below the tiled terrace was a rockery and then the big lawn. Across each end of this were set out stalls. Here the ladies of the village, turned traders for the day, were busy selling their wares and gossiping nineteen to the dozen all the while. The heavily-laden trestles were piled high with home-made jams and preserves, mouth-watering cakes and local honey, bread and even sweets. The farmers' wives had a stall for cheeses and butter made in their own farm kitchens. Trade was brisk among the milling crowd, while choir boys with raffle tickets pursued victims around the grounds. Children dragged mums towards a bran-tub, in to which they plunged hot, sticky hands in search of treasure.

Beyond the lawn and the tennis court there was bowling for the pig. In a pen of hurdles, the prize lay contentedly snoring, a wisp of straw across his nose oblivious of his future. Meanwhile dads with jackets off and sleeves rolled up, were getting down to the serious job of knocking over wooden skittles with three large balls. The ground was uneven and the grass a little long: the sexton had forgotten to scythe the field. To us boys watching, it was obvious that a wide variety of methods were employed to send the skittles flying. Some considered speed essential for the best results and hurled the balls down so fast that they went bouncing over the skittles and across the field, a horde of small boys scampering in pursuit. Others preferred a more studied approach of rebound and effect and, after spitting on their hands and wiping them on their corduroys, they squinted down the course and bowled cunning spinners. One year the pig was won by the local carpenter, a master bowler, though he it was who had made the particular skittles in use!

Later in the afternoon, the local school mistress would begin to collect her little charges for the country dancing display. The centre of the lawn was cleared and the boys and girls, watched by their proud parents, began to skip and dance around the maypole, weaving in and out between one another to the faint sounds of the piano coming from the vicarage library, where the junior teacher hammered the keys as she watched the children through the open french window. What clapping and smiles greeted the performance!

So the long day came to an end. The vicar's garden and the mums all looked a little tired, but all had enjoyed the Fête. The following day in church the vicar was able to announce the grand total taken at the Fête towards the church restoration fund. Yes, it was worth it after all.

The Farmhouse

The River Thames, brook-like and insignificant but for the golden glory of the Marsh Marigolds that grew beside the infant flow, marked the boundary of a small but ancient farm. It was the home of gentle Shires and roan Shorthorns, of white ducks on the pond and geese in the rick-yard.

The farm-house stood apart from the stables, cow sheds and barns, being on higher ground on the other side of a narrow lane. A tall square house of Cotswold stone built in about 1689, it had carved drip-sills and mullioned windows and to the front a walled garden. A gateway in the wall opened into the home meadow

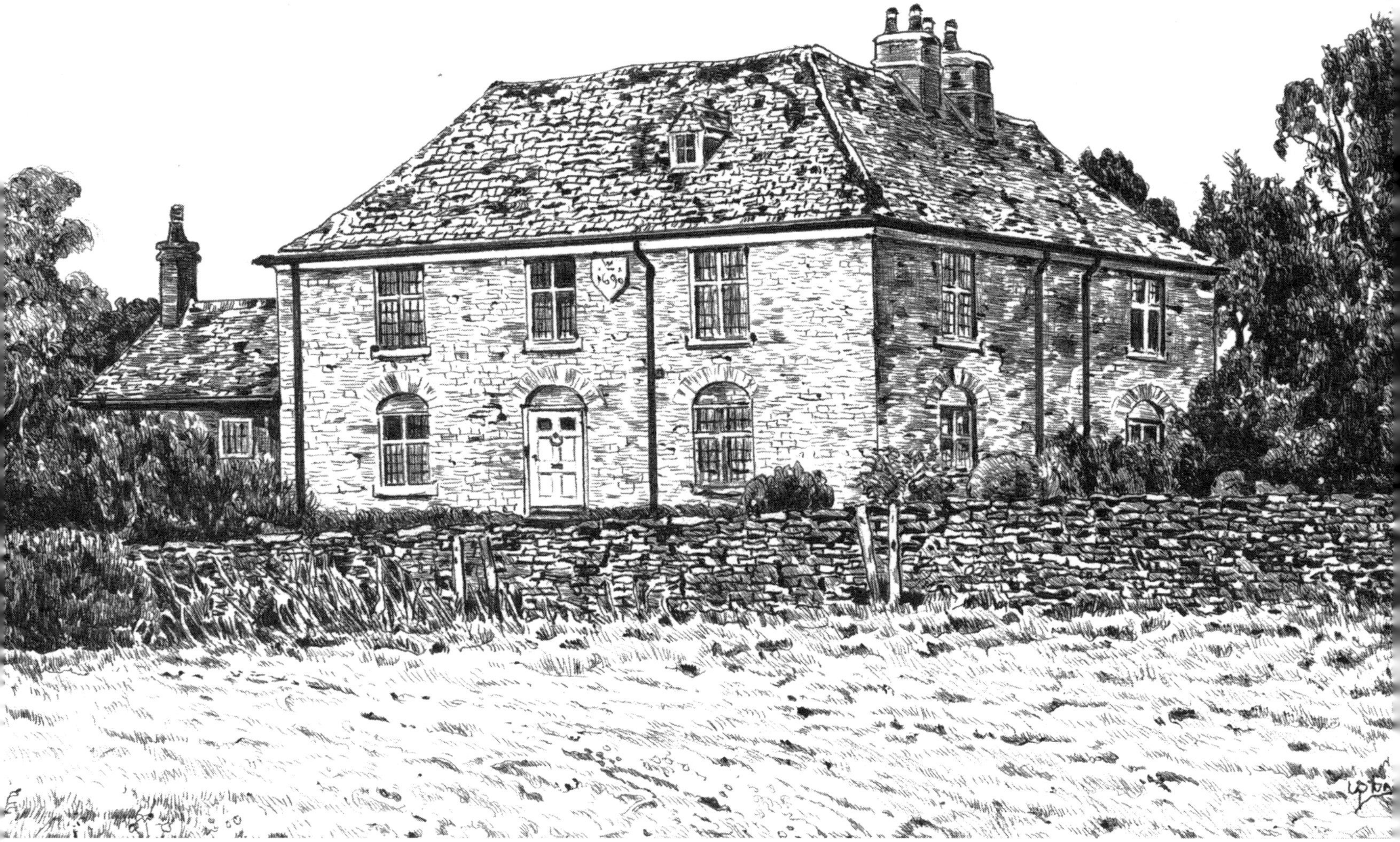

where a footpath meandered between cowslips and buttercups, its hedges of blackthorn with dog-roses a-blush and blackberry blossoms. Across the meadow among sombre yews and tombstones, stood the little church, brooding and damp. A vicar came but once a month, and as no other house stood near, the church was always considered to be the farm's church. But for Sundays and the rare visits of relatives, the front of the house was little seen, except when passing along the land. It was the back of the house that was the hub of the farm's daily life. The door always stood open, the flagstones in the doorway worn and bare.

Twice a day, every day the cows were milked. The men, each with two pails of milk,would pass across the lane, the heavy yoke across broad shoulders, to go up the cobbled path to the dairy door. In the cold room a long stone trough brimmed with water flowing from a pipe. In the trough were six churns and on one a muslin cloth, through which the milk was filtered. The other churns stood with lids a'cock. Later, following the afternoon milking, each full churn of ten gallons would be lifted from one trough to stand in another just outside the door. This tank also overflowed with cold water, filled through a channel from the trough in the dairy. Ferns hid the inlet and curled their heads in every crevice and their oscillating reflections moved across an indigo sky. The inner trough stood empty save for one

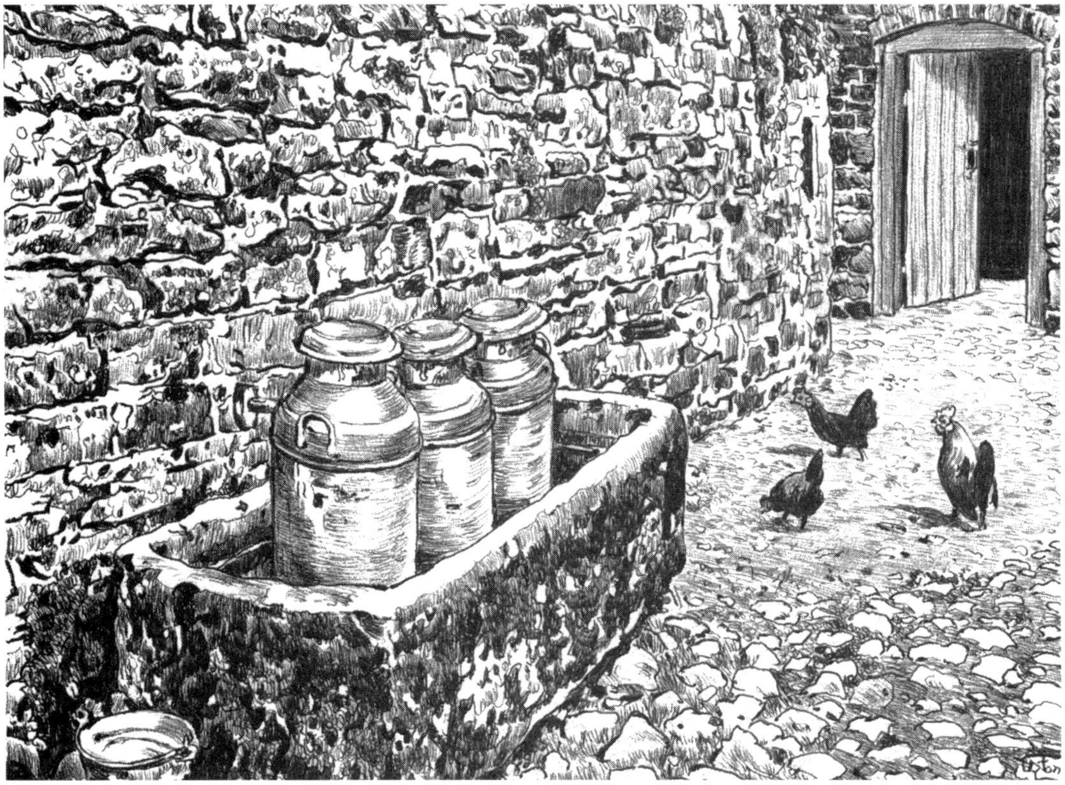

half-filled churn. Then, as the milking pails were scoured and dipped, the clear clean water ran cloudy and opaque. The up-turned pails dripped on the stone ledge, and the three-legged stools. White coats and hats were hung upon wooden pegs.

Across the other side of the dairy ran a long flagstone shelf built above little arched alcoves. Along the shelf were ranged jugs, large skim-pans and a butter churn. To the left on crucks, near the doorway where three stone steps led up to the kitchen, were two barrels of cider with wooden taps and a crock beneath each to catch the drips. Above these, two large sides of bacon hung from hooks in a beam, and on further hooks there were lanterns and a very old lanthorn.

The kitchen was the centre of the house. Here the family lived and the women did most of their work. It was a large warm room, for a fire always burned in the black range set in a cavernous opening of worn bricks. An iron kettle and large copper saucepans clustered round the flames, and an old saw-toothed pot crane hung down,soot-blackened in the chimney. Heavy flat irons, tongs and long-handled bellows stood beside the range, while above on the slate mantle-shelf there were brass candlesticks with square pans and decorated snuffers, two large coloured coronation mugs of King George V, containing matches and spills, and a lacquer tea-caddy and finally, a posset pot of Bristol Delft, some pewter tankards and an old horn mug.

From the rafters hung a number of wicker baskets and along the chimney-breast, resting on wooden pegs, an old 12-bore shot gun with a calendar from an agricultural merchant tied to its barrel.

The wall opposite the range was entirely taken up by an enormous oak dresser, its shelves heavy with blue and white Willow Pattern china, Lowestoft cream jugs and earthenware storage jars. A bunch of large keys dangled from a hook, and

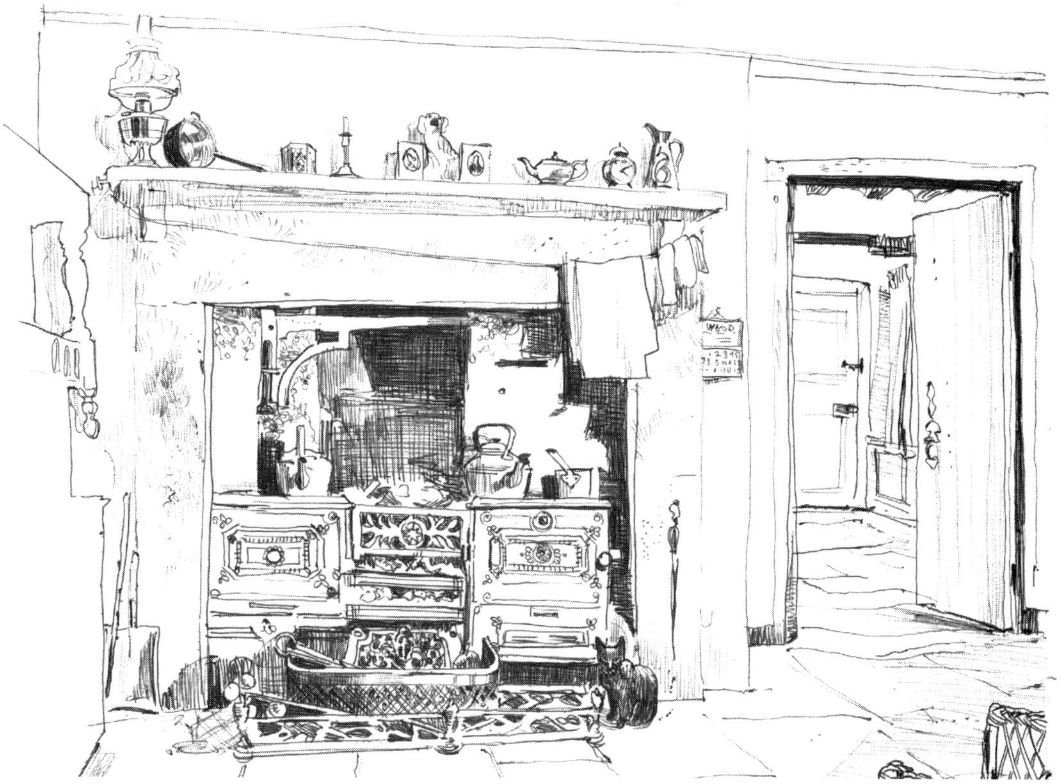

papers and letters were tucked behind big breakfast cups, decorated with hunting scenes. Drawers held baskets of cutlery and other kitchen utensils, the knives bone-handled and thin from constant sharpening. In the larger middle drawers there were crisp white and checked linen table cloths and napkins. One last drawer was full of string, tacks, wicks, spare candles and every possible object which may be of use, while the worn board was cluttered with a basket of fresh brown eggs, a pestle and mortar, pots, bowls and tins and a jug of violets.

In the centre of the scrubbed flag floor stood a large table with chairs about it and under the window a settle, piled with odd cushions and two cats asleep.

It was a busy room full of life and activity, quite unlike the parlour. For the front room was kept for guests and those rare occasions when the family gathered for Christmas and birthdays. If one peeped in at the door the room appeared cold and ill-lit, for its only window stayed shadowed by the huge old yew tree outside. Brass fire-dogs supported a heap of logs in the stone fireplace and behind these was a cracked iron fire-back with a coat-of-arms engraved on it, dated 1646.

On the walls maple-framed daguerreotypes of great-grandfather and other early Victorian ancestors hung alongside prints of prize Shire horses and cattle. On a heavy sideboard rows of large silver cups reflected the successes of the Shires bred by the family, including two great winners: 'March Majesty', Champion Stallion RAS 1912 and 'March Major', Champion Stallion and Best of Breed 1919. Old cane-backed armchairs and a leather couch were placed around the fireplace.

Between the kitchen and the parlour was the hall with a tiled floor on which stood a great oak chest decorated with carvings of badgers and pigeons and next to it the grandfather clock whose deep voice spelled out the passing hours. Beside the seldom-used front door, thumb sticks, crooks and whips were clustered together in a large earthen pot, while a selection of bowler hats and a variety of other head gear hung on the antlers of a red deer stag, a trophy which some earlier member of the family had stalked in Scotland many years before.

Leading off the hall on the other side of the kitchen was the dining room, a long low pleasant room with a heavy mahogany table and chairs, a side-table and a large glass-fronted bookcase containing many sporting volumes together with The Badminton Library, Baileys, some early veterinary books on horse ailments, Dickens and a complete set of Shire horse stud books. On its top there stood a domed glass case, and within a beady-eyed woodcock. Although such a special room, it—like the parlour—only came into its own for Sunday lunches and other special occasions.

Finally a broad oak staircase, lit by a tall window on the quarter landing, divided two ways to the rooms upstairs. Here bare oaken boards, which creaked as one walked on them, led by passages and further flights of stairs to bedrooms and bathrooms. Each bedroom was sparsely furnished with great soft beds, a rug and a washstand.

On this floor there was the secret room, its doorway cleverly disguised as panelling, where it is said that Royalist sympathisers had once safely hidden. The entrance, now sealed up and forgotten, added to its mystery and the house's long history.

In the centre of the flagged yard at the back of the farmhouse a deep well, around which was a U-shaped dry stone wall topped with flat slabs. Across the end of the U is a large upright stone. If you lifted up the bleached wooden lid, the rough circular well appeared bottomless, the water so still and clear that its level was difficult to judge until a bucket was lowered on a crooked stick. On touching the water a flashing of reflected sunspots revolved about the curved sides, where minute ferns and lichens clung—a sweet-smelling dampness arose.

The laundry always brought out to the garden in a big willow-work basket was taken through a small gate, and up a cinder path to the orchard where the washing-line was attached to the old apple and pear trees. Sheets, shirts and coloured clothes soon flopped in the wind like loosened sails, and a prop kept them above the soft fruit below. Check table-cloths were laid out over the gooseberry bushes to dry in the sun.

Beyond the trees, the vegetable garden where rows of potatoes, greens, carrots and parsnips grew. Beans climbed in profusion up brittle sticks, their tendrils reaching up to the light. Beneath the wall, rhubarb sprouted up through bottomless old buckets loosely packed with straw and their huge leaves shaded wild violets. Tall hollyhocks overlooked the wall. Here the handsome bumble-bees inspected each flower and busy honey bees from the hives searched for nectar.

A moss-grown path between two clipped bay trees led to a quiet shaded alcove where herbs entangled with convolvulus scented the air; and beyond a small stone-tiled building, overgrown with ivy and red-veined creeper in which wrens built a nest each year. Over its latched door draped a rambler rose, its perfume quite overwhelming.

Within this quiet retreat, two earth closets, communal in well-scrubbed board,

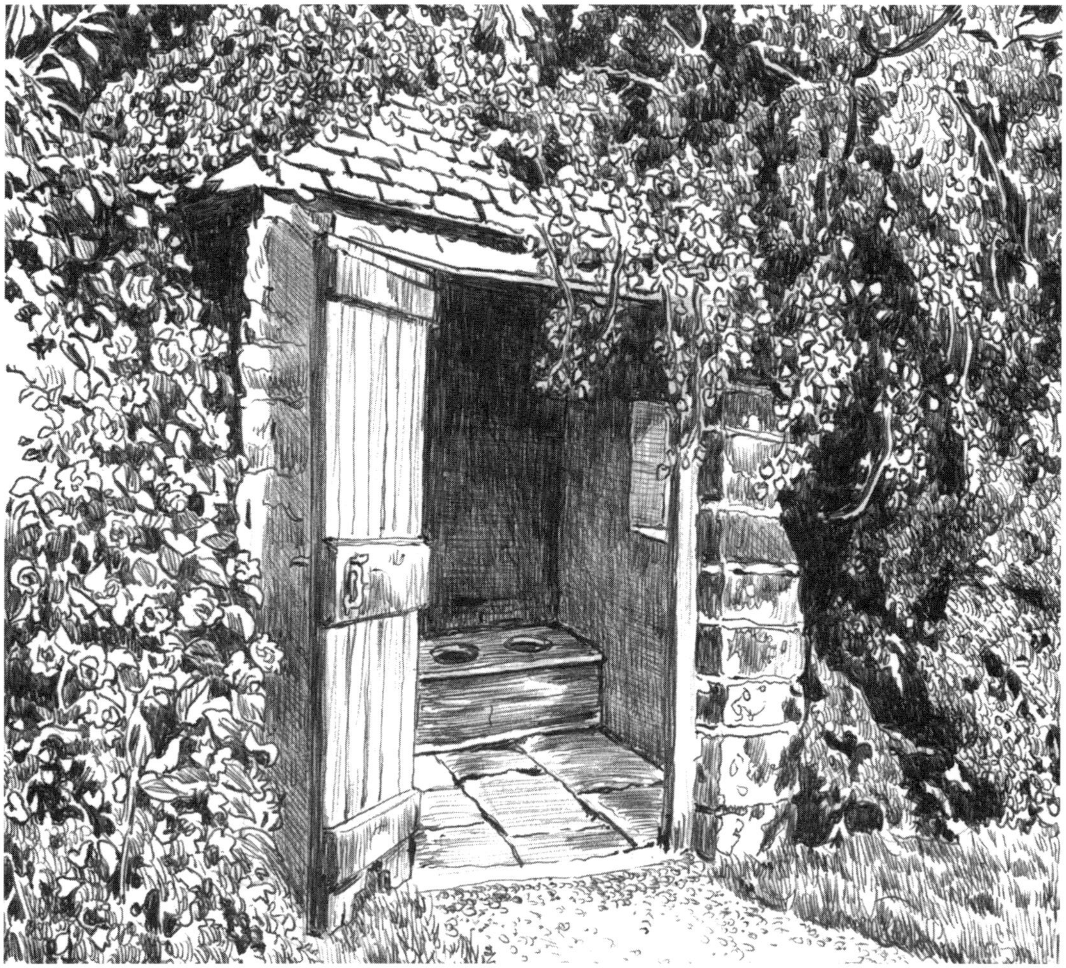

The privy

where to sit was to watch through cracks the wind-rocked flowers and to hear the innumerable sounds of birds. A place for dreaming!

Back by the kitchen yard there was a row of lean-to sheds which included a wood-shed and an old bothy where once a farm worker would have lived. Next to it a door through the wall gave entry to an old orchard where the hens and bantams lived and scratched about beneath Russet and Crab Apple trees.

We boys loved to visit this farm and when we were invited to tea, this was a rare treat. The journey by pony and trap to the farm was about ten miles, but the roads were quiet. Our interest as ever was the farmyard and the livestock, particularly the farm horses. But the place that most fascinated us twins was an old railway truck, for inside was kept the old show harness no longer in use. There were collars, mullins and breaching, all of shining black leather, and ribbons called butterflies with which the manes of the horses would have been dressed. One box was filled with horse brasses and cottle bells. Other boxes contained the iron work, bits and chains, covered in bran to stop them from rusting. Along the walls old rosettes, prize cards and stallion cards were nailed up: records of past successes at agricultural shows.

Recalling our farm visits provides a magical reminder of an age now mostly forgotten.

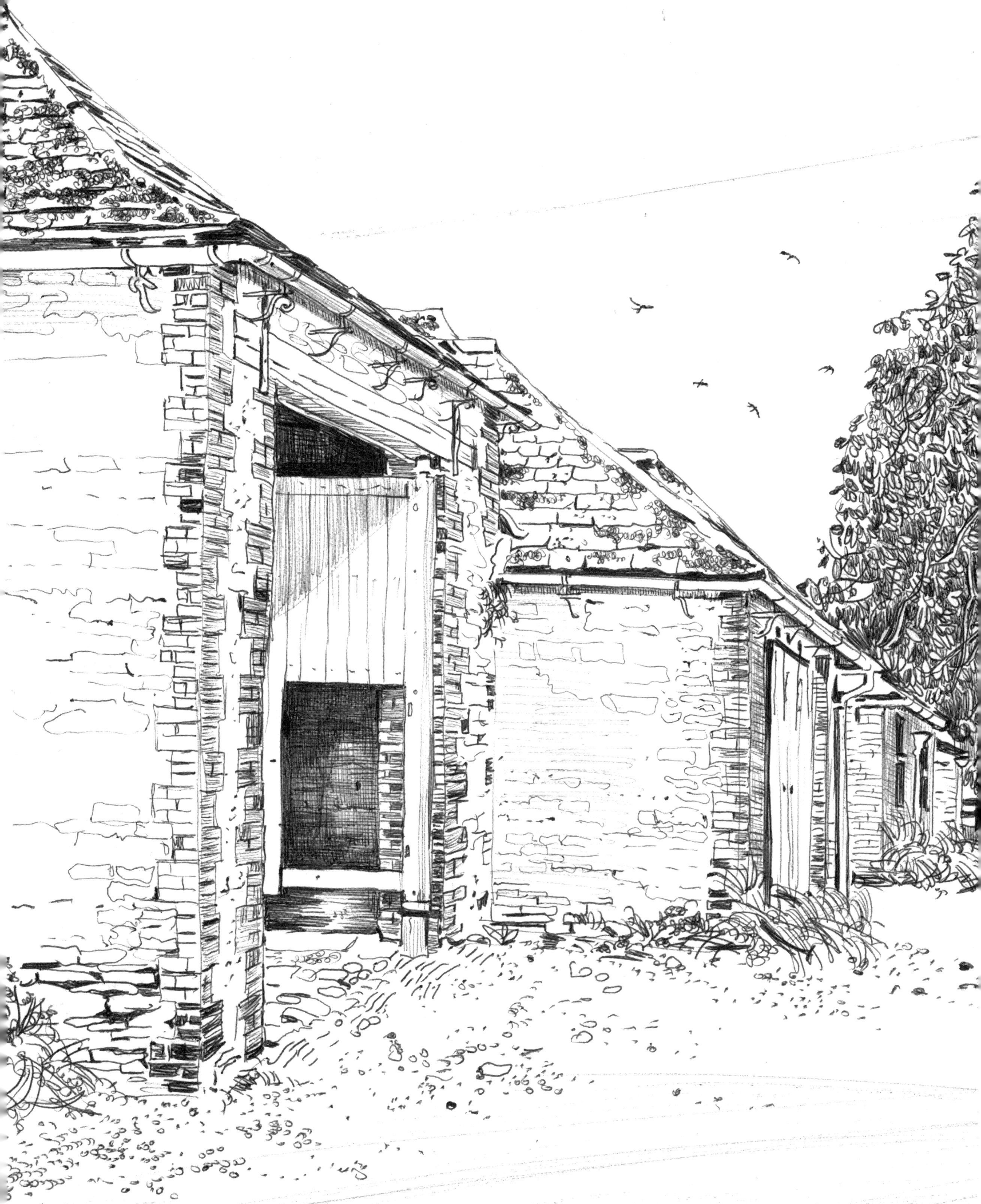

The Barn

To enter the barn by the small door set within the large double doors was rather like stepping into some forgotten Gothic church. It had that mood of quietly dreaming through the years, old as time itself. Beams of ancient sunlight filtered the dust of ages. Its spell fell upon us boys at our intrusion, and we were hushed.

Great oaken posts like pillars, resting on sarcen stone slabs, soared upwards supporting beams, raflers and king-posts like the ribs of a ship, braced and strutted to take the enormous weight of the steeply pitched Cotswold stone roof. The worm-holed timbers, festooned in cobwebs, were visited in April by the swallows newly arrived from abroad. Here they built their cups of mud, collected from the verges of the farm pond, and tirelessly hunted the summer skies to feed their young.

On the oak timbers one could still find the builders' marks incised at the joints, all held by wooden pegs. Throughout the great length of the barn, dimly seen save for the shafts of light and motes of dust, were an old wagon, tumbrils, spare wheels and some broken wooden rakes, a plough and many other discarded tools of the farming past.

Two massive porches, opposite one another, gave light ard air to the centre of the barn. Here on a raised wooden platform the threshing and winnowing once took place. Then the big doors were opened wide to let in the breeze and the thump of flails would have been heard, as men beat the sheaves of corn. I only remember picking up an old worm-eaten flail hung on a nail in the barn and asking one of the old labourers what it had been used for.

Above the great doors on the southern side in the gable apex were serried rows of arched holes with projecting sills where doves nested in the spring. In medieval times these had been a valuable source of fresh meat in the winter months. Many estates and farms then had dovecotes especially for the breeding of squabs for the pot. Indeed an old man I knew kept Mondain pigeons for the table in an ancient 'doo-cot'.

Today the stone gables stand stark and bare against the sky. The roof is gone and rotting beams lie tumbled among nettles and honeysuckle. No swallows nest there, but now build their homes in the farmbuildings still in use. The barn's life is over, no grant will save it now: its day is done.

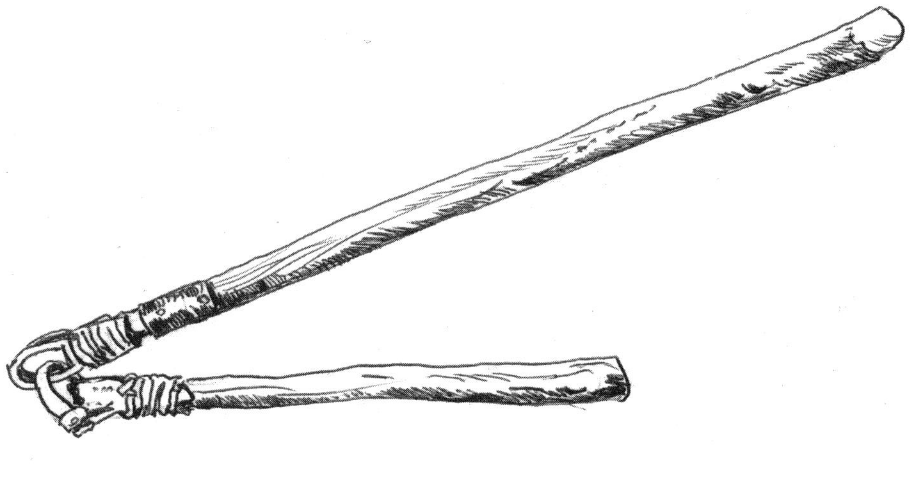

The flail

The Manor

The Manor could be approached from two directions. By entering the long beech wood through the wicket gate, the world of farming was shut out and we felt hushed by the expectancy of adventure. The impact was always there, always fresh, a heightened thrill for we were trespassing. We crept through the saplings, briars and soft willow herb to The Duke's Walk. Here an avenue of massive grey beech trees marked the bank where the wood sloped downhill. They were old trees of considerable girth with down-sweeping branches across the flinty causeway, their roots laid bare.

The pathway was flanked on the right by a wall of younger trees beyond the beeches and then the track lost itself among alders and pale larches, a more recent plantation. Skirting the edge of the spinney, the way zig-zagged down to a stream. Here the trees again were more mature and mostly oaks with dense undergrowth, through which we moved, alert and intoxicated.

Then, stepping out from the trees, before us was the lake, calm, serene with its twin islands reflected in deeper tones, and beyond The Manor House. The sudden view of the lake never lost its magic. Each time the sensation was there, a deep-throated feeling of beauty—all our own. Hidden by a belt of tall reeds, we would wait and watch, alert and excited. There was movement of wildfowl under the far bank or the proud cob swan and his mate near their nest site. A moorhen would slip out near the bank, her jerky progress marked as outward light-touched ripples mirroring her movements, gently rocked the reed blades by our feet. Slipping quietly to our usual spot, alarm caught us for a second as from beneath our feet a heron lurched upwards into the airways. It was not the gamekeeper as we had feared.

Like a magnet the lake would draw us to its banks, and the Manor House on the hill became the backdrop to the scenery, untouchable and dream-like.

Poaching had always held a special interest for us boys and we spent many an hour learning the skills from one who knew. It had a certain excitement all its own. To beat the keeper at his own game gave an added thrill, as tense and furtive we helped to set his nets or watched his dog slip silently down the hedge in the dark. Our poacher was a shy and silent gypsy lad who talked little of his 'work' in the fields and woods, but he had an intimate knowledge of the ways of the wildlife and the countryside, for he shared their world out under the stars.

Back in the woods, the steep bank beyond the beeches was our poaching ground, for rabbits abounded there. We learned how to catch rabbits with purse-nets, pegged over the burrows. A yellowy-white ferret was sent underground while we lay listening, listening for the warning thump of a rabbit. Expectancy is rewarded as one of the purse-nets is kicked upwards and a rabbit enmeshed in the nets rolls on the bank, then another: what excitement!

The heap of limp and furry bodies would be harled, then the hind legs slit at the sinew and one threaded through the other so that they could be carried on a stick over the shoulder. Then in the dark, back by silent ways to our home with a couple of rabbits for the pot.

Gypsies we knew liked nothing better than to run their long-dogs after the big brown hares of the Marlborough Downs:

"Mush, hows about yur jook'avin a plastra wi mande? She do run shoshoi an' the kanengro."

"Have you some kushti land, brother?"

"When the gorgio ain't about."

"Tacho pal."

So the conversation would go. A good lurcher, whatever her breeding, is silent and shy.

Pheasants, those gaudy foreigners, have long been the quarry

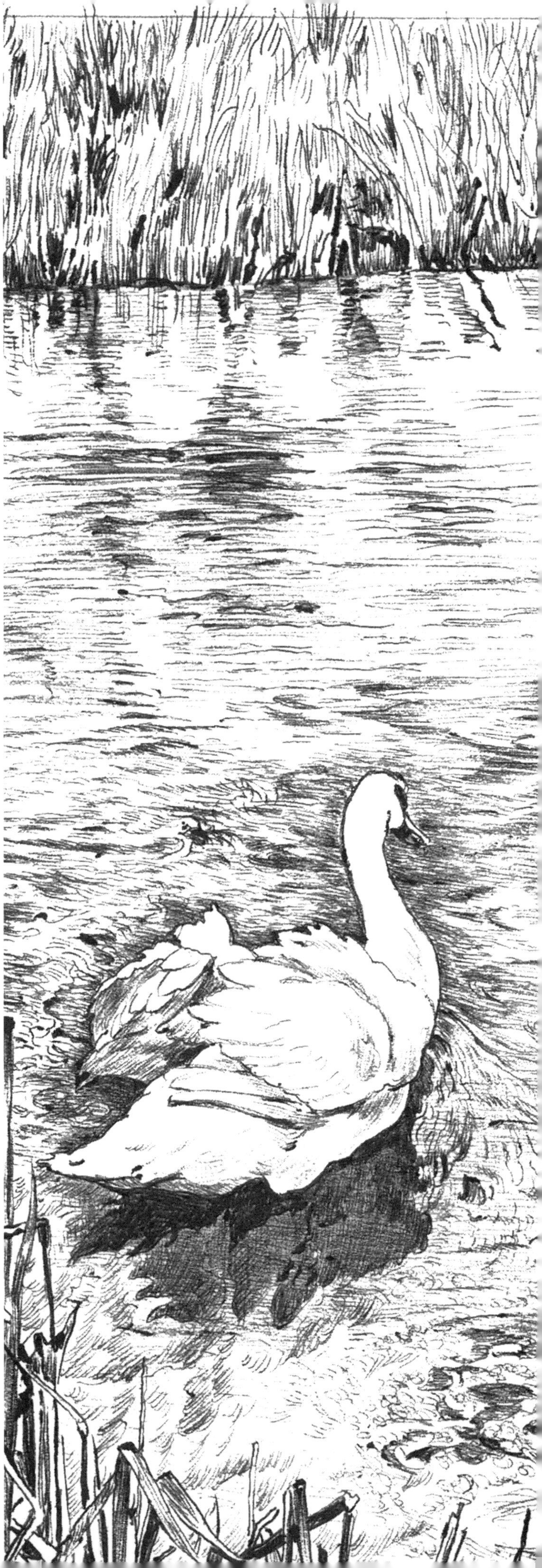

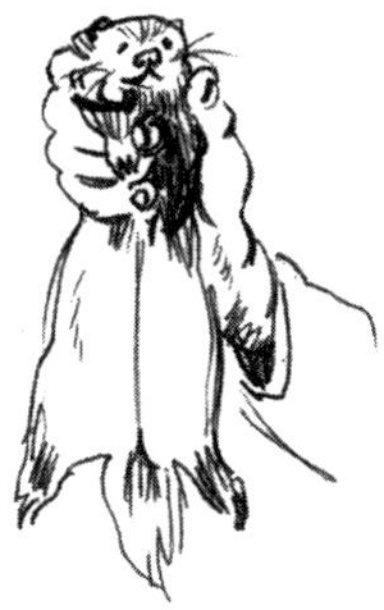

A ferret

of poachers. Indeed our Great Aunt Millie still 'took' a pheasant or two in the woods when she was over eighty years old. One day, she told us boys, she passed the owner of these game preserves when returning from such a foray and stopped to say a word. Only when she got back to her cottage did she realise that the long tail-feathers of the cock Ring-neck had been sticking out of the top of her bag!

My first shot was with an old single-barrel twelve-bore. I remember it, for surprise and indignation was the result. Below the wooded bank the fields began and I stopped by an old hedgerow oak to climb the two rails beside the tree. Halfway over I froze for there, not ten yards distant, sat a rabbit. Very, very slowly I moved back behind the tree and with trembling fingers cocked the gun. I fired and was knocked over by the recoil. Smoke drifted away as I looked expectantly, anxiously—but the field was empty, no rabbit.

The other way to approach the Manor was by following the lane which led to the entrance to the house. There were well-trimmed holly hedges on either side and grass verges then, on the right, a large tythe barn built in timber standing on a sarsen stone base, its roof of thatch well maintained. Beyond it a driveway led to wrought-iron gates set in a high lime-stone wall. Through the gates you could see the most beautiful of manor houses, low and many-gabled. Stone drip-sills and mullions set in golden walls dressed in lichens. Many chimneys and dormers gave an intricate skyline to its roof of stone tiles..

Here, before the gates of the manor, the hounds met to draw Great Wood. What a view of Old England! Fine horses, clipped out and fit, the riders in red coats and toppers, the farmers in more workman-like black. The Duke in the livery of blue and buff astride the chestnut gelding Limerick, and the hunt servants in green. Near the holly hedge two boys, full of suppressed excitement, one on Tamerisk, a roan mare, the other on Sir Ivor a 15 hands bay cob with hogged mane and a docked tail.

Soon the gossiping crowds lined up, leaving a gap as the hounds moved off to the sound of the horn. Horsemen and ladies side-saddle stream behind, followed by people on foot. Beyond the railway line lies Great Wood, and as we approached, jays in the bushes screeched out their harsh alarm as hounds and field arrived. The Major, hunting the dog pack, disappeared into the wood with the hounds all around his horse. The field waited. Soon a whimper was heard, then more sound as hounds race to the scent. One is seen to cross a ride then, thrusting back into cover, more voices are heard. A first whip on his grey came galloping up the hill. "Gone away, gone away". The boys waited for the Field Master's signal, the cob alert and the roan fidgeting and sweating a little. Hounds broke out of the wood and all was movement. We joined in the stampede, the roan mare bursting forward was hard to hold, such is her excitement at the hunt.

So the hours go past. Hounds lost the scent, but when cast forward picked it up again. While hedges and fences were jumped by the bold riders, others made for the gates as they tried to stay with the hounds. We lost them some time later and decided to make our way home, but looked forward to another day out with the hounds.

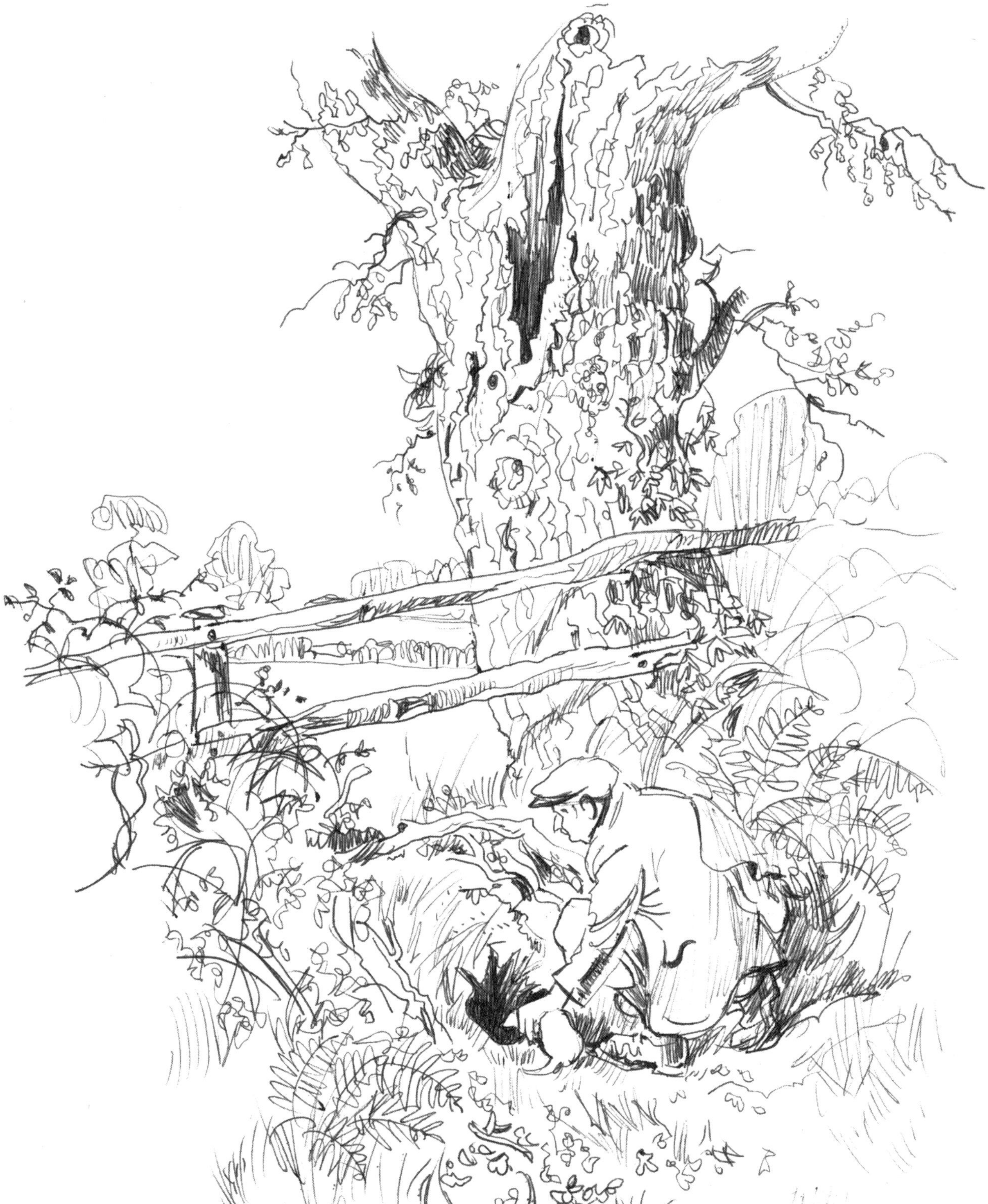

Ferreting

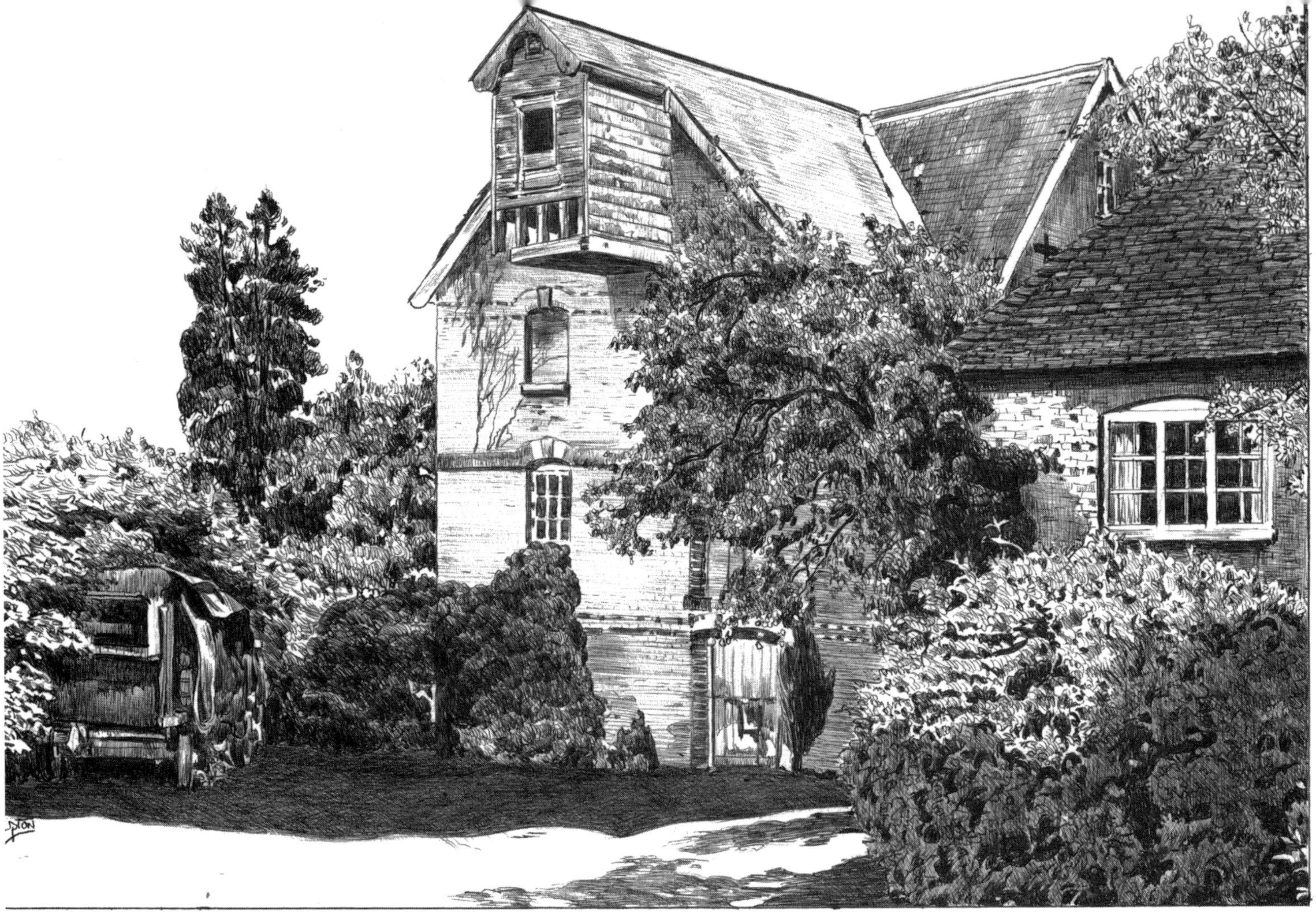

The Mill

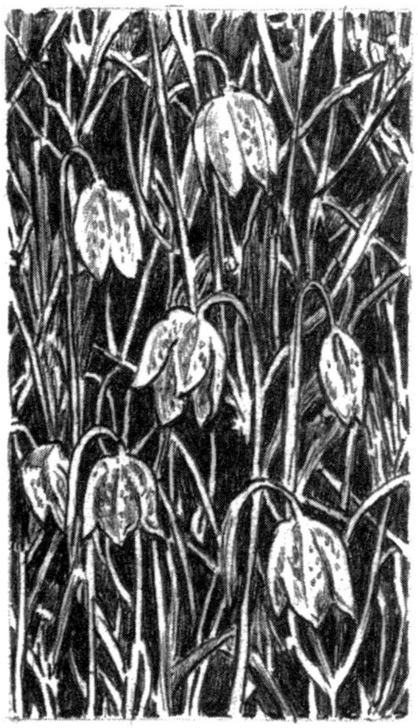

I don't remember the miller, but I do recollect the mill near Stanford End. Today, from the lane one sees neglect; the mill and the threshing machine or drum in its yard are both relics, no longer living. The old overshot wheel is gone, the sluices rotten and the water talks no more. Go over the hump bridge, as we did as boys, and walk through the meadow of buttercups, cowslips and, in season, masses of snake's head fritillaries. Butterflies and damselflies are everywhere and grasshoppers jump as your feet brush through the grasses. Near the end of the meadows you come to the mill pool behind a high bank, still reflective and shrouded in lilies. There is some white water at the grill, but silence, for no longer is there the thunder and vibration of the big wheel running, churning. Cross the narrow wooden plank over the sluice, with a green-slimed brick wall below and walk down the sloping bank to the pool below where the water-run spends itself in a gentle flow beneath the alders, a canopy of green, dappled by sunlight.

No longer does the miller appear at his door, and come into the yard where once came wagons, loaded with sacks of corn.

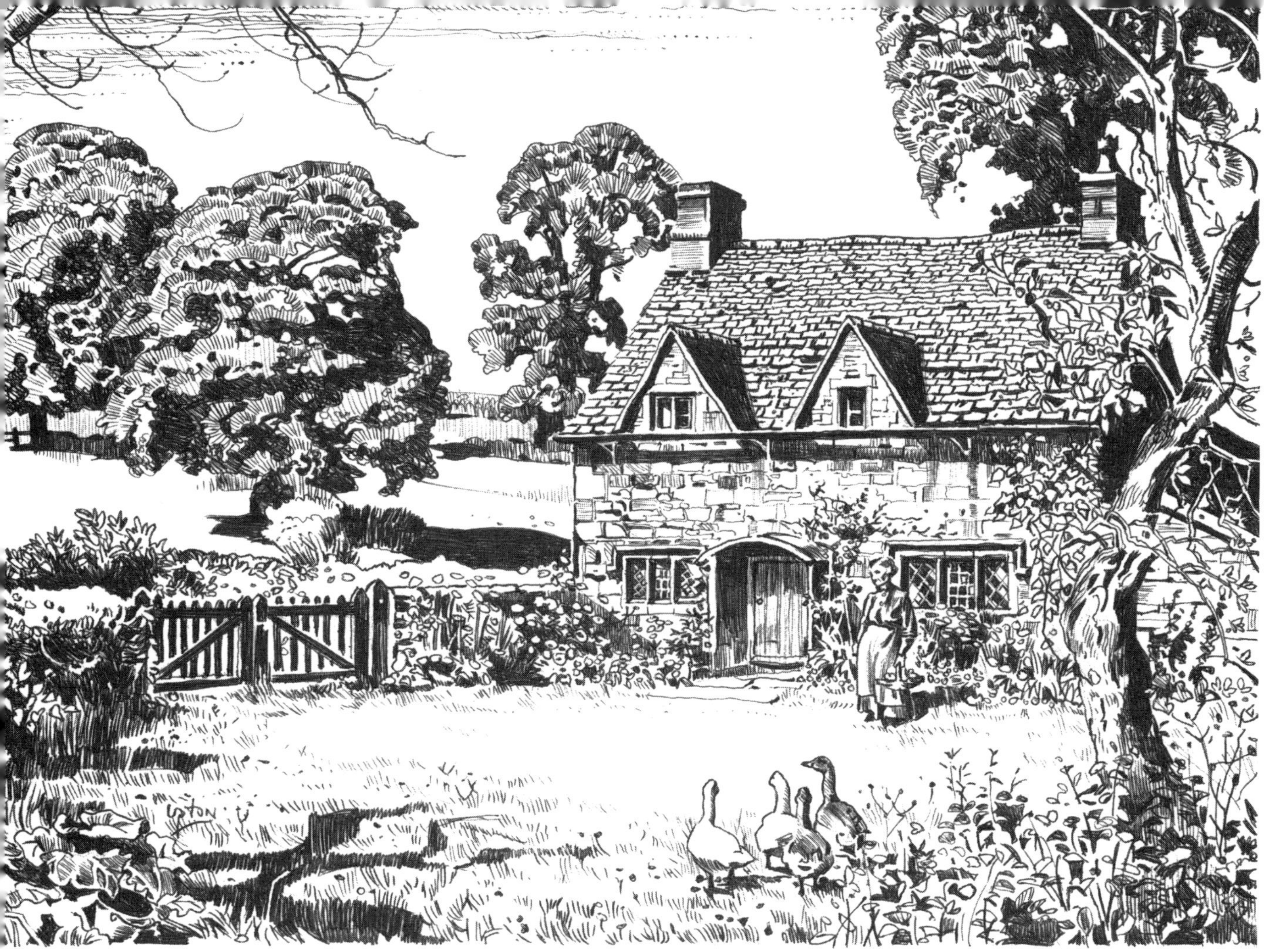

Cherry Orchard

Halfway up the deer park, a small lane came to a stop by tall deer gates and a little cottage where an old lady lived alone. She rarely moved far from her home now, except in the warm days of summer. Sometimes we would come upon her as she searched the hedgerows and woodlands for berries and wild plants. A little soul, bent double and dressed in faded black, but for a poke bonnet and white apron.

Shyly she would say a word or two, as if to converse was now an effort in her loneliness, yet she displayed a quiet dignity and gentleness. Often she would sit outside her door, still busy with one job or another, for her old hands were rarely idle; her only companion a big tabby cat.

The cottage seemed to radiate tranquillity and contentment as if it were at peace with the world. Built of Cotswold stone, mellowed with the years. Rosettes of houseleek, pennywort and yellow stonecrop had invaded the stone tiles on the roof, where busy wagtails bobbed and raced about the ridge.

Its small walled garden ran riot with blossom, visited by bees and later there was the fruit harvest to look forward to. Among the leaves and boughs all manner of small birds, twinks and nettle creepers chirruped in constant harmony from morn to night when the ghost-like barn owl glided silently hunting for voles.

Whenever we went that way and came to the infant stream which flowed past the garden wall, we would pause at her garden gate. We were also shy, but often had an errand to fulfil, for we came bearing a basket of little gifts of food from the neighbouring farmer's wife.

Yet we also longed to enter the little parlour. So, lifting the latch to the garden gate, we went up to the open door. Quietly she would greet us and thank us for the gifts and remind us to be sure to thank the mistress for her kindness.

Too soon it would be time to leave the enchanting cottage and, as we said goodbye, in our basket would be some sweets for us, or honey-comb from her bees, and a little gift of lace which she had made.

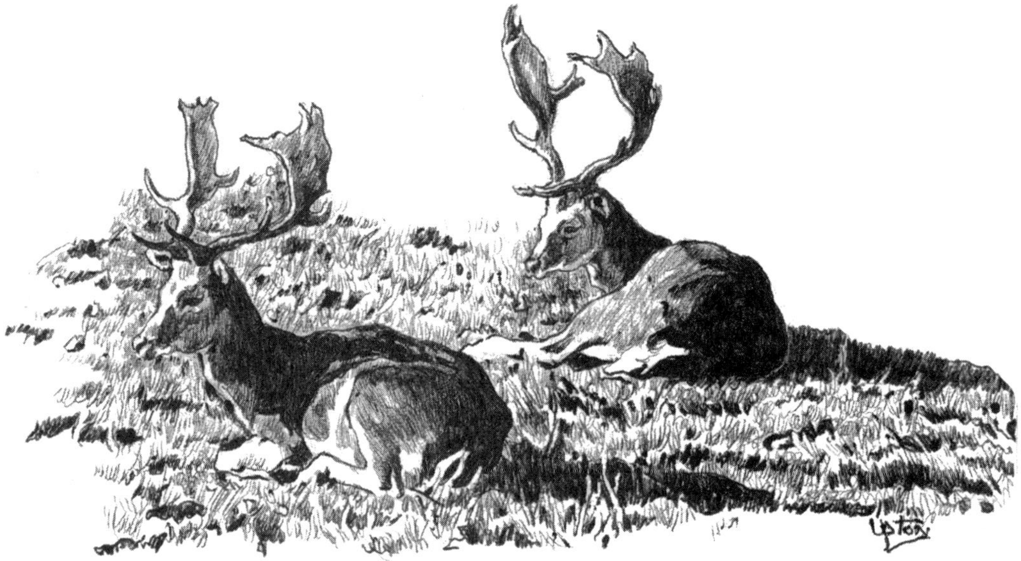

Countrymen All

The Farmer

IN THE OLD room, the soft light of the spring afternoon just touched the heavy sideboard with its many silver cups and trophies. The grandfather clock in the hall wheezed out the half hour and the old farmer in the armchair by the fire stirred and relit his pipe.

Soon he took up again the telling of his story, a remarkable life that had started almost a century ago. In that quiet room his gentle voice spoke so vividly of times past that it was as if it was only yesterday that he had taken over his father's acres. Now at 94, still farming in the same village where his family had lived since before Queen Elizabeth I, he can rightly be proud of his heritage. I can only tell it as I heard it from this grand old farmer who still describes himself as 'a bit of a rebel'.

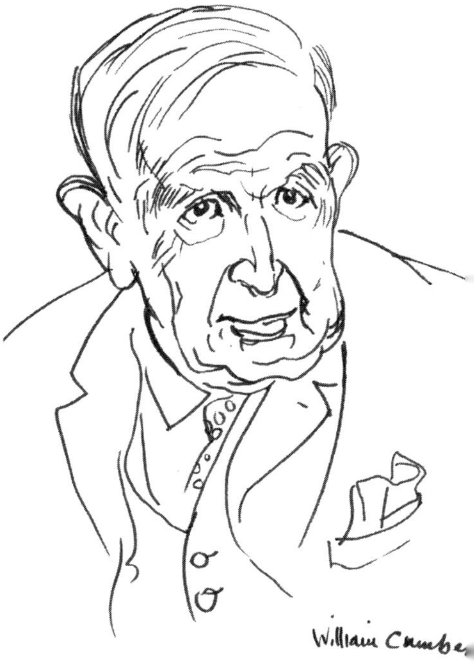

Mr Cumber

He took over his father's farms in 1904, the same year that he married. Eight years later he had taken on a further 1,372 acres on £8,000 capital so that by 1913 he was farming 3,000 acres in four counties. He also owned his own Fowler steam engines and cable plough tackle. 1910 was a year he remembered well for the summer was so wet that all the corn was laid. They had to harvest it with sickles and one of the men he employed that year was still working for him until a few years ago. In 1911 he started milk recording, then a new idea, and has continued to do so ever since.

At that time he had six carters with fourteen horses, most of the ploughing being done in those days with a single-furrow plough, but he had two teams of three drawing two-furrow ploughs.

He smiles as he tells of a conversation he had, when paying his men, with the old carter who worked his last team of horses. He who came in 1910 and worked for nearly fifty years on the farm, 'Boss', he said, 'Oi han't earnt this yer money'. 'But it's yours, that's what you're entitled to,' replied the farmer. 'Now, look yer Gov'nor, how much did us'ave tew plough en a day, cum dirty weather or foine in they old days?' 'An acre a day whatever the weather,' the farmer replied. 'Roight; now'ow much does oi plough these days? Well, oill tell yew, Boss. It do take oi, an they tew ol horses, three days tew plough an acre now. You see, oi baint be worth this your money, snow you!'

Shire horses were of course his real love and most of the cups on the mahogany sideboard were won by horses of his breeding. The first pedigree mare was bought in 1902. Then in 1913 he moved the stud to Wiltshire, under John Slorah, the stud groom who died in 1970 just three years off a hundred.

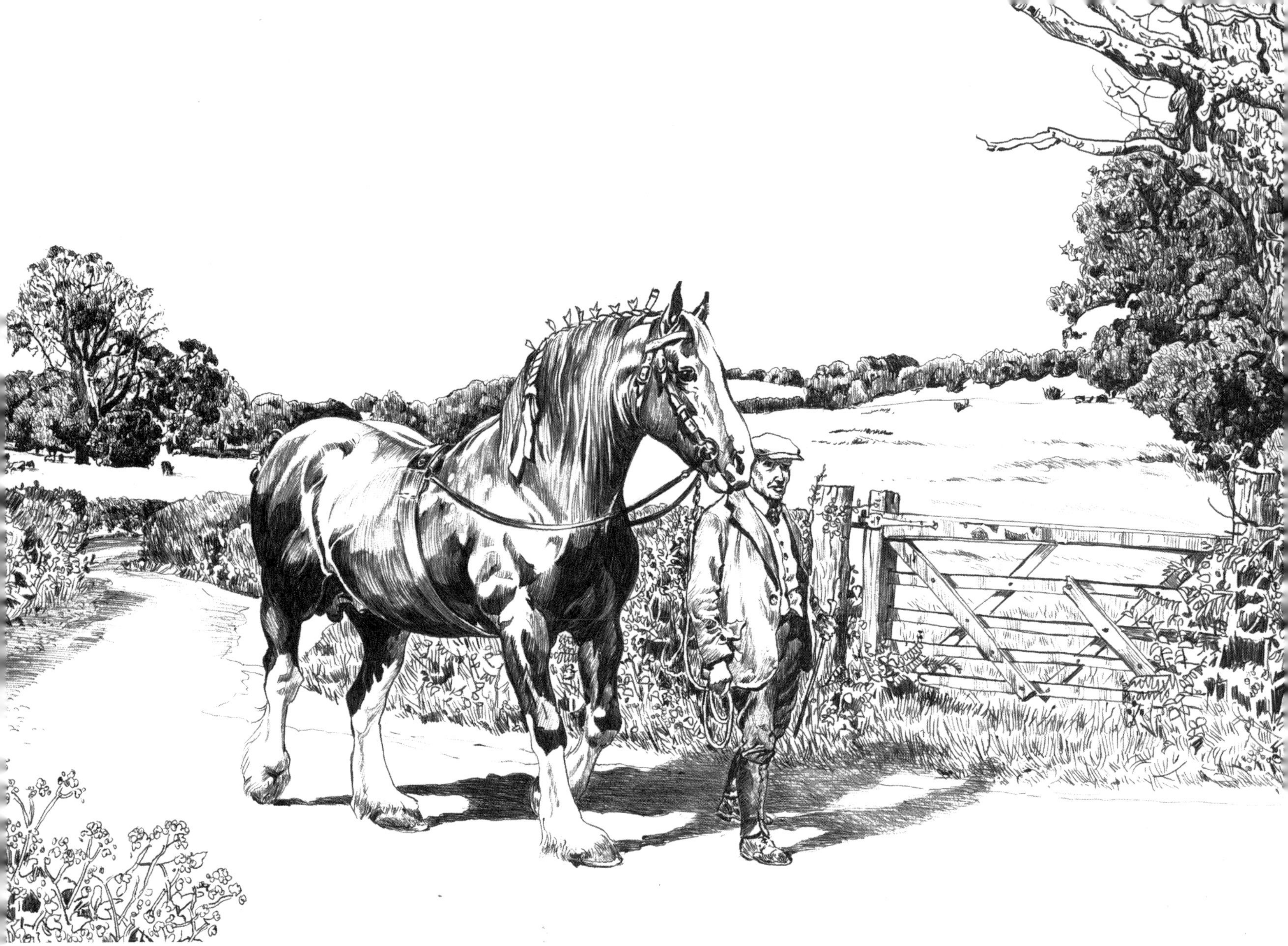

The Shire Stallion

The Agricultural Show held annually at Islington was in those days one of the most important horse shows in the country and many were the prizes won there and brought home to the farm.

By 1936, the stud had seventy-two Shire stallions, an enormous number, many of them being 'walked' throughout the country, from Anglesey to East Anglia in the covering season. Each Autumn he would buy in about twenty colt foals, by his own stallions; perhaps only three would eventually be kept as future stallions, and the rest would be gelded. These were broken in at three years old then sold on at six for commercial use.

There is an old photograph in the farmer's bedroom showing fifty-two of these great stallions. No more could be lined up for the picture as there were no more men available to hold them!

At the stud on the edge of the Downs all the stallions ran out at grass although this was contrary to the usual practice of those days. The fields were fenced off in paddocks of about eight acres each, and though the fences were made to keep the big horses in, they were high enough to allow the free passage of sheep beneath, so that they could graze over the whole field.

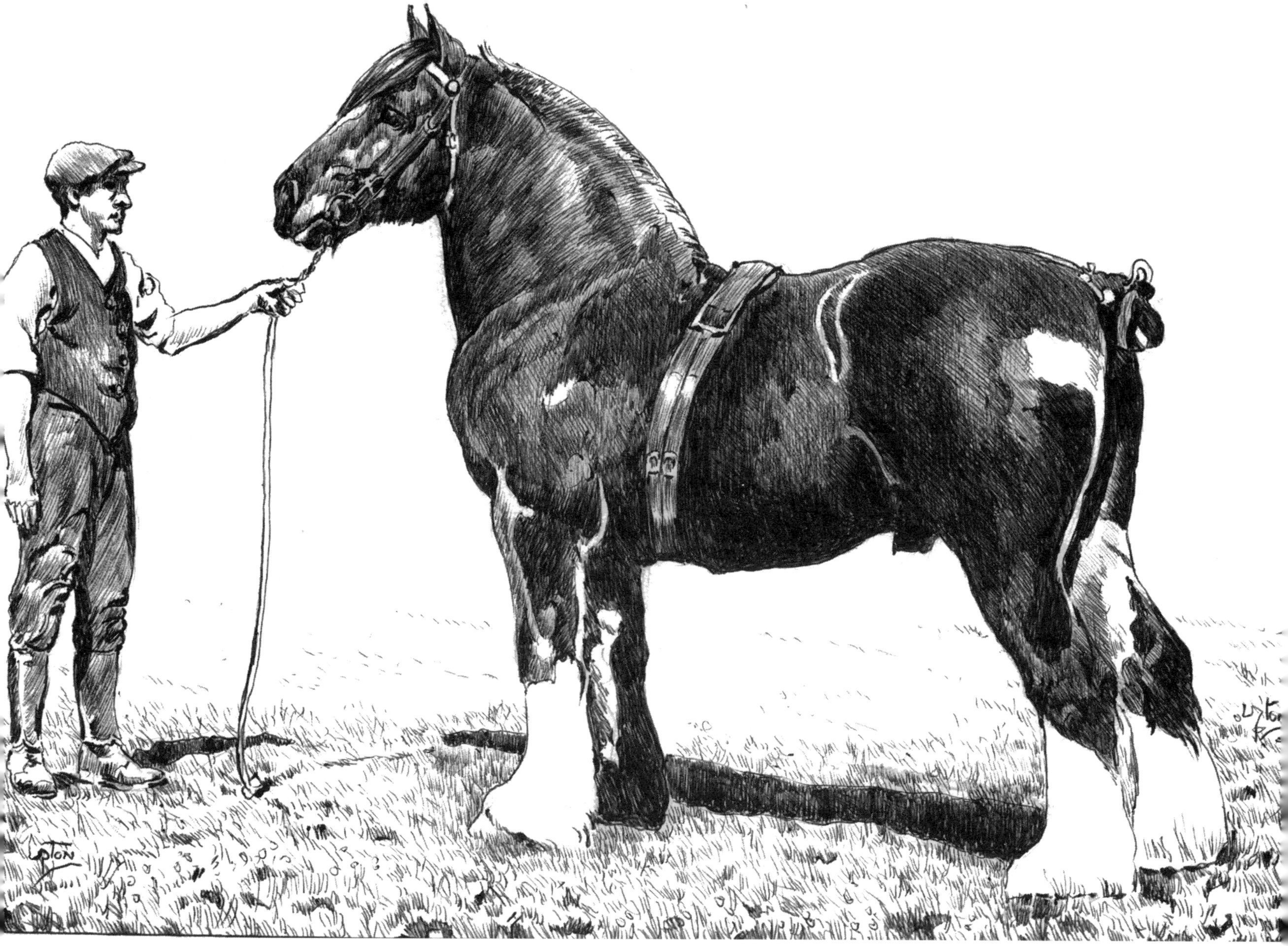

Mr Cumber's Shire Stallion

With the start of the Second World War the stud had to be severely reduced in numbers and most of the stallions were gelded and sold for £200 to £250 each. Many went to Westminster City Council to pull dust carts. Horses were in demand again as petrol was rationed. After the war he developed the stud again, though never to the pre-war scale. Now he has just one Shire left: for old times' sake.

The Shire Horse Society was fortunate to have had him as its President and as a member of Council. He in his time tried to arrange a link between the Shire and the Clydesdale Horse Societies. He even took some of his stallions to The Royal Highland Show once classes were introduced for Shires.

In answer to the question of Clydesdale blood in Shires, he firmly believed that these two breeds are of the same stock, a theory vigorously denied by many, particularly among the breeders of the Shire horses.

Such an expert has naturally been sought as a judge of horses and cattle. In this capacity he has been to all the major shows in Britain, and even abroad including Chicago in 1938—it must have been quite a journey then. He also remembers visiting the Royal Show back in 1882 as a very small boy when it was held at nearby Reading.

Not only was he known for his Shire horses, but also for Dairy Shorthorns which he also bred. Now, he has only twelve left, having gone over to 'Black and Whites' for, "We don't keep cows: cows keep us". In the 1900's most cows in Wiltshire and Berkshire were Shorthorns, especially the preferred Strawberry Roans, though they came in all colours. One silver cup of which the old farmer was particularly proud, and justifiably so, was won by Duchess Barrington 2nd, a Shorthorn of his breeding, when she won the Dairy Show Championship, the only time this had been achieved by a Shorthorn. Moreover, she gave ninety-six lbs. of milk.

In public life he has served his country well for over half a century as a member of many committees. He has made money and lost it, over twenty-eight thousand pounds in two years of depression in the 20's , but he survived when many did not. At ninety-four, he still farmed his land.

I like to remember him as on that spring afternoon, reminiscing over the years with such clarity while yet apologising for forgetting a date or two about good harvests and bad, the stock he had bred and the changes that have come in agriculture during his life. Just as I was about to leave, he got up and said, "You must meet my lad who helps on the farm". His lad was seventy years old!

So, a true yeoman and great character in whose company spending an hour or two was a rare pleasure.

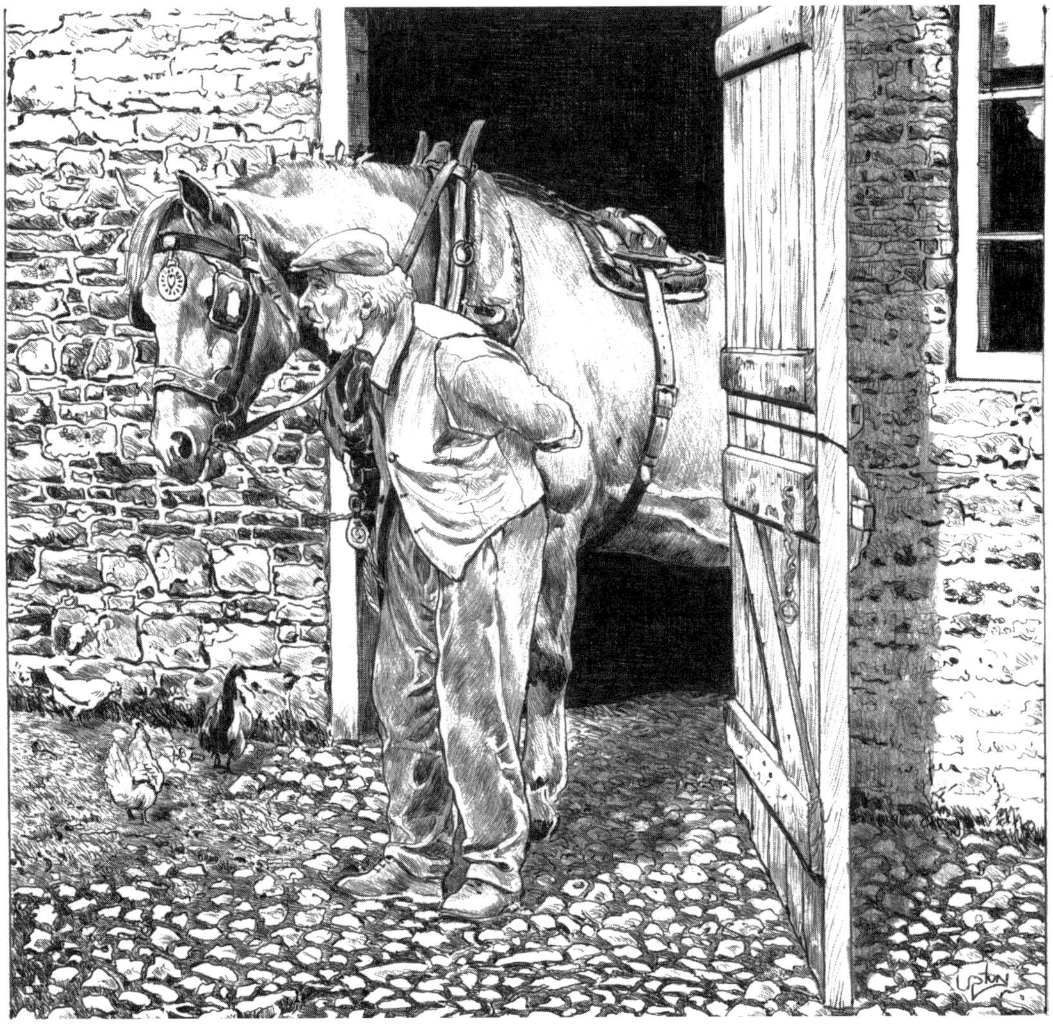

The Old Horseman

The Valley Farmer

Many of the farmers of the Vale were men whose acres were moderate compared with the big farmers on the Downs.

Mr C was typical of the Vale. He had about one hundred and eighty acres on which he kept a fine pedigree milking herd of Ayrshires and a few pigs and chickens. The rest of the land was arable producing oats and straw for the stock plus at least one field for a root crop such as turnips.

He was a regular church-goer. Every Sunday morning, dressed in his black suit with a large flower in the buttonhole, he would take his wife, the most gentle of ladies, down the farm track to the highway, past the manor gates and the timber mill, over Thunderbrook, a small stream, to the church on the hill. He was lame and getting on in years, but rosy of countenance and with three stalwart sons, all in farming.

After the church service he would be in much demand with the ladies to tell one of his stories, for he was renowned for his tales, although some of them would have shocked his good wife. Here is one I remember.

A neighbouring farmer had working for him a new lad. On market day, the governor called for the boy and told him to keep a close watch on the sow as she was due to farrow and he had to go to market. In those days it was thought necessary to pick up all the piglets as they were born and put them into a large wicker basket with a lamp to keep them warm. Then, when all were produced the litter could be put back with the sow. "Now, take care," said the farmer, "tew catch they liddle piglets quick, afore the sow do eat'em –'cos her will!" Some hours later the farmer returned and went to the pig cote. Opening the basket, he found it empty. Just then another piglet was born, "Quick, do grab he", urged the farmer, but the lad made no effort and the sow ate it. The farmer, now extremely cross, turned to the boy, "Yew gurt vool, what have yew got tew zay for yerself?" "Don't worry nuffin, Govnor," replied the boy, "that little pig have been out eight times already. He'll be out again in a minute!"

Although of the old style, he was ready to try new methods in farming, and never too old to learn. His small farm was certainly a model of neatness and good husbandry. All his fields and hedges were kept clean and trim and the gates painted white.

He found pleasure in showing us boys the farming skills, whether it was carting manure to the fields with the old Shire mare, or milking the cows. His was a good life, measured by the seasons' ebb and flow. What greater satisfaction was there then working one's own land? He was a truly contented man, with the daily round of milking. He knew each cow by name and also understood their individual ways. His world did not extend much farther then the valley, its parish life and the annual Farmers' Hunt Dinner, a great opportunity for more tales.

When going to church or to the local shops he drove a large Austin car of 1930's vintage. It was tall and high off the ground, with running boards and small windows. The big leather seats and serge lining with tassels to the blinds reminded us of a coach . He rarely travelled faster than twenty-five miles an hour, which was probably just as well for he liked to view the neighbouring farmers' fields rather than the road ahead, not that there was much traffic in those days. One day, when he was giving us boys and our mother a lift, a 'modern' shiny black motor car shot past us sounding its horn. "Well," he said reflectively, "It do look loike an'earse, all square an' shiny-like, and I do reckon e'll need one before I!"

His farm is now gone like him. It has become a golf course.

The Shepherd

In his book, *A Shepherd's Life*, first published in 1910, W H Hudson writes of the Wiltshire Downs when each valley and hill held its flock of sheep. An ever-changing formation of white on green, echoing the clouds above on this wide landscape where, except for occasional clumps of beeches, the clean line of the down meets the sky. Each flock was watched over by a shepherd and his dog, the silence broken only by skylarks on high and the toll of sheep bells.

The shepherd's life was quite a lonely one tending his flock, but at certain times of the year as the seasons progressed the flocks would be taken to the farm buildings for shearing and dipping, and there was tupping and lambing too.

On the Marlborough Downs, one large farm ran a flock of Blackface and first-cross ewes, so that jobs such as drenching or butting-out were day-long and tiring work. The sheep had to be fetched in off the downs and into pens. The dogs, hot from bringing in the sheep, would usually jump into a water-trough to cool themselves while they slaked their thirst, then they would lie in the shade of a hedge or building until called to do more work. The shepherd and some helpers, laden with bagpipe-like drenching bags, if that was what was to be the day's task, would trap each sheep against the fencing with their knees, lift its head up and squirt the liquid into the mouth of each protesting sheep.

Shearing, which took place in the Spring, was often known as the 'first crop' of the farming year. It is a back-breaking job, catching up sheep after sheep, sitting them up against your legs and clipping off the fleece cleanly without nicking the skin; a nick required recourse to the pot of Stockholm Tar which would be smeared over the wound. The sheered sheep, looking very different minus its coat, was released and galloped off to join the members of the flock already shorn.

Tupping in Gloucestershire, a new young Suffolk ram was taken out in a Land Rover to forty Clun ewes. Stopping in the field, he was let out and sat up to be daubed with red raddle on his tummy which would mark the ewes he eventually covered. While this was going on the ewes, ears forward and inquisitive came nearer—forward hussies! They gathered round expectantly, but he scurried off, then walked more slowly trying to regain his ruffled composure in the face of such odds. They rushed him and he, losing his head, leapt back into the back of the Land Rover. Eventually we got him to stay!

Lambing—how best to paint the scene? I walk up to Park Piece under the

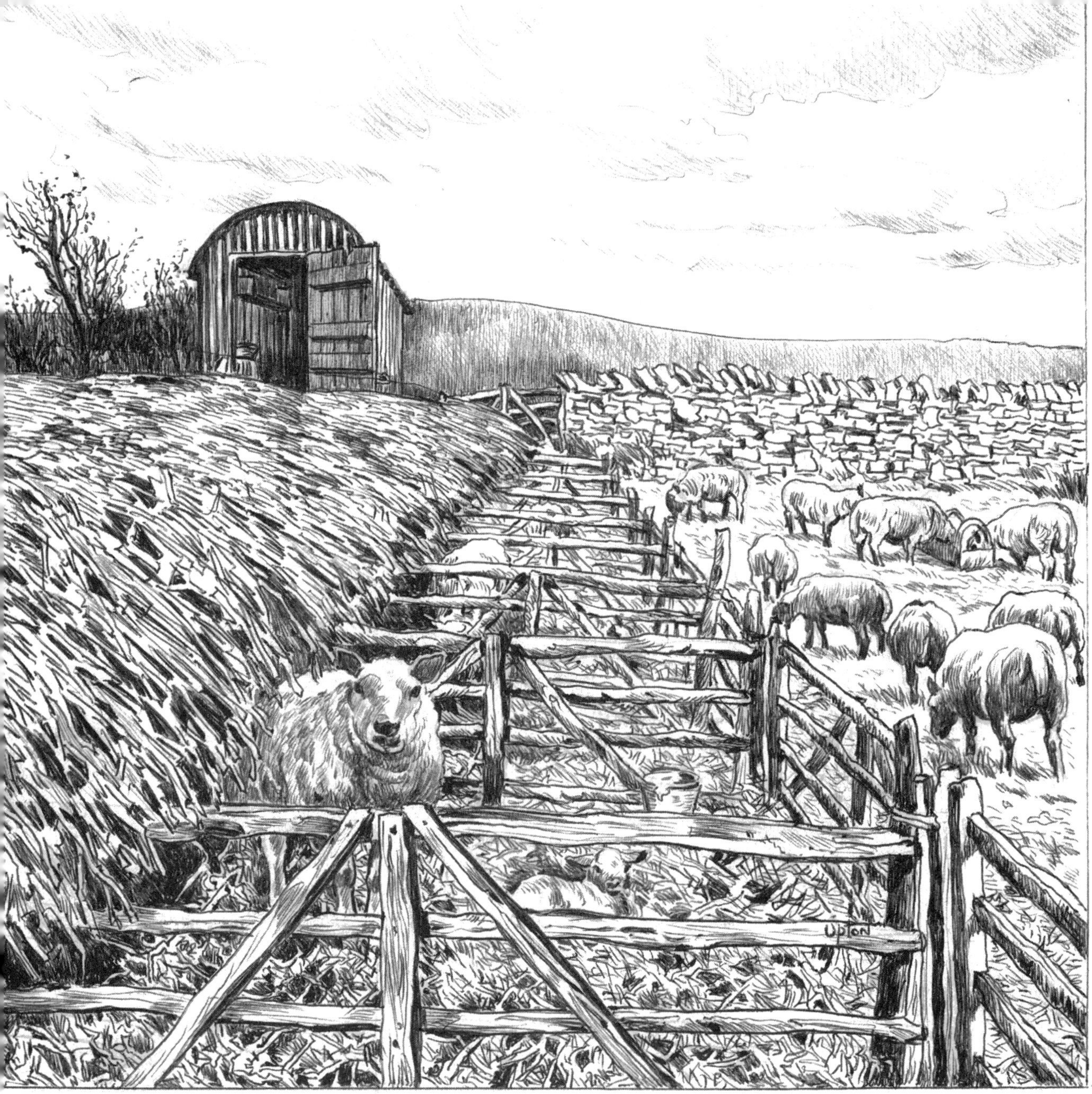

Lambing

darkening elms, and see a moving lantern glow. It is the shepherd checking the new-born lambs. Two large pens built of hurdles and thatched with straw, and along three sides smaller pens, a hurdle in length and half a hurdle in width, have been constructed with the back half under the thatched roof. Inside each pen a deep bed of straw, and a ewe whose pale amber eyes catch the lantern light as she mothers a new-born lamb or two. They with tightly curled coats and legs braced are busy wriggling and suckling, or fast asleep. In the centre of the yard of hurdles is an open area where more ewes move about, or eat at cribs full of hay. Outside the yard are the older lambs with their mothers.

"How many lambs tonight, shepherd?" He stops to pull at the ears of his dog who is loving the attention, and does not need to say, but he does, "Lambing hasn't finished yet and we don't want bad luck with the tooties". We go into his temporary abode, a wooden hut on wheels, where he stays during lambing time. He brews a cup of tea then takes up a dead lamb which he skins. It seems harsh, but one dead one may save another death, for if he has an orphan lamb he will dress it in the skin and the ewe who had the dead lamb will usually adopt the orphan, fooled by the scent of the skin. The dogs creep in to lie beside the hot stove.

I walk back home thinking of the warmth and peace and the wonder of new-born things.

This same shepherd was the first to teach me 'time and motion'. His ewes were folded on a field of turnips, and their lambs were forward fed each day. We, having been dropped off by the farm manager, trudged across 'The Plain', heavily rugged–up, he in an old army coat, for it was bitterly cold. A hundred yards short of the folds he stopped, put down his lunch bag and took off his coat. We then walked on, I somewhat puzzled.

At the pens we quickly went to work, driving in the piles and vossels (large and small sheep fencing stakes) then rolling out the netting, we tied it with binder-twine to the stakes. Overlapped gate-hurdles, held with a spring stake and twine, served as openings. We slowly worked our way up the field and, by lunch time, where were we? Right where Shep had left his lunch and coat. I had to walk back to where we had started to collect mine! Well, I had learnt something: think ahead. Sitting to the warmer side of the water bowser, out of the wind, on bales of straw we drank our cold tea and ate sandwiches of ham and cheese.

After lunch, the new pen was finished and he allowed the lambs to move onto the new piece while the ewes came up a pen and quickly settled to eating up what the lambs had left. Our last job consisted of re-rolling the wire of the vacated pen, bare now except for the shells of hollowed-out turnips. The shores were pulled and carried beyond the feeding lambs, then the rolls of wire and hurdles were moved too, carried on our backs held by stake thrust through them, all ready for the next move in a day or two.

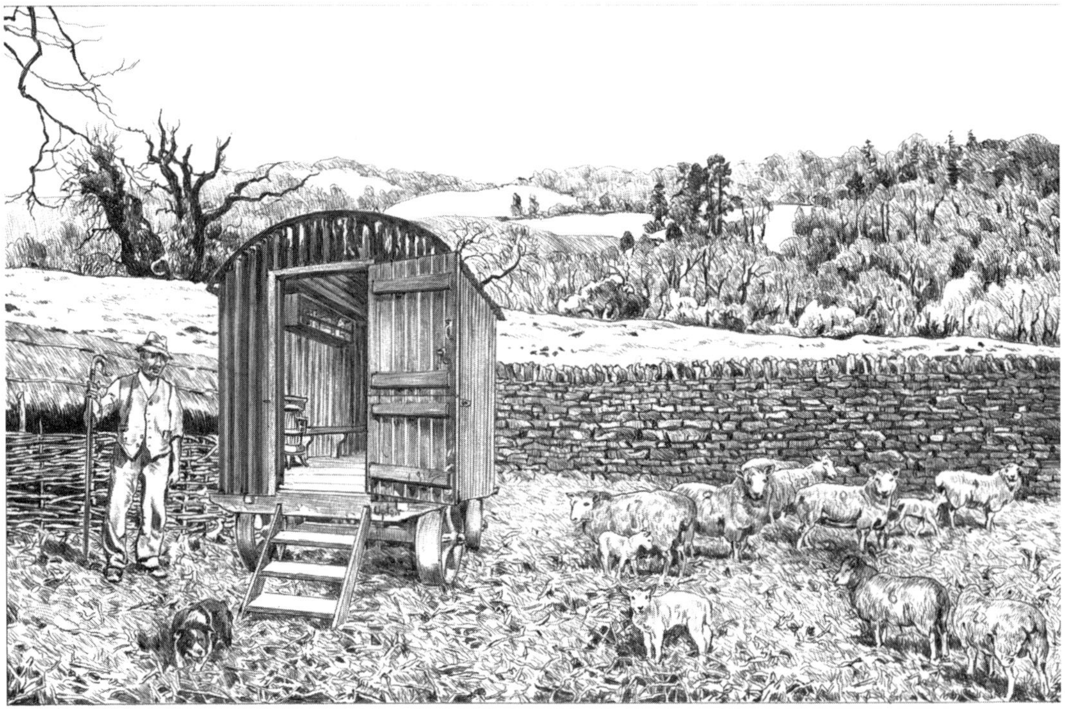

The Shepherd's Hut

The Horsemen

It's winter and still dark, except for a cold light beginning to show to the east. Into the yard come two labourers, lanterns a-glow and swinging as they pass the cart shed. The water trough is covered with a thin film of ice, the mud brittle on the cobbles underfoot.

One of the men unlatches the stable door, they enter and are greeted by a low whicker from the horses, who all cease their feeding on the hay in the rack and turn their heads. Each horse is given a short feed of rolled oats and chaff while the men skip out the beds of straw and put the clean bedding up under the manger. Then it's a quick rub down , the men meanwhile carrying on a one-way conversation with their charges, or whistle through their teeth a tuneless ditty.

As the day gets lighter, the horses are harnessed. Heavy collar lifted from wooden pegs on the wall behind each horse and slipped upside-down over lowered heads to be turned rightway-up and pushed back to their shoulders. The brass hames with their elegantly shaped tug hooks are fitted in their groove and the chain linked at the base. Two teams, or pairs, were wanted for ploughing so, except for bridle (mullin), backstrap, chain traces and plough lines, no other harness was required. The teams were led outside and the men would mount the loft steps from where they could sit sideways on the broad back of the near horse. So, down the frost-rimmed land under the trees would pass the two teams, each led horse a step or two behind the leaders, on their way to a day's work at the plough.

Within the stable meanwhile Major and Colonel, the last two horses, big bay Shire geldings were being prepared for shaft work in tandem. The names of farm horses after the Great War were often military such as Captain, Trooper and

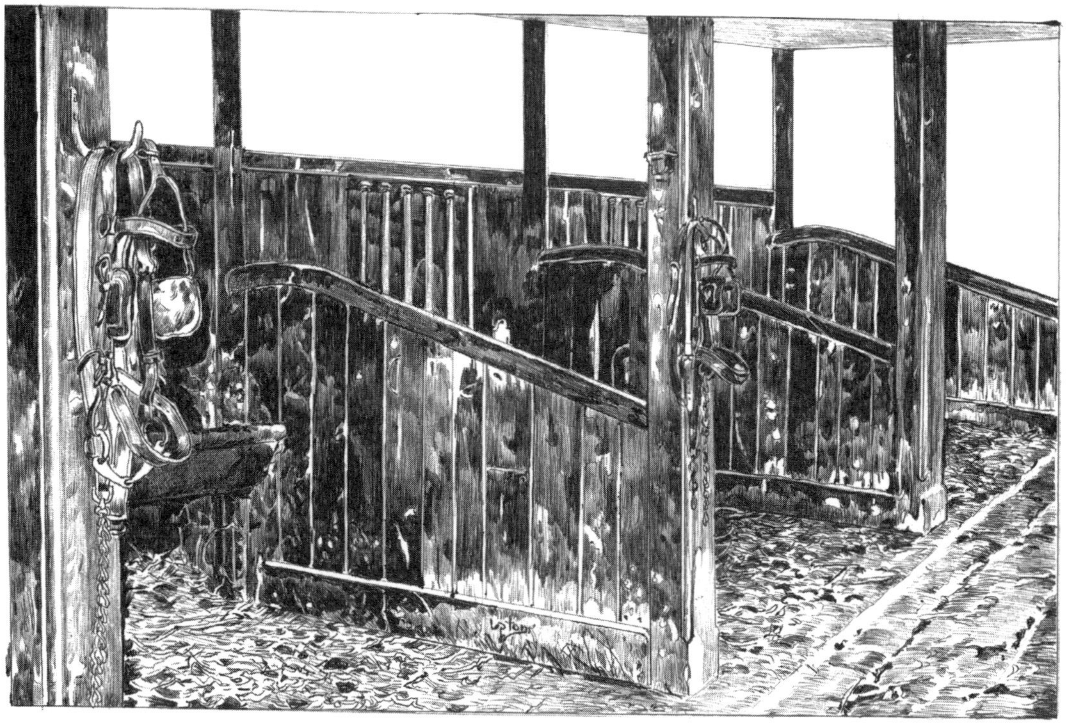

The Farm House Stables

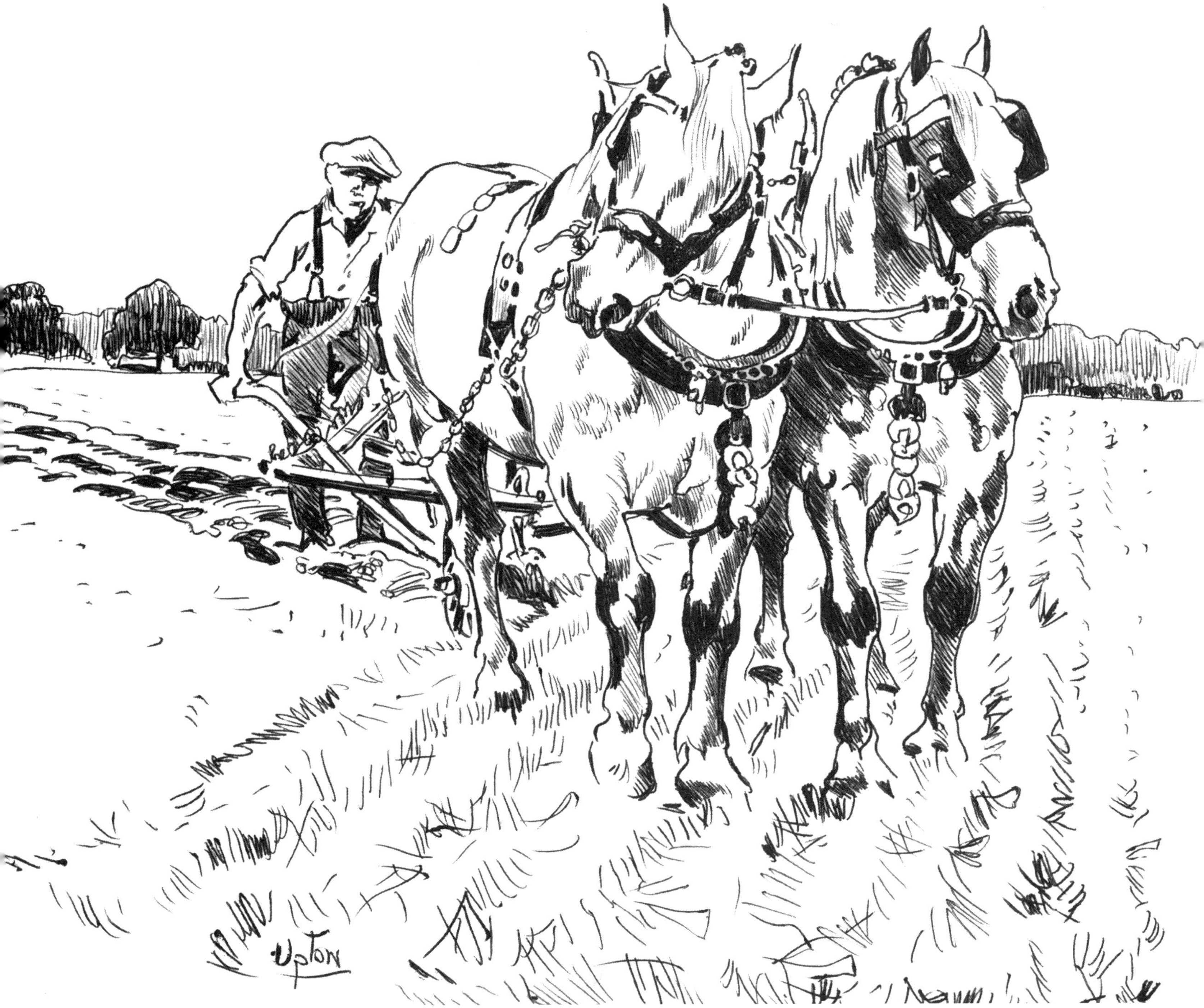

Sergeant. Today they are going to the station to collect bags of concentrate feed for the dairy herd. Ewart has even fetched out his sets of brasses on martingales and bells to add to the smartness of the turnout. Colonel is put into the shafts, and Major up front as the lead horse. Soon they are on the high road for their day out.

Up on the plain, straight sliced furrows turn the stubbles in broadening lands, as the two teams move slowly back and fore across the land. What better sight is there than horses at plough, the very essence of true husbandry! Shares cut deep and the earth rears up along the moleboards, the ploughs pass and fade in the morning mist. Birds follow the plough. At the headland, the teams come about and stop at the carter's voice, then once more steadily back across the field. They could plough about an acre a day, so they would be back at the same job for many days to come.

The Ploughing Match

On a blustery and cold November day we joined the gathering on the stubbles. For farmers and farm workers, their wives and children it was a day out to meet, talk and criticise, for it was the day of the ploughing match.

Perhaps the crowds were at their thickest around the beer tent near the gate, before making their way to where the horse teams worked slowly up and down the slope. Narrow strips of glistening furrows cut the remnants of last year's barley crop, straight and even, each entrant's bouts being appraised and compared by people in the crowd. Old ploughmen, leaning heavily on their thumb sticks would eye the lines and study the set of coulter and turnfurrow. Some nodded in approval at a team of fine black Shires, well-matched and turned out to perfection, their manes and tails dressed in straw plaits and red and green ribbons.

Purposefully and rhythmically the horses strode up the slope towards the spectators, the plough lines slack in the horseman's hands as he leaned to the right to steady the plough. At the end of the furrow, just a quiet 'wey' and the horses stopped. Carefully he would scrape the mole-board with his spud and check his setting while the team stood idle.

Then at a word and a slight tug to the near-side line, those great horses would come about, while the ploughman put his weight on the right handle of the plough so that it swivelled round on the turnfurrow. After carefully lining up his team, off they would stride again, down the slope of the field, the off-side horses appearing slightly the shorter being in the last furrow.

Further along the stubbles, a trim team of dapple grey Percherons made a pretty picture, their decorated hame-caps and ear covers with tassels a-bob adding to the image.

Another entry was a mixed pair. A black and a grey, then another team of Shires, this time greys. All along the field ploughmen called to their teams and proved their skill with straight, well-turned furrows.

At two o'clock the horse ploughing finished, after four hours of work, to await the judges' decisions. Meanwhile an auction of produce could be heard taking place in the second marquee by the gate. Near the hedge the horse teams ate their fill from feed-bags. Patiently they stood at rest, angular old heads free of their bridles, while the ploughs were man-handled into the backs of wagons and the decorations and harness carefully packed into iron-bound carters' boxes.

The senior judge then gave a short speech and awarded the prizes. The day's events over, the crowd began to drift away and the horses were driven slowly homewards. Then, as a stormy early sunset filled the westering sky, the muddied gateways and empty tents were all that was left of the Ploughing Match, save for the endless furrows above which the pewits flew.

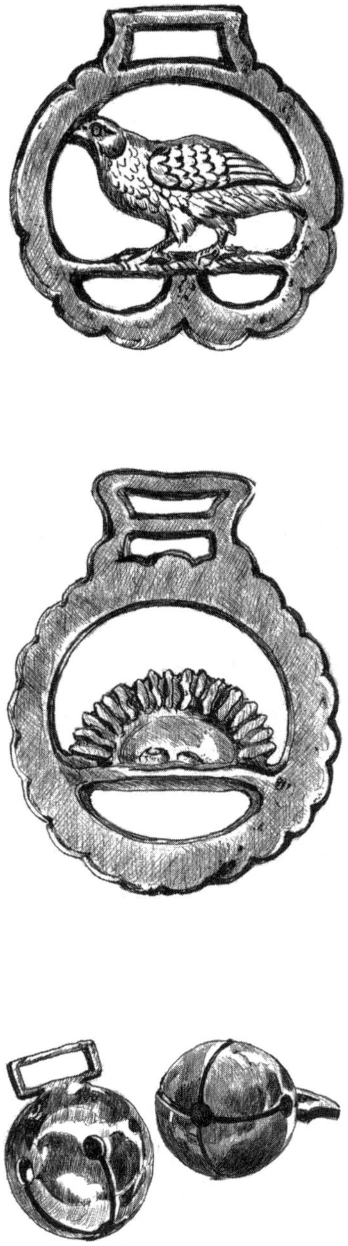

Bells and Brasses

The Blacksmith

Many a time we would go with Old Jack to take the farm horses, Diamond and Blackie, to be shod. We felt quite superior astride their broad backs, for the short journey up the hill to The Cross Keys Inn. Once there, you turned through the old archway where a century before the stage coaches had entered for a change of horses. Behind the inn there were the old stables and the blacksmith's yard which was next to a large open-fronted barn with ring-bolts in the wall. Here we slid off their backs and tied up the horses with their halter ropes.

After a short wait, the blacksmith appeared from the inn and went into his forge where we joined him for we found his place fascinating. First, however, it was back to the horses, the smith carrying his tools in a worn iron-handled box containing nails, hammer, pincers, pritchel and rasp. Setting it down, he grasps the hairy heel of the bay's near foreleg. With a click of his tongue, the mare lifts her foot and stands up on the hind leg which she had been resting. He quickly removes the old shoes by cutting the clenches and withdrawing the nails with the pincers, levering up the shoe. With hammer and buffer he cuts back the hoof and pares the wall level. He cleans up the sole and frog, cuts a groove for the claws and rasps the surface. So each foot is prepared.

Back in the forge, his fire is smouldering beneath a soot-blackened chimney, but as the great leathern bellow—the handle an old cow's horn—is worked up and down the fire begins to spark and blaze, lighting the dark interior. Beside the fire is a narrow metal tank full of water and one iron rack on which hang the tools of his trade. Like a sacrificial stone in the centre of the room, stands the anvil. Hanging round the wall, and stacked in heaps in the yard, are iron rods, old shoes, hoops,

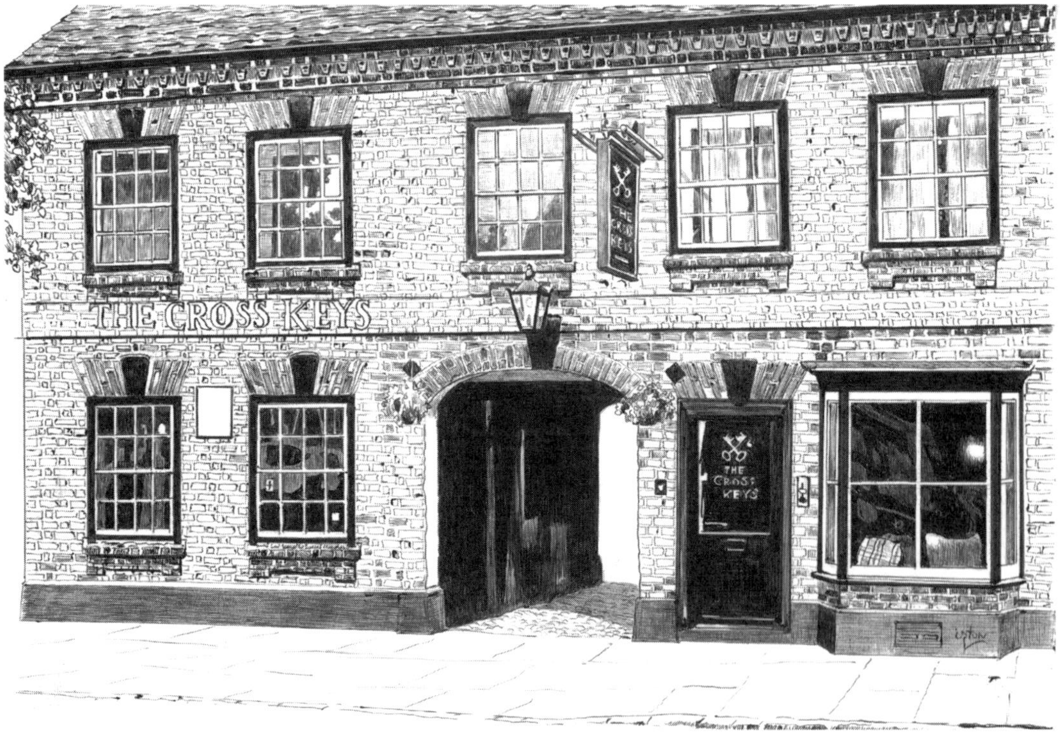

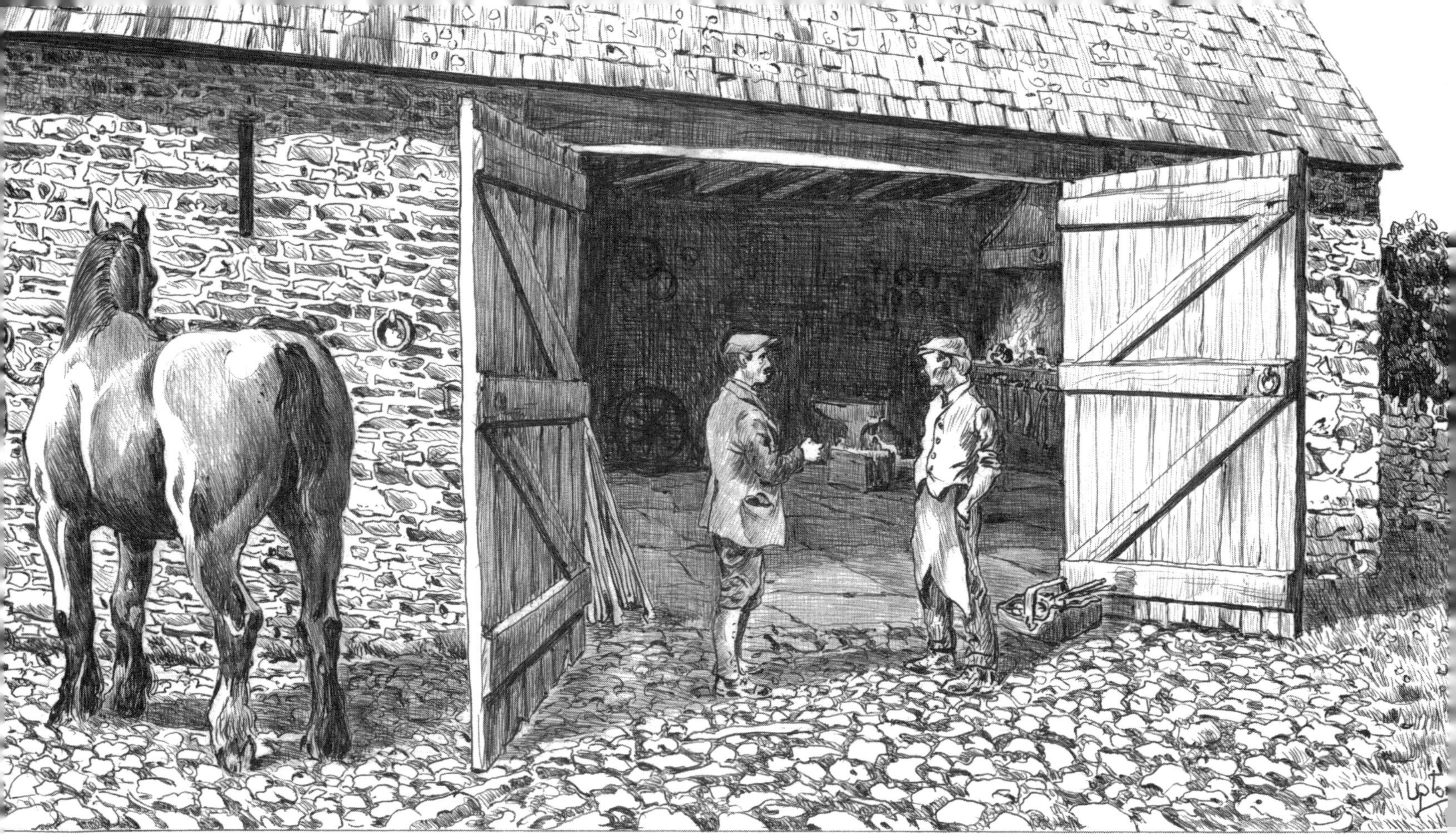

wheels and parts of agricultural machinery. The smith cuts lengths of iron and pushes them into the fire and, once red-hot, he brings one out with long-handled tongs and takes them to the anvil. Soon the forge rings to the double tap of his hammer as he shapes the glowing iron. When complete the shoe is plunged into the water tank and clouds of steam slowly disperse.

Once all the new shoes have been made, the blacksmith would disappear into the inn to return some minutes later, wiping his mouth on the back of his hand. "I sweats beer", he would explain.

Each shoe was then reheated in turn and carried out to the horse barn on his long-handled pritchel hammered into one of the nail holes. Putting down his box, he talks to the mare and picks up a foot, which he holds between his legs, tucked around his leathern apron. Against the prepared foot he then places the hot shoe, holding it firmly down with his rasp, as he hisses through his teeth and he peers each way through enveloping clouds of steam. This tells him where a little more shaping may be required. Once all four shoes have been checked, they are cooled in the water again, brought back in his box and nailed to each foot in turn. Five nails to the outside, four to the inside, starting with a double tap, they are driven home with the pincer head held against their tips. The points are then twisted off with the claw hammer, the leg is then drawn forward with the shoe resting on the apron while the clenches are hammered down, the hoof lightly rasped and a lick of oil all round.

A dog comes into the barn and chews at a piece of the frog, lying on the barn floor.

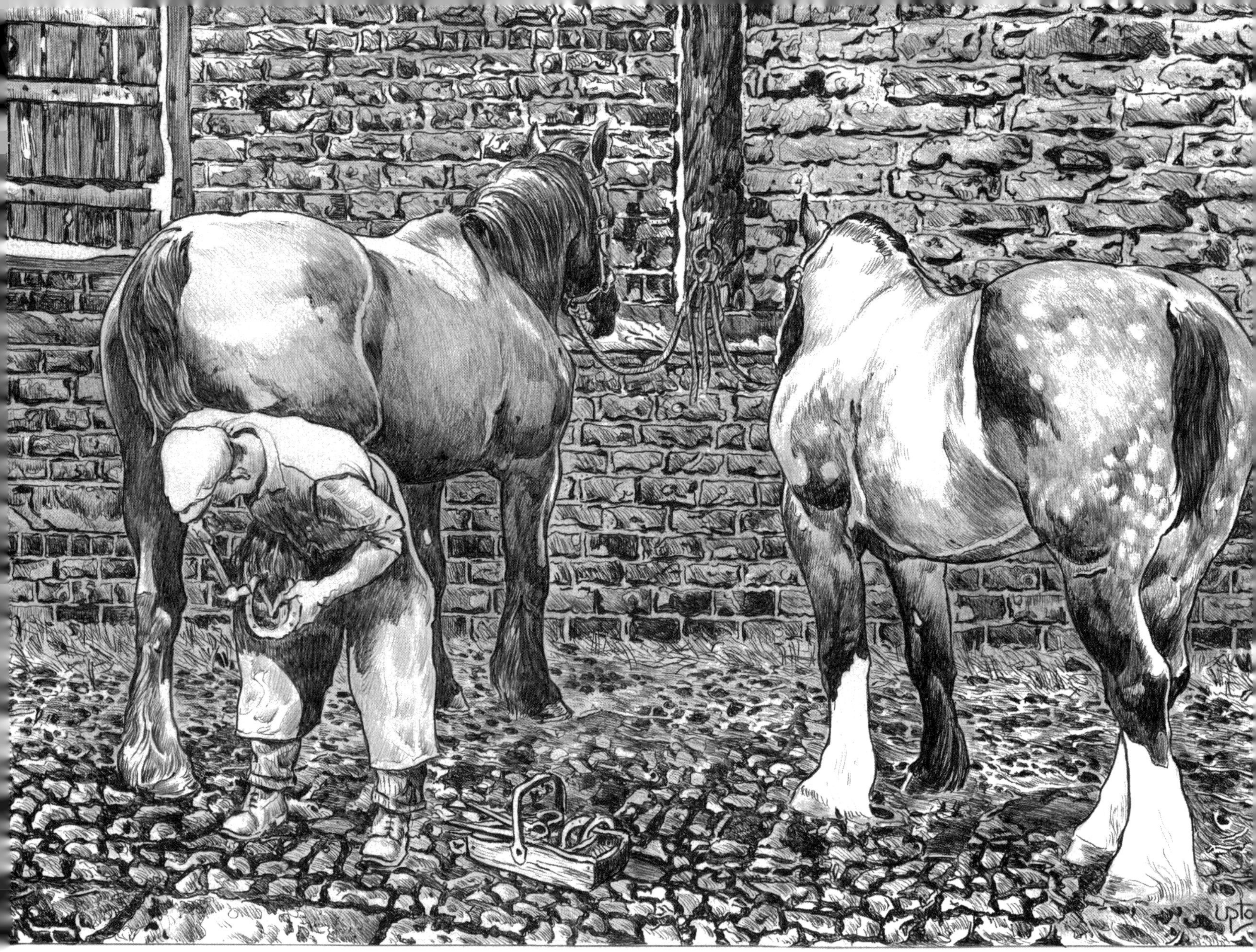

The Smithy

Later we were to take our ponies to be shod behind The Cross Keys, but eventually we had to ride some six miles to another farrier. Why? Because the forge I describe above was no longer there. Instead the yard, heaped with rusted iron,was obscured by brambles and nettles, while the rest became a car park. The blacksmith now did part-time work at a petrol station on the other side of the High Street. The age of the work horse had gone.

In those early days, the blacksmith did not only shoe horses, for that was the farrier's job, he worked in iron and made many of the tools and implements used on the farm.

The plough must be the most fundamental agricultural implement and as early 1533, Fitzherbert in his book *The Book of Husbandrie* describes the plough. He writes of its parts, the main beam, the sheath of oak which held the iron share and the plough-tayle. Also the groundwrest and the mould-board, which he calls the Sheldbrede, then just a simple flat piece of wood.

Obviously the weight of large wooden ploughs had a lot do with the choice of

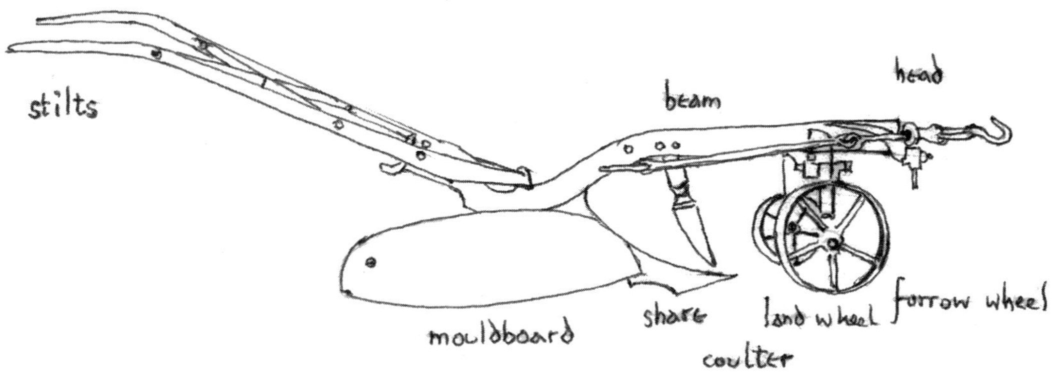

The Plough

draught animal and, in many counties, ox teams continued in use right up until the 19th century. One team of Herefords still worked the land for Lord Bathhurst in the 20th century.

By the 1800s, firms such as Ransome and Jeffries were making iron ploughs and horses took over the job of ploughing from oxen.

Many of the hand tools used about the farm, and those implements necessary for cultivations and harvesting, were made by village blacksmiths and , as with the wagon and the plough, local needs were to influence the construction. At the anvil, the blacksmith would hammer heated iron and fashion it into two-tined forks, cromes, and blades of sickles, scythes and hay knives. He also had a hand in making winnowing machines, barley hummerlers and drowels for turning straw ropes. For the wheelwright he produced the iron hoops for wheels, or strakes and chains, but by the end of he 19th century more and more of his work had gone to the large agricultural firms. He was left to repair the tools and implements brought in by the farmers and to shoe the horses.

Methods of harvesting the corn crops had changed little for hundreds of years, being cut with serrated sickles or hooks, until efforts were made to mechanise the job. John Common, a Northumberland man, invented a reaper in about 1812, but not until the 1850s did his design catch on, partly due to the antagonism of labourers concerned about loss of work.

Later a mowing machine was produced incorporating the same cutting action as the reaper, a knife moving rapidly back and fore in the cutter bar. These rattling iron inventions, including tedders and rakes, disturbed the old peace of the haysel, and were the start of the complete mechanisation of farm work and the beginning of factory farms. Today, we are but cogs in the technical wheel: the only thing that hasn't changed is the weather.

The Wheelwright

I still remember the wonderful sight of great four-wheeled wagons, loaded high with sweet-smelling hay, each pulled by a pair of Shires riding over the sunlit fields in the valley of my youth. I remember also the thatched barn, beside the mill by

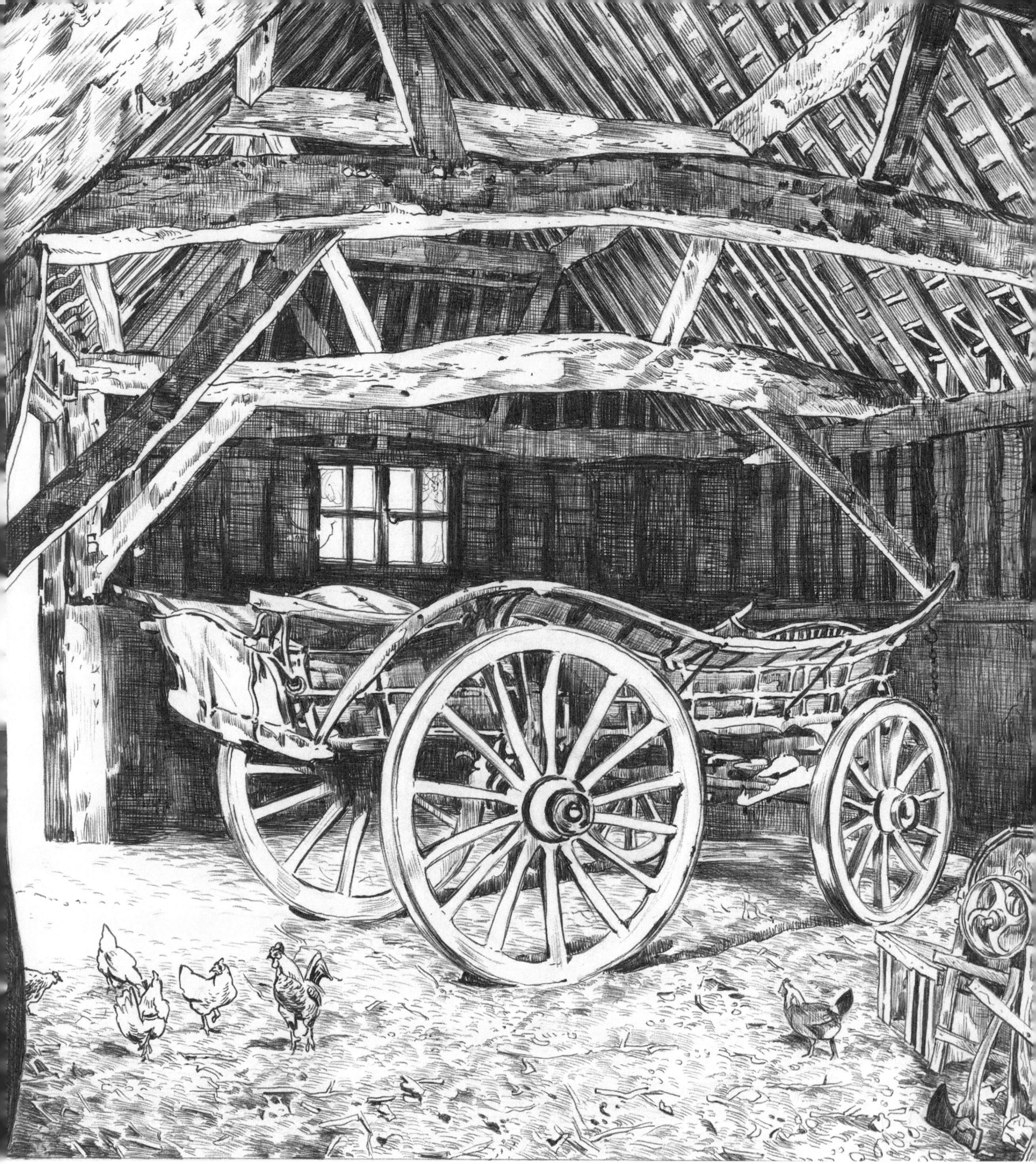

A Wiltshire hoop-rave hay wain

Thunderbrook, where a Wiltshire hoop-rave hay wain rested derelict and worm-eaten. It cast a spell a sort of spell on me in that quiet place. Its image has always remained, and I see it still, a symbol of rural pride.

The functional beauty of this old wain displayed the wheelwright's craft, built with simple tools and based on the local tradition, it had evolved through years of practical experience. For this work the wheelwright probably received little profit, yet today over one hundred years later it still stands, even if forgotten, as a monument to its village maker.

So much was I drawn to this old wain that I visited it again to do some sketches and to take its measurements. Later, I wrote my very first article, which was published in *The Young Farmers' Club Magazine*, in—I believe—1948 when I was eleven years old. So, I include it now.

> The Wiltshire Hoop-Rave Wain
>
> For many generations there have been wheelwrights in Wiltshire who have laboured most of their lives to improve their wagons, learning by experience from former errors, and of these wagons, the king of all is certainly the Wiltshire hoop-rave.
>
> This three ton haywain of Wiltshire is, alas, no longer seen in our fields with two straining Shires with corded muscles and sweating flanks being urged by tired stalwarts to draw their swaying ship over the meads to the yard where other men await to build the load onto the squat mushroom-like staddle stones.
>
> But now, if you look in the most unused corner of the crumbling stavel barn, it will be seen keeping company with broken drashels, worm-ridden cider presses, cobwebs and dust. If you have time to linger until your eyes become accustomed to the darkness, you will notice the graceful curve of the rave as it dips in the middle and rises again over the large back wheel. These curves are not only beautiful but they are very practicable and in fact most of the wagon timbers are curved. The wheels are set at the traditional width of five feet eight inches which was determined by the distance between the ruts in our chalk roads, for Macadam was as yet unheard of. The wheels are large so that the axle-bed and wheel stocks are well clear of the mud into which the chalk was churned by the passing of many wagons and the poaching of the feet of horses and cattle. The front wheels are 3' 9" across and the large back wheels 4' 9"; they also 'dish' so that the load is correctly distributed on them and if some of the paint, if all has not already disappeared, is scratched away it will be noticed that the stocks are of well-seasoned elm, the spokes of oak and the felleys of ash or oak, for a strong wheel was the pride of its maker.
>
> The out-rave dips down in the middle so that pitchers will not have to lift their loads so high, for where they would have to lift it a full 5' they now only need lift it 4' 5". The bed of the wagon also dips here and it is 1¼" narrower in the middle so that the front wheels can lock over further without damaging the sides of the wagon. As you idly run your hand over her fine old wood you will notice that there is hardly a timber in her that hasn't been shaved or chamfered, for the wheelwright, like so many of other country craftsmen of his day, was an artist and he lessened the weight of his wagon without losing any of her strength, and also added to

> her beauty. The paint will be mostly gone, but some bright yellows, reds and blues might be seen, and perhaps the remains of fancy scrolls. Her maker's name and the year of her birth may be seen faintly inscribed on her headboard.
>
> As you linger in the darkness looking at and fingering the other forgotten memories of the past, ending their days among the cobwebs on the bed of the wain, you can see a drashel with an apple-wood handle worn smooth by countless hands and its iron-hard thorn swingel, a wooden cider press which was used every fall for making cider and perry for the farmer's household and his labourers, and a cracked beer horn with the letters V A crudely carved on the side. You dream of the life of those simple labourers who used them. But, 'what a sentimental old fool I am becoming!' you say to yourself, so you clamber out into the sparkling light of day with a strange feeling of sadness for the old hoop-rave and its companions who are lost forever to the green fields of our Wiltshire countryside.

It was not until the middle of the eighteenth century, when the enclosure of land was almost complete, that the wagons began to be built for use on farms, and slowly the different types evolved according to the farmers' needs.

In the South-West the hooped-rave bow wagons were built, whereas in the Midlands and East, box wagons were constructed. In Devon, sledges were used instead as much of the terrain was unsuitable for wheeled carts and, in more remote areas, panniers carried by ponies were more practical. Many of the spindle-sided wagons of rural Surrey were built by George Sturt of The Bourne, Farnham. His story is told in his book *The Wheelwright's Shop*.

Later, as local craftsmanship died, individual characteristics were submerged by mass-production, the last remnants of wagon building being barge and boat wagons which were still being constructed in the 1940's.

For many of the smaller jobs about the farm, such as dung-spreading and root-carting, the tumbril was used. These two-wheeled carts were more easily drawn through muddy gateways in winter, even so it sometimes required a trace-horse in front of the thiller, or shaft-horse. Most tumbrils were built to tip so that loads could easily be emptied.

There is no doubt that a horse and tumbril could often get onto the land when a tractor would get hopelessly bogged down. Sometimes four feet could keep a load moving, where wheels would only spin whatever their horse-power! The horse would also walk on, when told, without a driver at the wheel, and he would not have a problem starting on a cold morning. True, he cannot work all day without a rest, but nor can a man, and the horse offers companionship of the nicest sort and works at a pace equable to both.

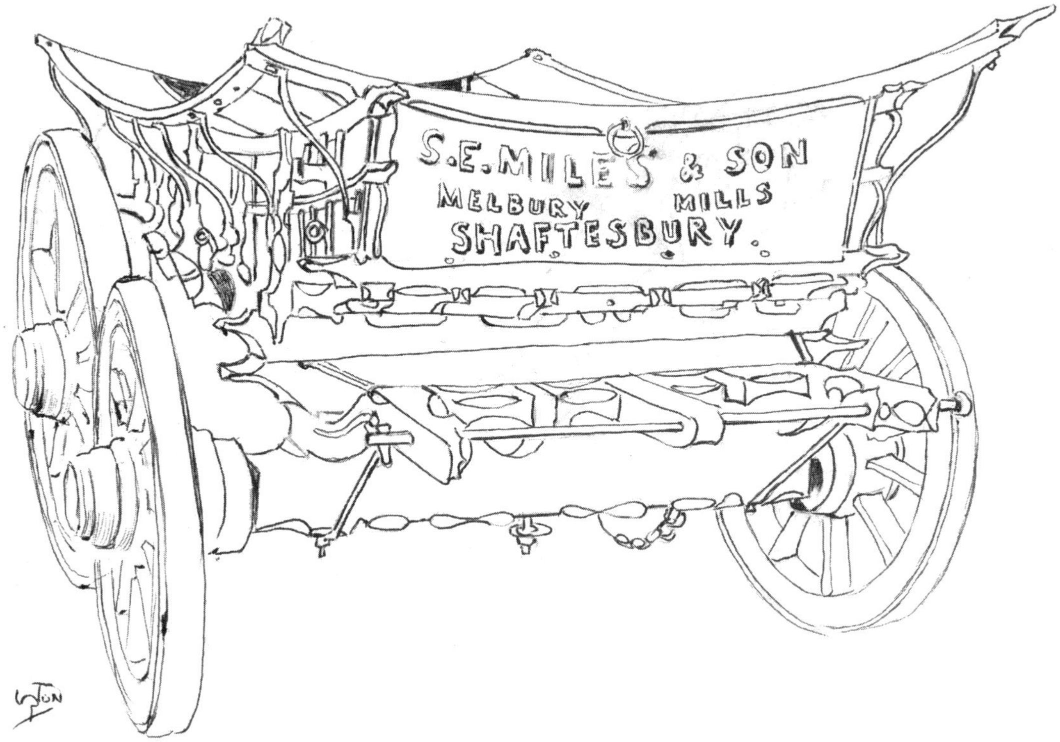

A Dorset Box Wagon

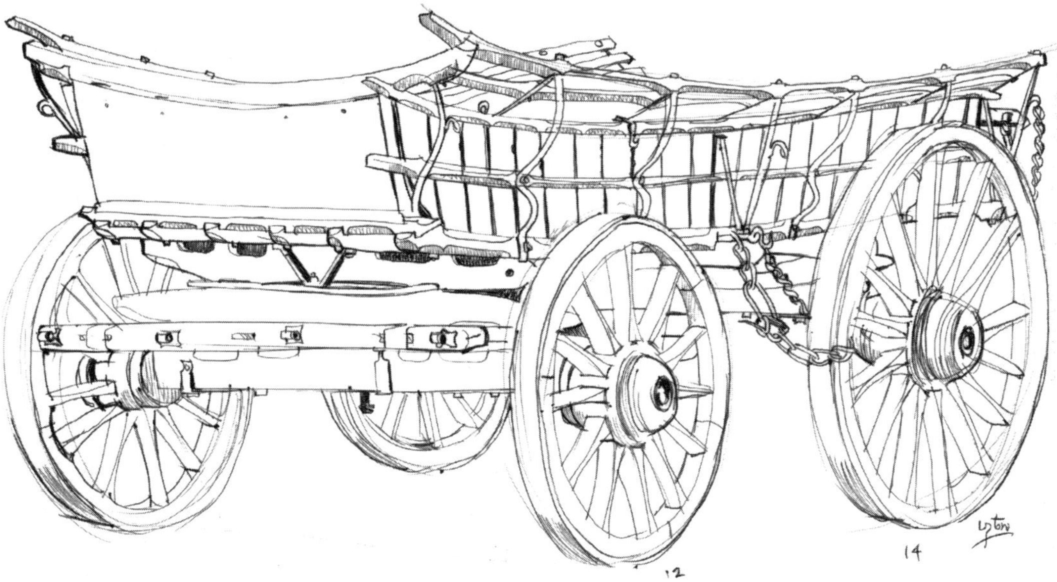

A Surrey Box Wagon

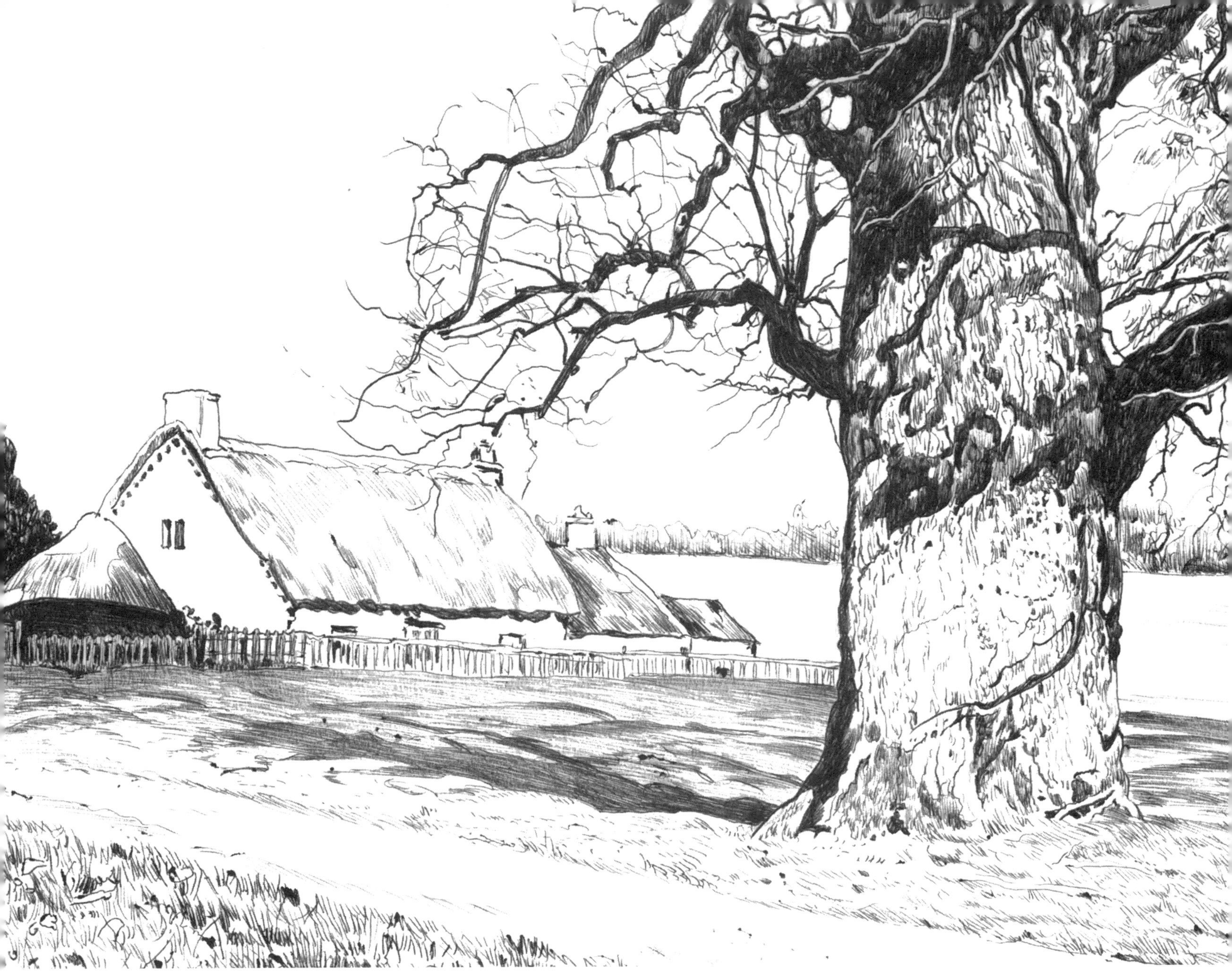

The Gamekeeper's Cottage

The Gamekeeper

Halfway up the Park near the avenue nestled the Gamekeeper's cottage. Beyond its door ran the infant Avon, and an ancient elm shadowed the buildings. The cottage stood low, and to the front the thatched roof overhung to form a continuous porch the length of the dwelling, supported on rough-cut wooden pillars. A pathway of uneven brickwork led past outbuildings to the kennels where two black labradors and a spaniel come up to the railings to greet you. The antlers of red and fallow deer were attached to the gable-end of the game larder, and around the back some ferrets' huts were fixed to the wall. In the spring, striped pheasant chicks would dart with clockwork motion back to the bantam 'mums' who were clucking in concern, trapped in their coops.

It was here that we first met the keeper who was feeding his birds. Tall and spare, he stooped a little as he came under the trees to meet us. He was dressed in faded brown tweeds, the plus-fours baggy and loose. This, we were to discover, was what he appeared to wear come snow or sunshine. His face, shaded by a fore-and-aft hat, was weather-beaten with clear blue eyes, which suggested a certain authority and contentment in his occupation.

Standing under the porch, we waited while he disappeared into his cottage, soon to return bearing a very large stuffed bird which he put down before us. It was a good example of a cock capercaillie and obviously brought out to test our knowledge and interest in wildlife, as he asked us to say what it was. This we did, although at that time we had never seen a live caper. He then told us that many people didn't know, or thought it was a Golden Eagle!

One reason for our visit was to enquire about sparrow-hawks. He right away said, "Come with me", so off we set across the Park to the woods at Hinnager. Beyond the beeches there was a good stand of tall larches and, in one of them the keeper pointed out to us signs of nesting activity against the trunk and near the top. It was decided that we should come back again in a fortnight's time when the young could possibly be about. As we walked back, a female sparrow-hawk flew towards the Slait and away over the young corn. Things looked quite positive.

Standing at the base of the tall larch, two weeks later, we looked up for the tell-tale signs of young hawks. No mute stains marked the branches, and no noise was heard of the young, nor were there distraught parents about, but there was definitely a large nest up there, so it was decided to make the climb.

Roger it was who strapped on the boot hooks—he was after all seven minutes older than me—and with a rope around his waist and the tree, he stood ready to ascend. After looking up repeatedly to assess, and perhaps to visualise the climb, he took his first steps. The bark of larches is loose so that the climbing hooks often slipped on the trunk, but using knees and arms he slowly moved upwards, with few branches barring his way. Dust and particles spiralled downward into our upturned faces. He appeared small as he got higher, clinging to the rough trunk, and the fast-moving cloudscape beyond made us watchers dizzy and our necks ache. After what seemed an age, he reached the first large branch and took a rest; but soon he resumed his upward course, now moving Tree-creeper like around the tree from branch to branch. To him, how far away we must have appeared when he looked down, and how small, for up there perspective is reversed which adds to insecurity. The nest now looked very big, only some ten feet away. Upwards he still struggled, now dubious of finding nestlings at all, as no sight or sound had rewarded him so far. Lesser larches now lay below his position, but the wind cooled his heated brow and trembled through the tree top. Slowly he eased his way around the pile of twigs, full of hope again, for this moment needed its reward. Blank: the nest was empty, not even complete. What a bitter disappointment!

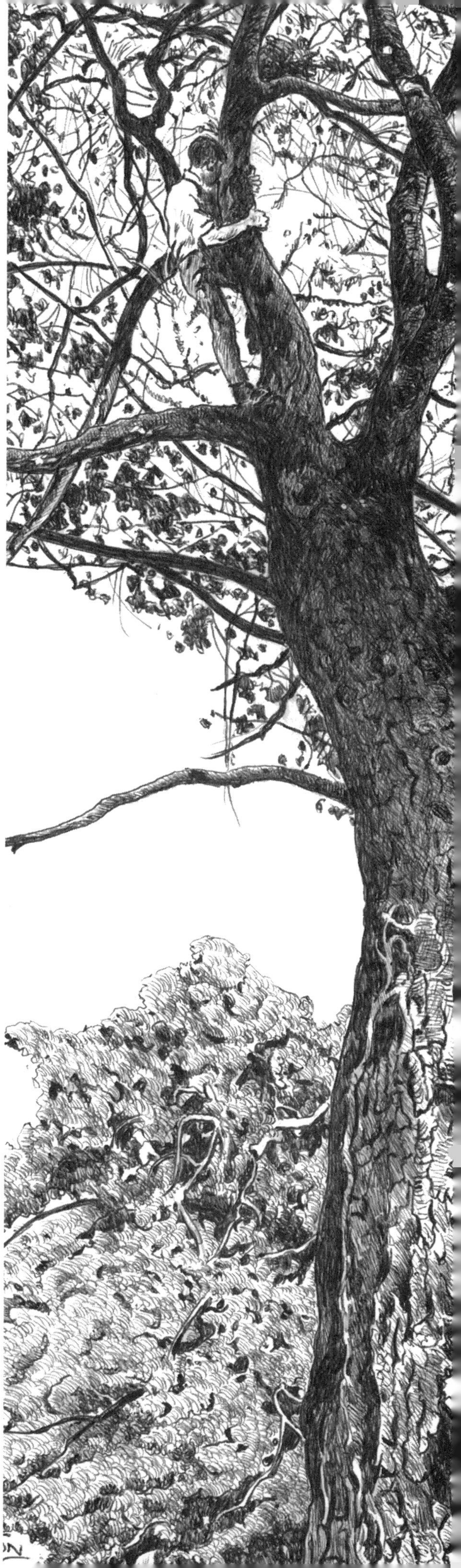

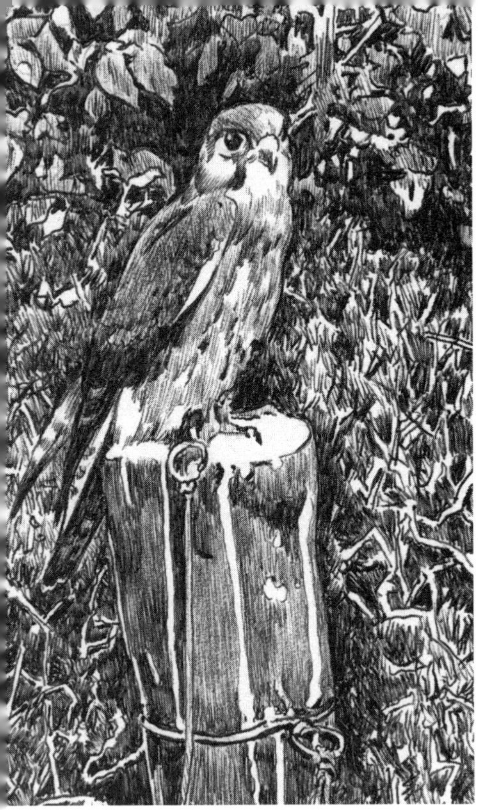

Back on the ground again, his hands dirty and scratched, his clothes full of bits of bark and leaves, yet nothing to show the others as evidence of his climb, nothing. However, I know that his feeling of anti-climax was softened by something achieved, for it had been quite a climb.

But we had no sparrow-hawk.

Sometimes things do change for the better and only a week or so later there was a knock on the door and there stood a young farmer friend who handed us a cardboard box. In this, he explained, there was a young spar-hawk, as he knew that were keen to get one. Quickly we set down the box and carefully lifted the lid: crouched back in a corner and clutching pieces of straw in its claws was a young… kestrel. The dark eyes of a member of the falcon family were watching us.

That night it slept in our bedroom.

We named the kestrel Kee and set about training her, for she was a female. Eventually, we reached the stage when we could fly her from one of us to the other on the creance, a long string, and then to the point where she was flying free. She had no interest in hunting. We caught mice for her, but it was her delight to be able to go for walks with us and our dog. She would leave the fist and race off into the air, wonderful to watch as she circled about above our heads. After a while, she would come gliding in to land on our shoulders or even on our heads. She stayed with us for a number of years, eventually to go back to the wild. About three years later we were able to purchase a goshawk from Germany.

Above: Kee the Kestrel
Right: the goshawk from Germany

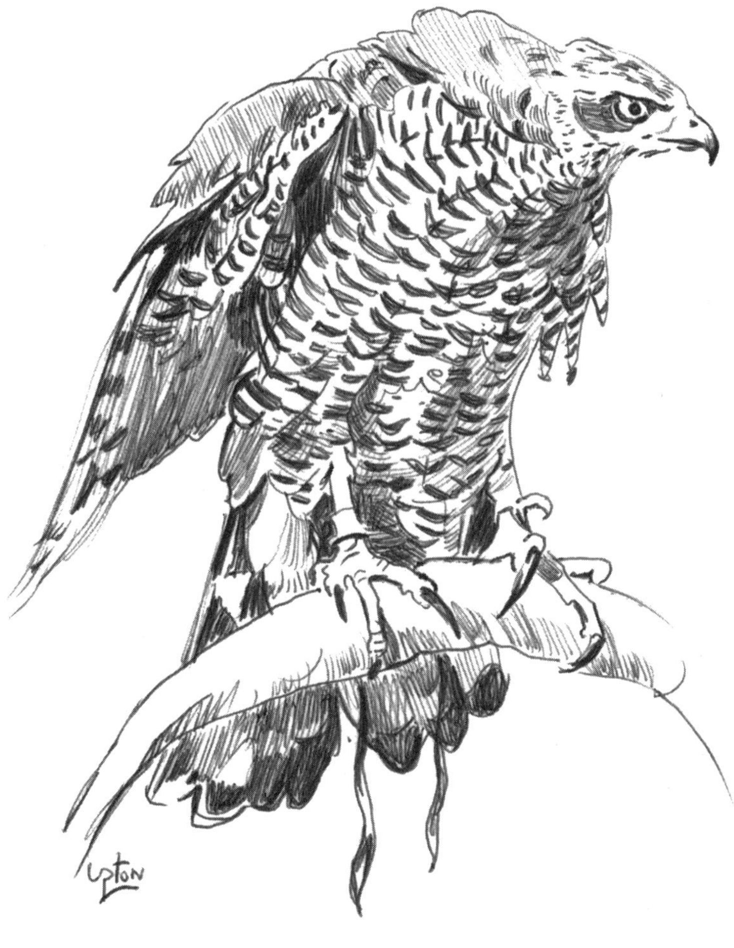

Seasons' Toil

Muck Spreading and Harrowing

As BOYS, MY brother and I earned pocket-money by muck spreading. Believe it or not, a pleasant enough and rewarding task.

Judy, the old bay mare, would be put-to in a tumbril. She would be backed up carefully between the shafts, she feeling her way with her hairy hind feet. Then she stood quietly while the shafts were lifted and the chain slung across the pad to be hooked up on the near side. The tugs on the collar were next attached and lastly the breeching.

"Walk on, Judy", then the old mare wrested into her collar and the tumbril rumbled forward on its two huge wooden wheels towards the dung heap. It was a wellington-boot, ammonia-scented job, lifting the heavy slugs on a four-tined crome. When the cart was filled, out to the field we would go, twin wheel ruts

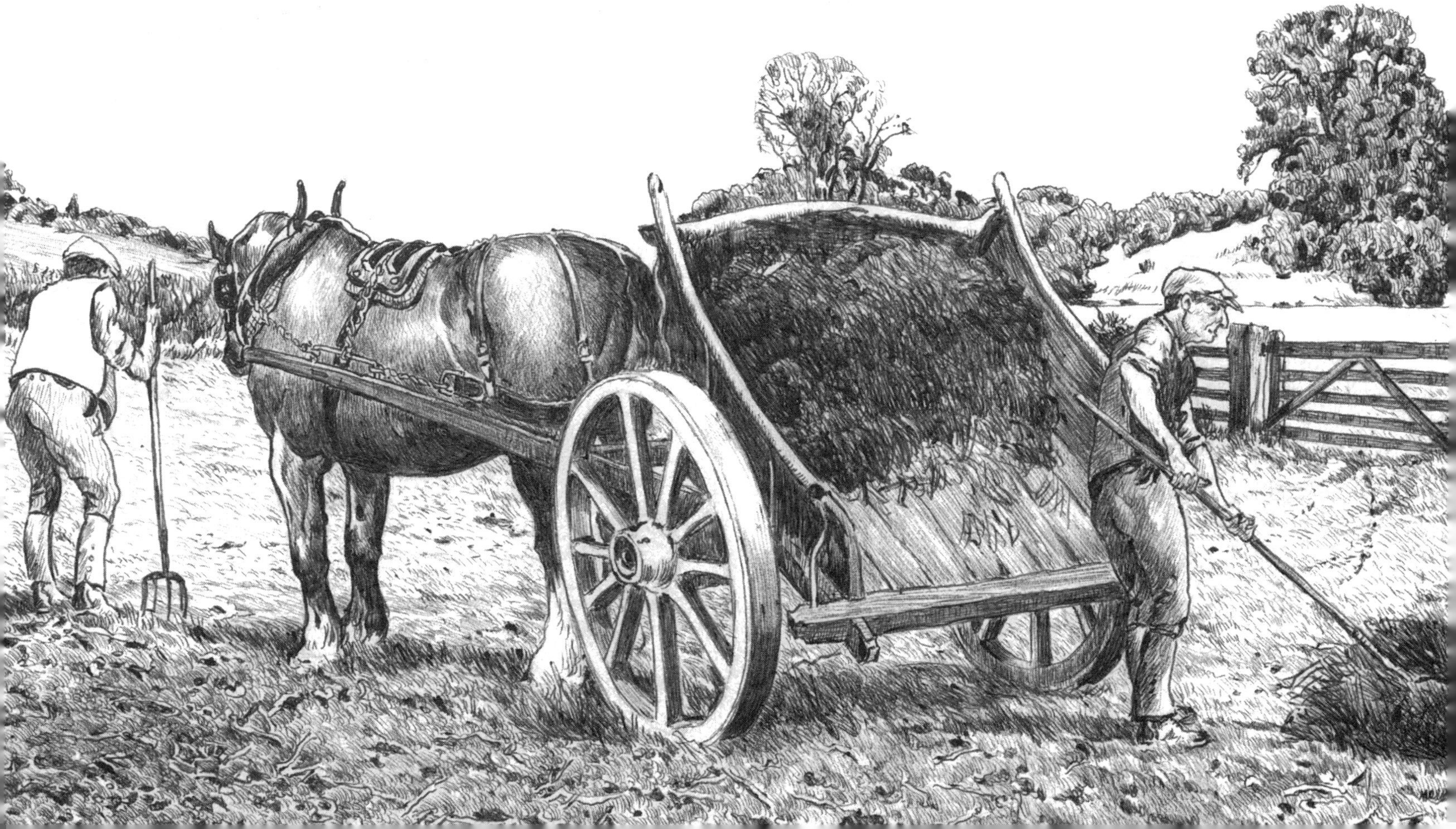

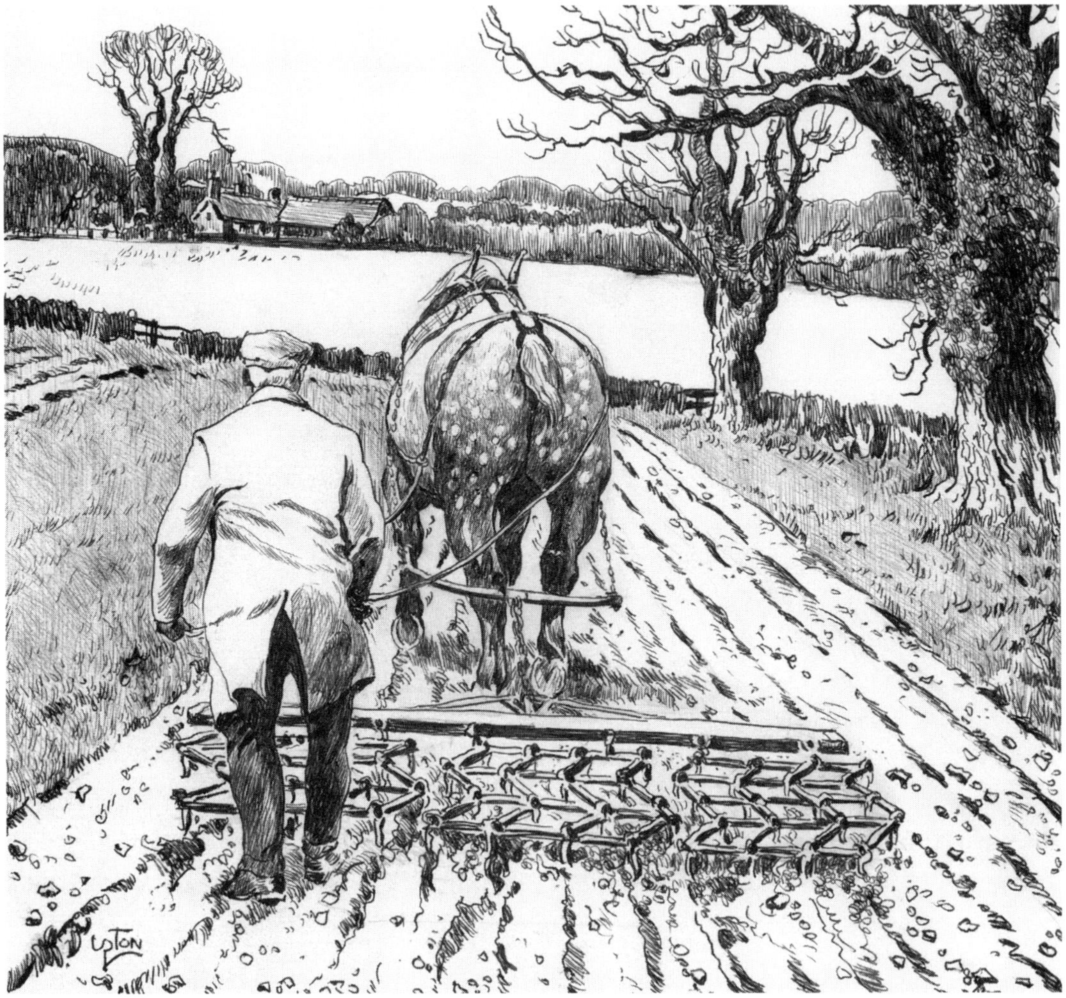

Harrowing after the Plough

radiating out from the muddy gateway, marking previous journeys. The field is partly covered with regimented piles of dung in rows. So Judy plods to the last heap and stops of her own accord: she has done this job for years.

The tail-board is dropped and a small pile of steaming muck is dragged out of the tumbril to fall in line with the other heaps. The mare walks on a few paces and stops again for the next heap, and so we slowly progress across the field until the tumbril is empty and we return to the yard. So the work goes on, taking back to the land what came from the land.

Later the heaps are spread evenly over the grass to lie, rain washed, frozen hard, snow-covered until it soaks into the soil. The field rests then,but as the days begin to lengthen, the grasses respond with strong growth for early bite or summer's crop.

In April, the chance of more pocket-money brings us boys back to the fields with Judy. Behind she drags the chain harrows to scratch the field's back. Up and down the brightening green she goes, leaving wide strips of pale green and dark green. You don't drive Judy, you walk with her and tell her what to do, though she probably knows better than you do. So, at the field's end you call "Gee-ower" and Judy turns sharp left, crossing her legs as she does so. She then straightens and comes back with the harrow's width just overlapping the last journey up. The field, when finished, looks well cared for.

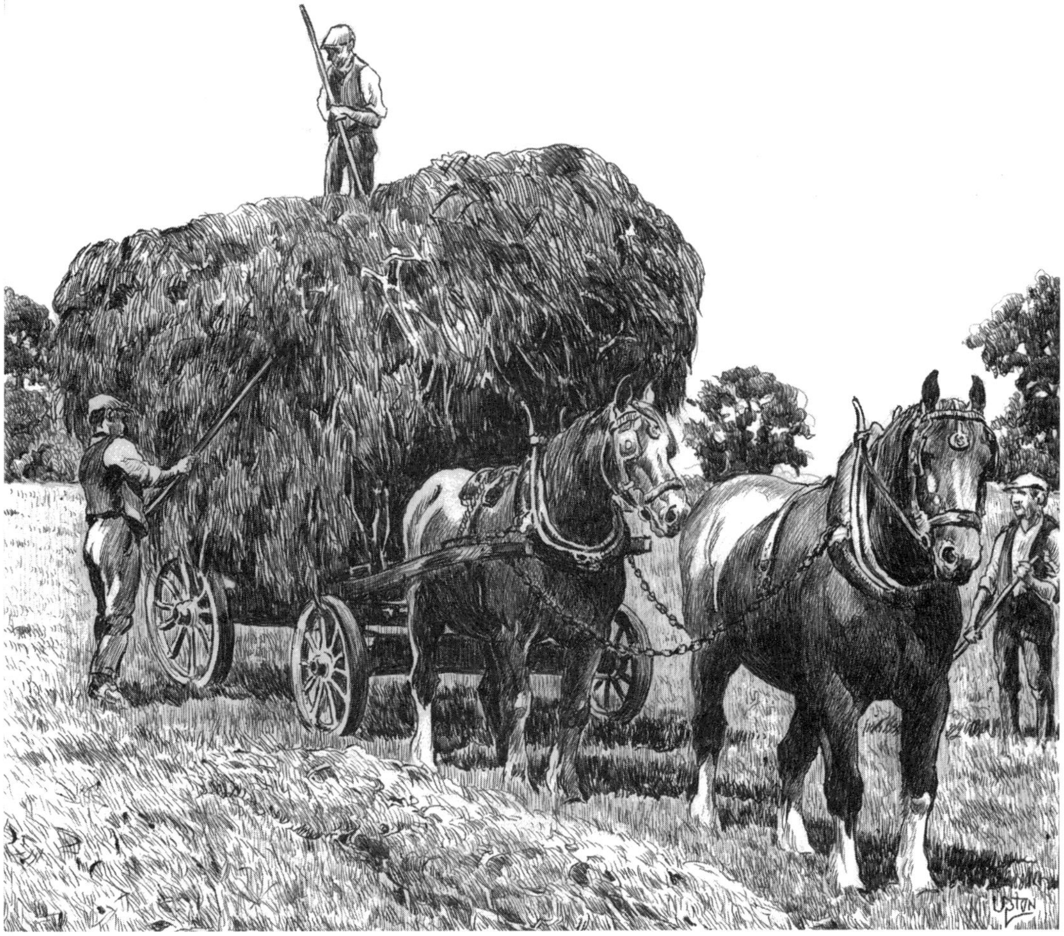

Haysel

Haysel

Getting in the summer's grass crop, brings to mind sun-warmed backs or rain-sodden fields and a worried farmer. In our youth most hay was meadow hay, mixed grasses, tall timothy, slender rye and buttercups and sorrel. In the fields of the Vale of the White Horse, grasses grew lush and rich. The fields lay waiting until, at last, the June days heralded the haysel.

The gate to the field was opened wide and a back-swath cut by scythe, a reminder of the mowing teams of an earlier age. Then through the grass-grown gateway into the field come Diamond and Blackie drawing the mowing machine. The low-slung pole between the horses is attached to their collars and their traces are fixed back to twin swingles. They stand, heads nodding against the flies, as the cutter bar is lowered and the sharp blade, carried in a grooved wooden board, is slid into place. The lines are taken up, George climbs onto the iron seat and haysel is underway; the hope being that it will stay dry for a few days.

The clatter of the machine marks the beginning of ceaseless toil to make hay while the sun shines for the winter feed. The long waving grasses fall to the vibrating blade. Anxiously, we look for partridge as the machine goes round and round and rabbits run to safety. The machine's blade is changed regularly, stops occur for field repairs and the oil-can is in constant use in an effort to keep the clattering machine on the move. Diamond snatches at tall grasses as she goes and both horses are lathered in sweat.

So the first field is laid, the swaths wilt and the clover turns brown. Next, the swaths are turned, damp and still green on the underside, now facing the sun. This work was mostly done with rakes, and was a job for the women and boys before the machine came and replaced the handwork. The sun still shines and swallows dip and slide across the sky, then rush down touching the grasses to fly beneath the horses' bellies after insects. Will it rain tonight?

So the work takes its course. Rain comes and the crop is twice turned, and the farmer frowns. The next day the weather is settled and the first wain comes through the field gate, Diamond in the shafts, Blackie in the traces. The horses are now hardened from the weeks of work, the men hardened and sunburnt too. The dried pale green swaths have been raked together in twos and the horses walk between the rows then stop. The pitchers slide their pikes forward sweeping up the hay, lift it and drop their loads on the bed of the wain. The man on the wagon places each forkful carefully building it up round the outside and onto the raves, later tying in towards the middle. As the load gets higher, more hay is placed against the ladders, always higher at the front. Diamond's quarters are by now partly hidden and in the shade. Every so often the horses are told to move on a bit, then halt again for more sweet-smelling hay to be tossed up to the wagon man who is catching it on his pike. He calls a stop, sticks in his fork, slides down the side of the load until he is hanging from the ferule, then he puts his foot onto the

Below: a Wiltshire haystack
Opposite: a West Country haystack

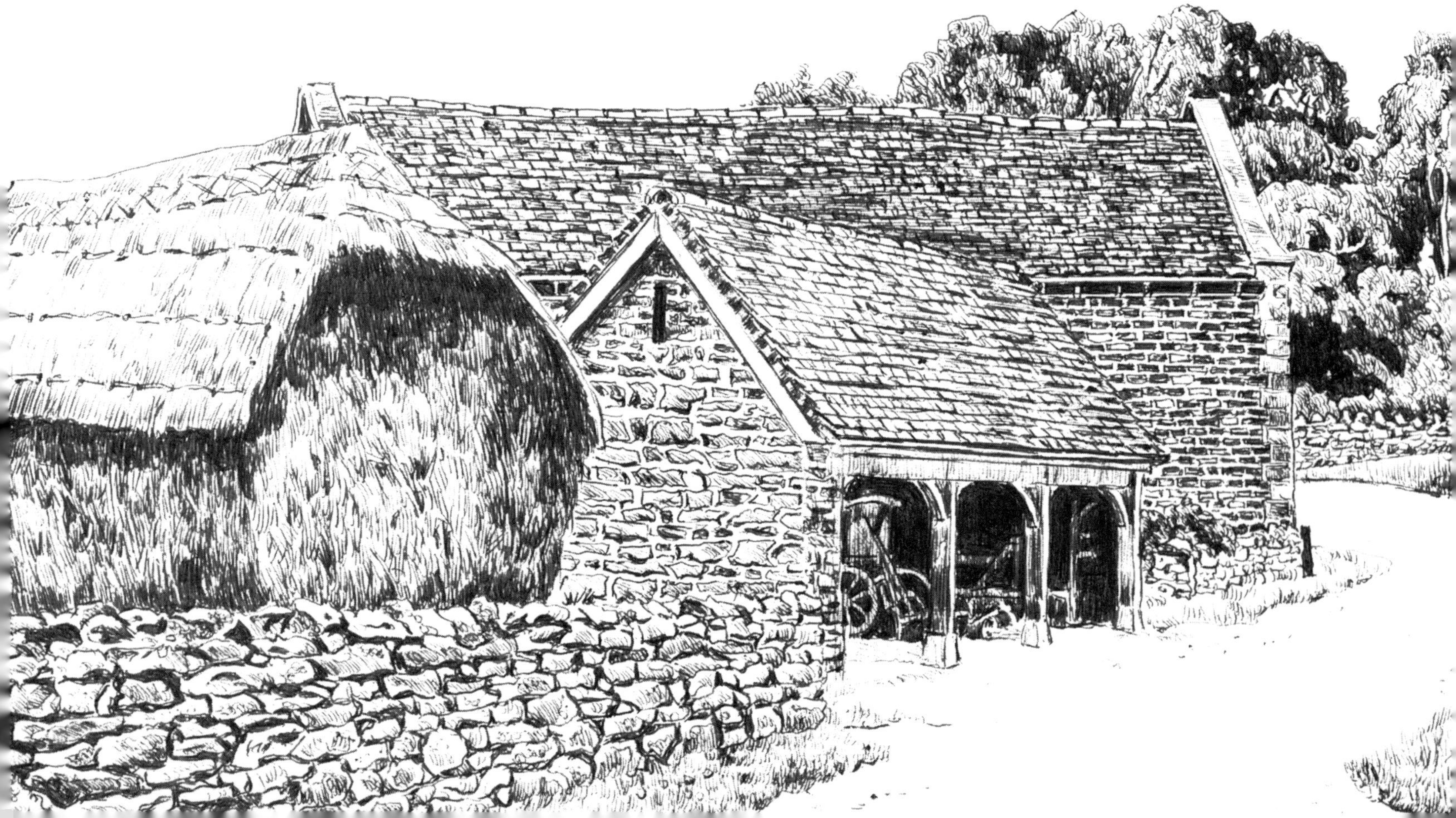

ferule of another fork stuck in the load and drops down onto the grass. We wait for the next empty wagon to arrive: some jokes are told and remarks made. Major and Colonel come across the field and the teams start again. We wake up the resting horses with the first load and start on our way to the stack yard and Dutch barn. Duchess and Blackie know how to use their power as the full swaying load turns for the gate. The shafts smack against Diamond's sides and the wheels meet the sun-baked ruts. She staggers and forces the wheels back. What strength! We walk alongside urging them on, although they know the way. Once in the yard, the wagon is pulled up beside the elevator which is driven by a chugging, spluttering engine, and the hay off the wagon travels up onto the haystack. Both horses' sides heave as they wait, with lowered heads, soon to start nodding and shaking as the flies gather around their eyes.

Haystacks, like cottages, differ in their making and style according to their district. In Wiltshire the stack, begun on a base of branches, is almost square, all sides sloping outwards until the low eaves are reached. Its building depends greatly on the skill of the man on the stack who moves around the edges, the hay being passed to him the man by the elevator whose job is also to keep the middle filled slightly higher than the edges. The stack will have a hipped roof, later to be thatched with a good weatherproof lid.

In the Eastern counties, stacks tend to be much higher and to have straight gable ends. Midland stacks usually are built with half-gable ends. Whatever the shape of stile, the good man builds fast and true with a pride in his work and a sure knowledge that his stacks will not need propping up before winter is through.

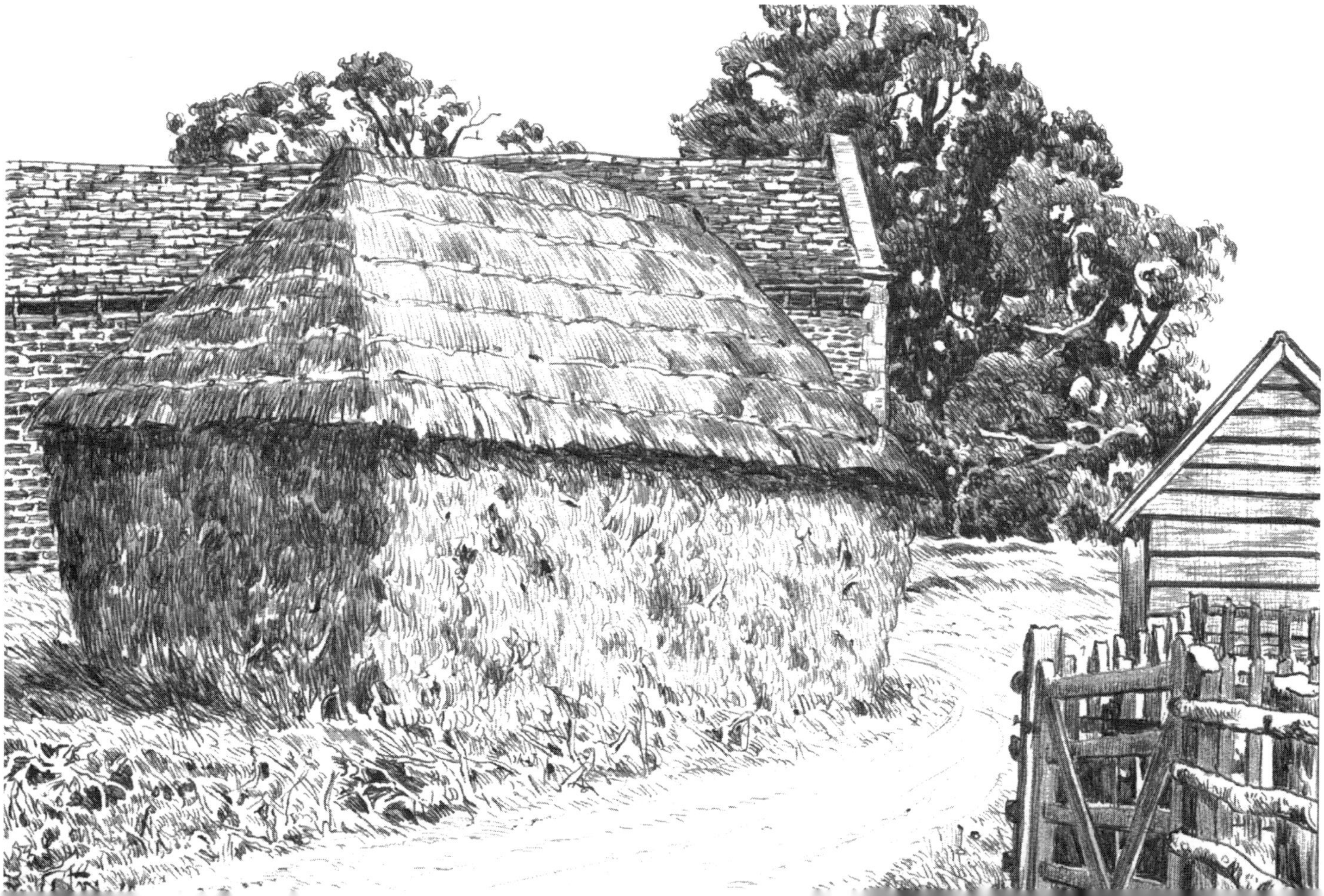

Thatching

Thatching is generally an autumn job, often done by one of the farm workers, for it is a far simpler business to thatch ricks or stacks, than to roof a cottage with straw or reed.

Once the stack has settled, a load of long straw is brought along with a ladder and the thatcher's tools. From the straw heap, handfuls are pulled out by the ends and laid out, then wetted. Next, the thatcher and his helper, often one of us boys, would take sections, or yelms, of the straw. About nine yelms were required to cover one strip from eaves to ridge. Up on the stack would be bundles of spars and rolls of binder-twine. So, once the yelms were in place, with heads down and overlapping, the spars would be pushed in and the twine running horizontally would be secured to the spars.

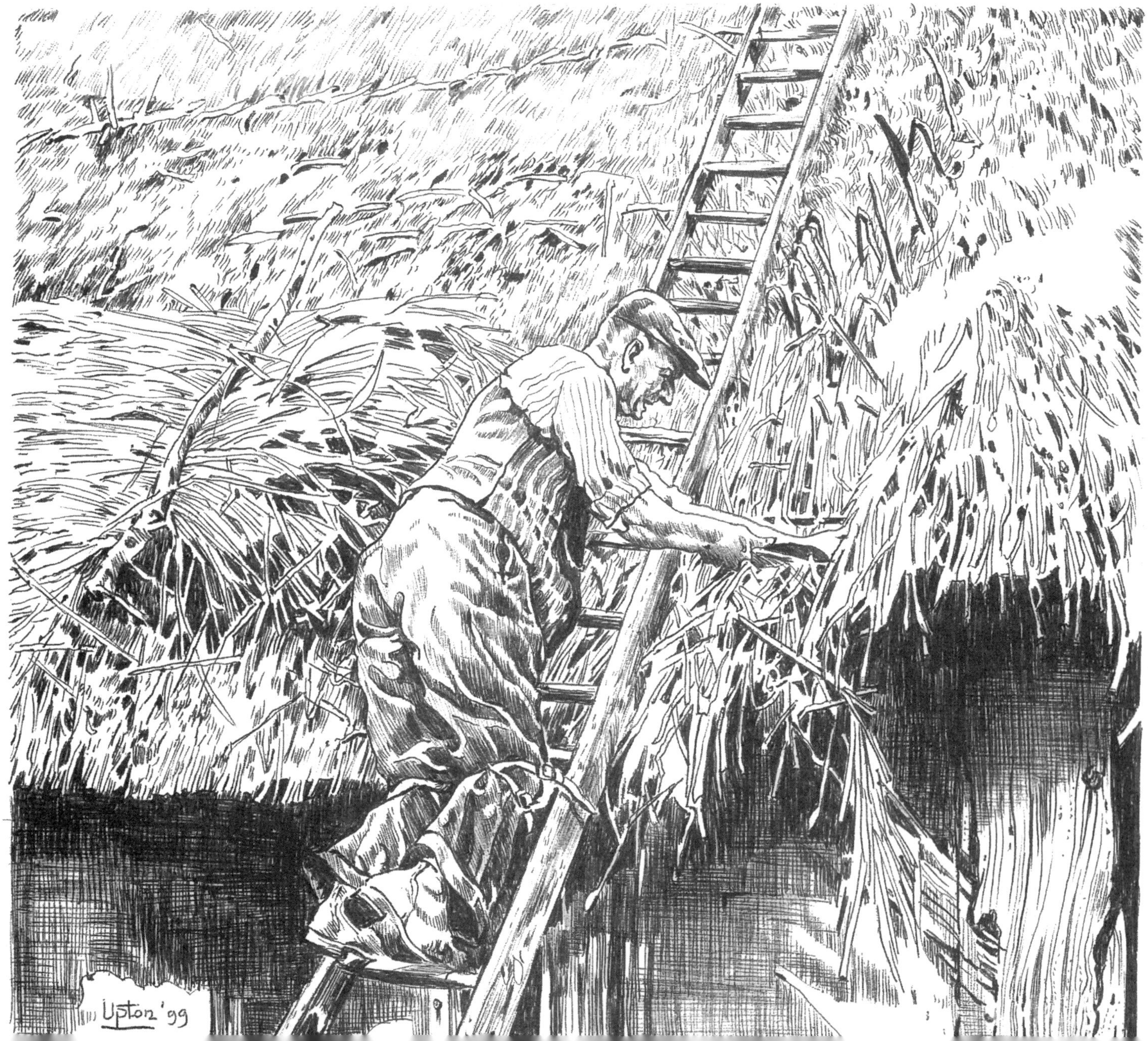

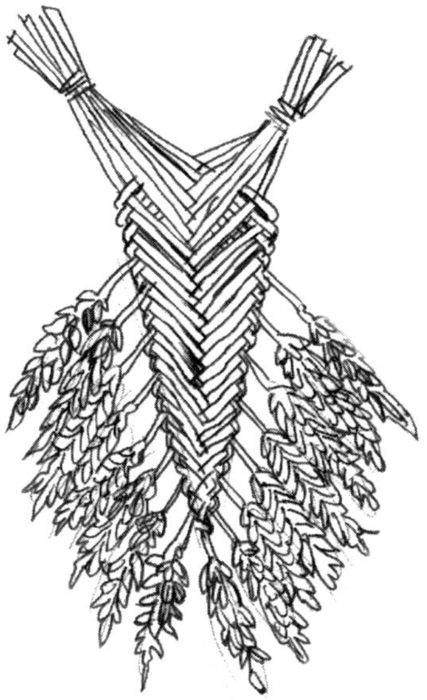

Once one strip was done the ladder was flipped over, ready for the next strip to be laid. When all was covered, the ridge and the eaves were clipped straight to make a clean job of it. In time, my brother and I were given the job of thatching.

So years later, we were up on a long straw rick, about halfway through the day's work when over the ridge we saw away in the distance a lone figure striding across the downs. We lost sight of him as he neared the belt of fir trees, then suddenly there he was, at the bottom of the ladder, a tramp. He addressed the two of us up on the rick, "Hail, brother beard-wearers!", for he had a large grey beard. He then proceeded to give us a somewhat incoherent discourse on philosophy. Once he had finished, he raised his hand to us, shouted farewell and turned about to leave. It was quite an unexpected sight for, despite the icy-cold wind, the seat of his trousers was worn out and there was his bare backside braving the elements.

Harvest

In the fields of the Valley, the heavy greens of summer bow to the deep ochre of the turning barley. Warm winds ripple in waves the heads of sun-grown grain, and whisper through the alders by the stream.

In the private world of the corn stalks weeds and flowers hide, the harvest mice live their acrobatic lives and the partridge seek for food under the golden canopy. In the skyways, swallows wing their way above the ripening corn. Poised on the wind, a kestrel, light as down, searches for shrew or mouse below while it rides the invisible tides.

Towards the gateway move in slow procession three horses, men, women and children. Disturbed, the kestrel slides across the sky to hunt another field. Harvest: the time has come and the weather is fine. Men at work will soon stir the field from summer's quiet.

A back swath is started to encircle the field, while the old binder is set up with serrated knife, canvas decks and wooden sails. Two rolls of binder-twine are put in the tin box. From one, the twine is pulled out and threaded up, rather like an outsize sewing-machine. An air of expectancy awaits the first sheaf. Into the track, made ready by men with sickles, the binder rattles and rocks its way, pulled by the three horses. Iron shoes and iron wheels bite into the dusty loam, flattening the cut stalks. The knife slides rapidly back and forth shearing the stems, whose ripened heads are bent by the slowly revolving sails towards the blade. In line it falls and rides the canvas to be caught against curved rods, where it builds up to be tied and disgorged—a sheaf of corn.

Women and children follow to pick up the sheaves, stand them on their butts in pairs, four down each side and one at each end: ten sheaves to a stook. Slowly the pattern develops as stooks, tent-like, dot the field.

The kestrel moving back, high up in cooler air, looks down on breeze-blown standing corn surrounded by lines of stubble on which stooks stand sentinel, each with its small shadow. He drifts down wind.

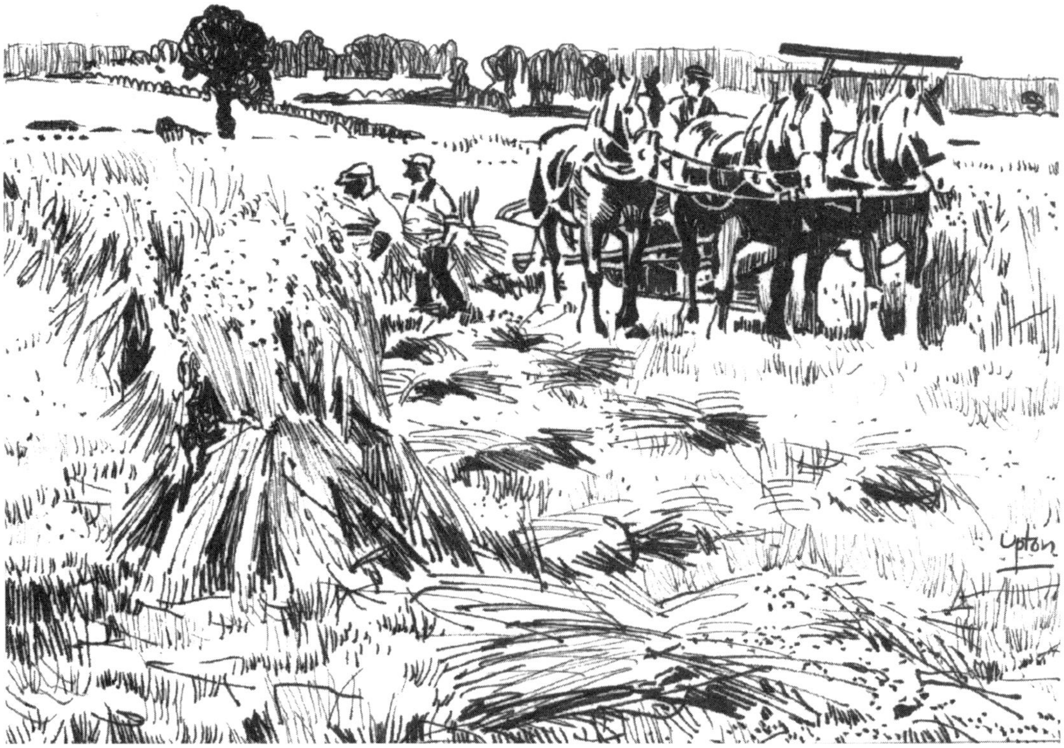

The shadows lengthen to ride the contours of the field. The sweat-stained horses cease their work. A tarpaulin is tied over the silent binder and tired mothers and children troop quietly to the waiting wagon in dimming light.

Soon, faint rustlings stir the waiting silence and a ghost-like form sails low across the afterglow. The barn owl lands on the top bar of the open gate, a shrew in its beak.

Each day while the sun lasts the work continues from field to field and the standing corn gets ever narrower, frightened rabbits begin to break cover. Small boys, armed with sticks, and the farm dogs chase the white scuts racing away to their warrens under the hedge. Suddenly a fox streaks away past a surprised sheep-dog who gives chase only to turn a somersault trying to grab Charlie's brush. The fox receives a blow from a stick wielded by an eager boy determined to be in at Charlie's kill. Crestfallen, the dog returns to loll in the shade of a stook after sub-merging himself in the cattle trough to cool off.

Wheat burnt golden, barley yellow and whiskered, lacy oats: all dot the fields, plundered in the dewy morn by flocks of fat wood pigeon. The winter-sown fields are now cleared by the gleaners, although carting the stooks continues unabated until all are in ricks at the farm. As at haysel, the wains are out, drawn by a pair who move from stook to stook, the sheaves tossed up to the wagon man. He lays them butts outward down each side, tied in by other sheaves down the centre. And, in turn, the high-loaded wains are taken down to the yard.

It's harvest home at last.

Threshing

Today the threshing tackle is coming to the farm. It is a cold, dry wintry day of low nimbus clouds and a watery sun.

In preparation, the first straw rick has had its thatch taken off and the farm terriers are hanging about on the lookout for rats. We soon hear a rumbling, and see drifts of smoke rising above the hedgerow and into the yard comes the steam engine, towing behind it the threshing machine. What an iron monster it is with its brass-bound chimney and great flywheel! It comes to a halt, and the men unhitch the 'drum', as the threshing machine is called and manoeuvre it into position close to the rick. Then the steam engine is moved so that its flywheel is in line with the one on the 'drum' to enable the web belt to be crossed in a figure of eight and slipped into place. One of the farm wagons arrives with heaps of hessian sacks to be filled with the threshed corn.

Some discussion and jobs are allocated, chains and cogs checked and oiled. The belt begins to move and the whole threshing machine begins to clack and shake off dust.

Boys on the rick-top toss sheaves to the side-man who throws them down to the man on the top of the drum. He deftly cuts the strings with a clasp knife and feeds the dusty stalks into the drum, which, as it revolves, knocks out the seed-heads and shakes back the straw to be disgorged. The corn falls downwards through sieves and runs through chutes into the hessian sacks. A small pall of dust

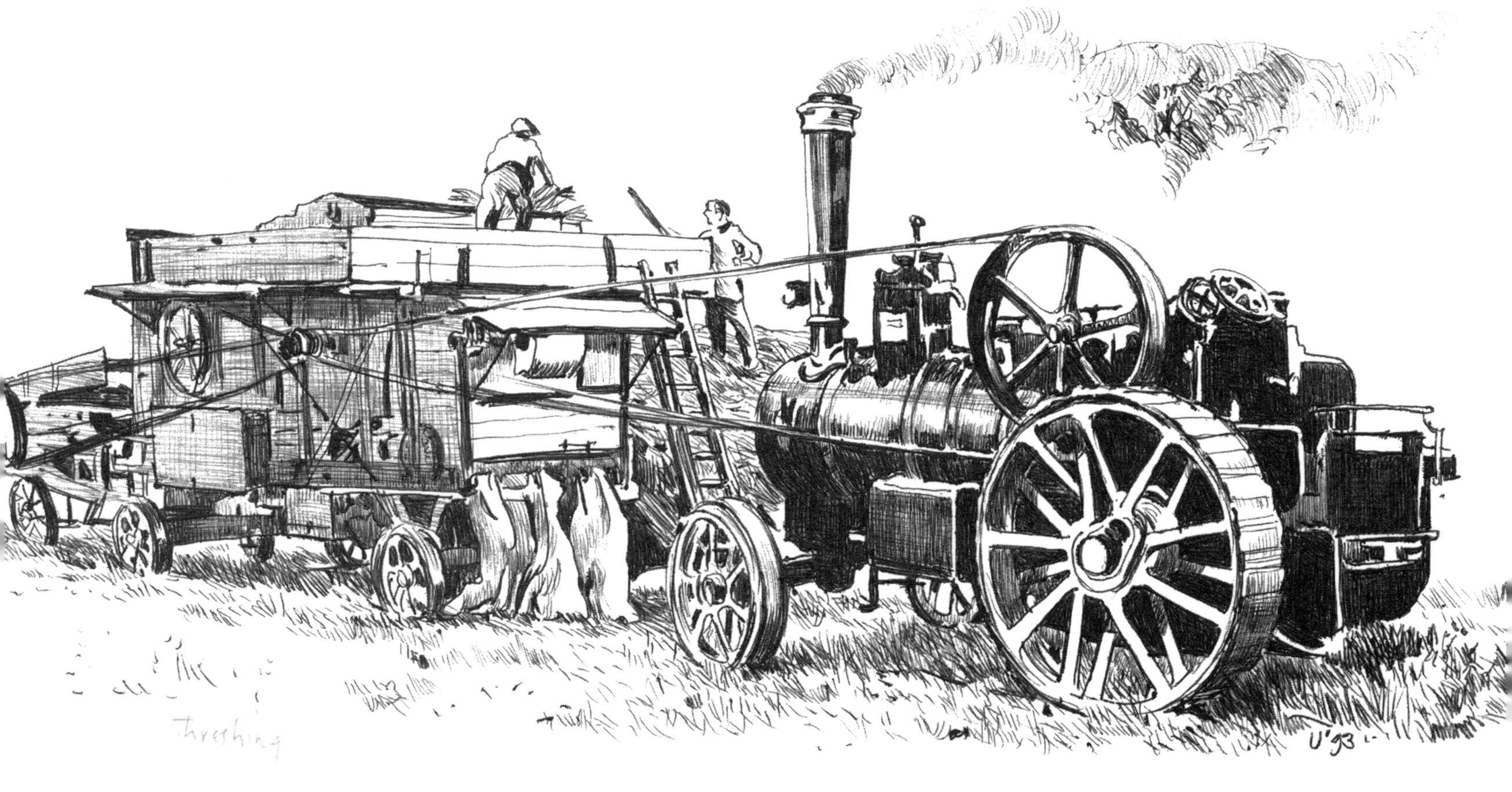

hangs over the sacks as the corn rattles down. The farmer takes a handful, holds it in his palm, sorts it and bites into one: a fair sample plump and hard. As one sack is filled, the corn flow is stopped by sliding a metal plate across. The sack is unhooked, the top gathered and tied with twine. The full sack of two and a quarter hundred-weight is swung up onto a man's shoulders. He walks across to the wagon, turns his back to it and deposits the sack onto a trolley, held by another man who stacks the bags up in the bed of the wagon.

The air is now full of dust, chaff and noise. The dust comes from the rick and the drum as the sheaves are fed into the machine. The rick gets lower and lower, while the dogs dart here and there amid the bustle, snatching at rats leaving the rick. So the hours go by. The engine driver keeps his charge full of fuel and water and walks around checking cogs and tapits, then wipes his hands with an oily rag.

At long last the rick is finished. Each man, his eyes red as he peers from a dust-grimed face, watches the fast and furious chase as the last rats and mice attempt escape from the two terriers and a sheep-dog who has joined in the fun. The great belt is flicked off the wheel and the thresher judders to a halt. The wagon heaped with bulging sacks is viewed with satisfaction: it's a good yield.

Soon, a general stir as the team prepares to move the engine and drum up to the next rick and the whole business begins again and again. So, until the evening light grows dim, the dust and toil goes on, then at last all is stilled. The engine lies couchant amid the heaps of chaff and straw. The threshing is over.

I clearly remember one day's threshing at Spratt's Barn Farm in the Vale of the White Horse. A new vicar had come to the parish and decided to pay a visit to the farmer. There being no reply at the farmhouse, he made his way to the rickyard, where all was noise and activity.

A rat, disturbed by the lifting of a corn sheaf, made a dash for a hiding place, two terriers in close pursuit. Being hard pressed, it found security, or so it thought, by going to ground up the inside of the vicar's trouser leg. He, no doubt horrified by the possibilities of its final refuge, clasped his hands in an iron grip around his leg and stood there not knowing what next to do. All work had stopped, as farmer, workers and two expectant terriers waited for the next act to the drama taking place before them. The vicar, it could clearly be seen, was in a dilemma: to let go or not to let go. After what seemed like an age, he carefully and slowly relaxed his grip and a very dead, strangled rat slid out to be snatched and shaken by one of the dogs. A clearly relieved man hastily bade goodbye to the farmer, no doubt to rush back to the vicarage bathroom to inspect his person for damage.

Clearly vicars' visits to farms were fraught with dangers—beyond the call of duty.

Hedges, Walls, Gates and Stiles

The hedger does his work during the long winter months when the sap is down. His job is with blackthorn and briar: these he tames and renews to form living boundaries to the fields. The hedges are full of variety and interest with feathery travellers' joy, scarlet rose-hips, hazel, elder and young trees which he leaves to grow into great hedgerow trees. Oaks and elms were the most common trees in the Vale and when the elm disease came it was a sorry sight. Dead trees everywhere—all gone.

Old Jack, who worked on the farm owned by 'Guts and Gaiters' was a born craftsman. Off he would go, clad in a leather coat and old army greatcoat, shouldering his lunch bag, and carrying a long slasher and bill hook. He wears upon his hands 'owl-catchers', hard leather gloves which even briars cannot penetrate.

Every so often he pauses in his work to hone the blades of his tools on a stone. As he goes, he piles up the discarded cuttings then, at lunchtime, he lights a fire and warms himself a while, and the store cattle in the field come to stand and stare in the smoke's haze.

The Hedger

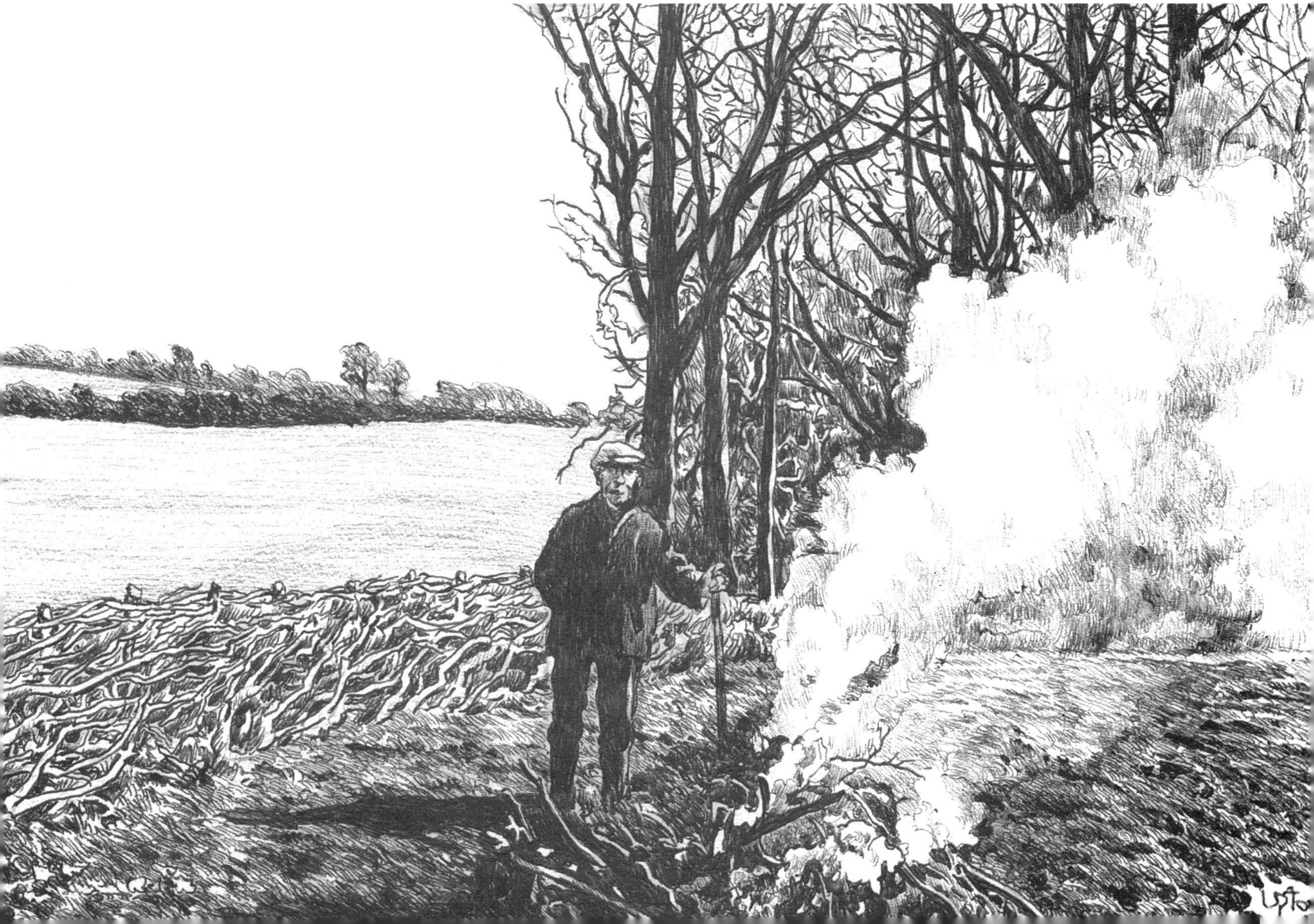

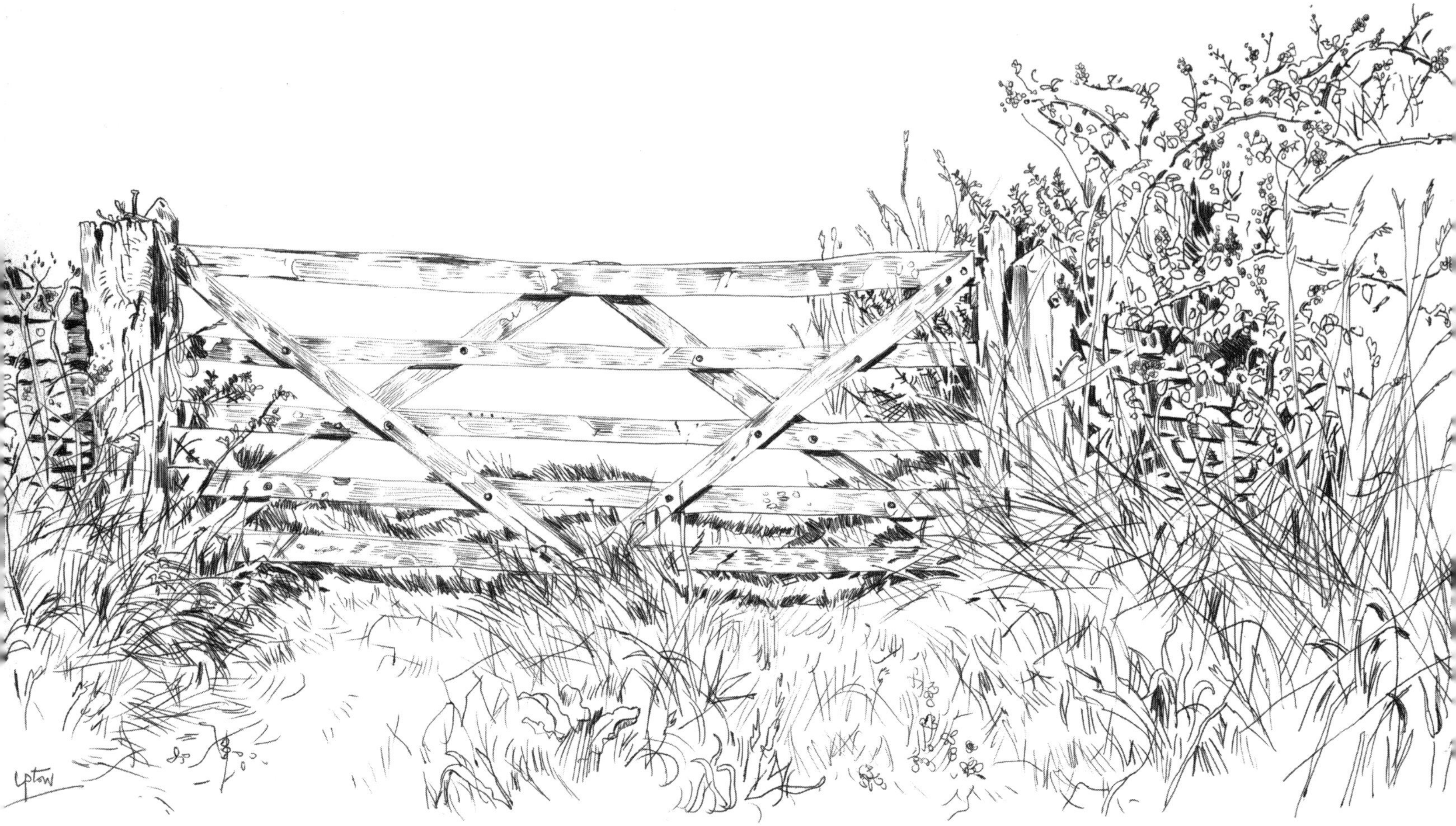

A field gate

What is left standing is partly cut, and each stem bent deftly over another. Stakes are then driven into the laid hedge every yard or so and the saplings interwoven between them. After this pleaching, the hedge is usually 'ethered', long rods of hazel or willow being woven along the top, and the job is finished. It will not require doing again for many years.

Although in the Vale of the White Horse hedges were the most common form of fencing, in the North and in the Cotswolds dry-stone walls were the norm. Here was another country craft, and a good wall would stand for years and years. Good hedges were there to keep the stock in, but they also provided shelter from the storm in winter weather.

At Avebury on the Wiltshire Downs, sarsen stones stand in that mighty circle as witness to our ancestors, but such stones were also used as solid gate pillars to field gates

The country methods of fencing differ according to the natural materials at hand and the inherited skills of the countrymen. So it is with field gates and stiles, showing distinct features in each locality.

Gates were mostly made of well-seasoned oak, a wood which weathers well over the years. In time the new timber turns to a silvery grey colour and is inhabited by gold and white lichens. The hard grain of the oak stands out as it ages, like the veins of an old man's hand. Rails riven, and not sawn, were the stronger for they followed the natural grain of the wood. Five-barred gates, the ones we see at field entrances, always had the lower bars placed closer together to keep lambs and other young stock in, and the head post was usually lighter than the harr, the name given to the hinge end of the gate. The major differences found in five-barred gates in different counties was the arrangement of the mid-staff and braces, and in types of gate catches. If a gate has to be climbed, it should always be done at the harr end to avoid undue strain, but many an old gate, through age or neglect, sags on its hinges and these days is replaced by a metal gate or by strands of barbed wire. No gate to lean on!

We all preferred to take the old ways, footpaths and narrow lanes set deep between banks and hedges. Where boundaries barred the way, a rich variety of stiles enabled the wayfarer to go on his journey. The simplest of stiles was the 'squeeze-belly', two posts set close together, often slightly wider at the top. Sometimes a low step or board was fixed across the base. Set in the hedgerows in many an English county, they provide a simple passage for all but the too-ample of girth, and at the same time do not allow livestock to get through. The 'squeeze-belly' can also be found in stone-wall country, but there a large slab of stone or slate set upright in the wall is more common. Another way of getting over a wall is steps. These are provided by the craftsman, for as he builds up the wall he places some stones so that they jut out on both sides. Then there is the 'kissing-gate' or 'swing-swong', usually in iron, but occasionally in wood, where only one can pass through at a time.

A Wiltshire field gate

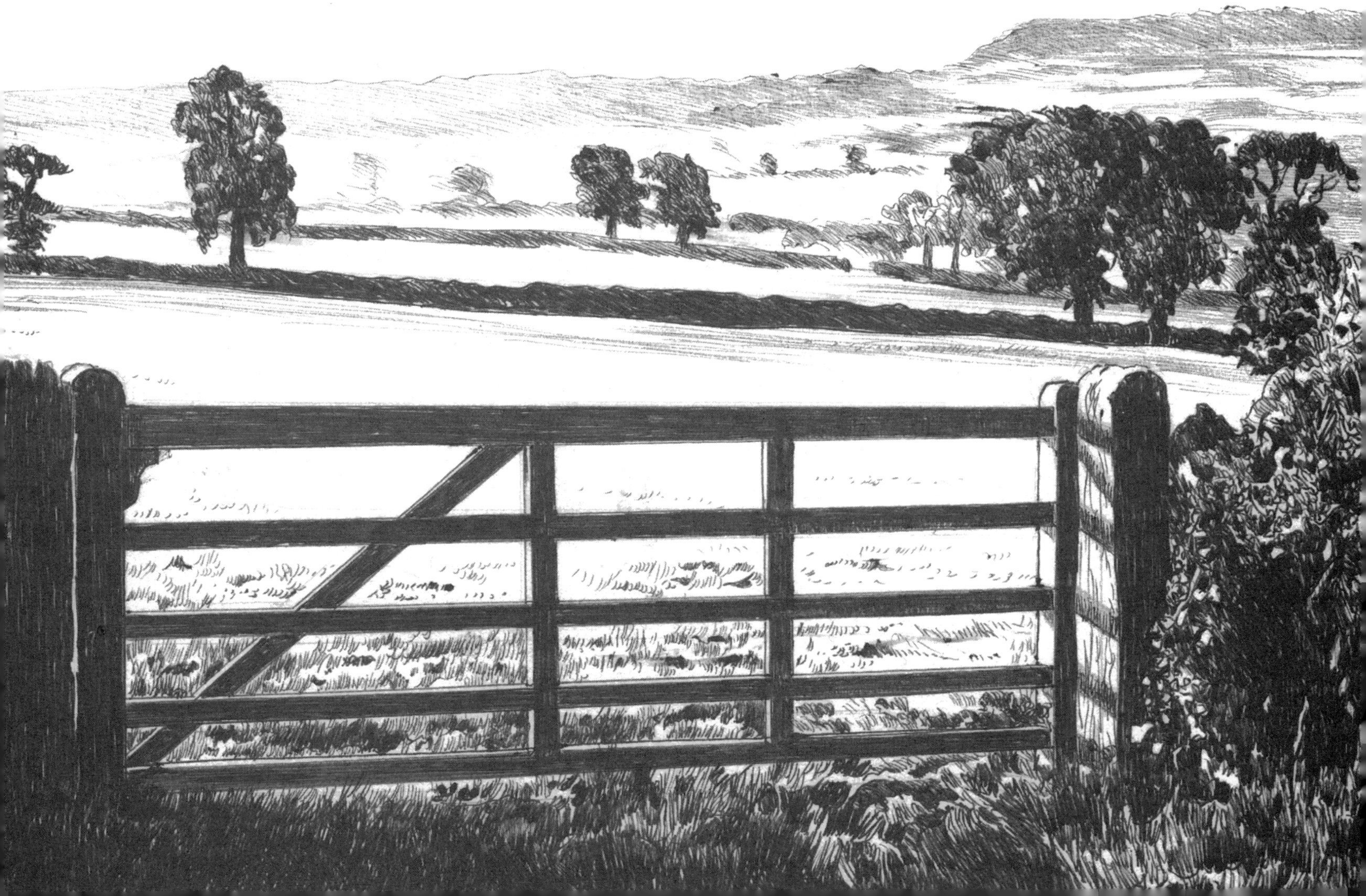

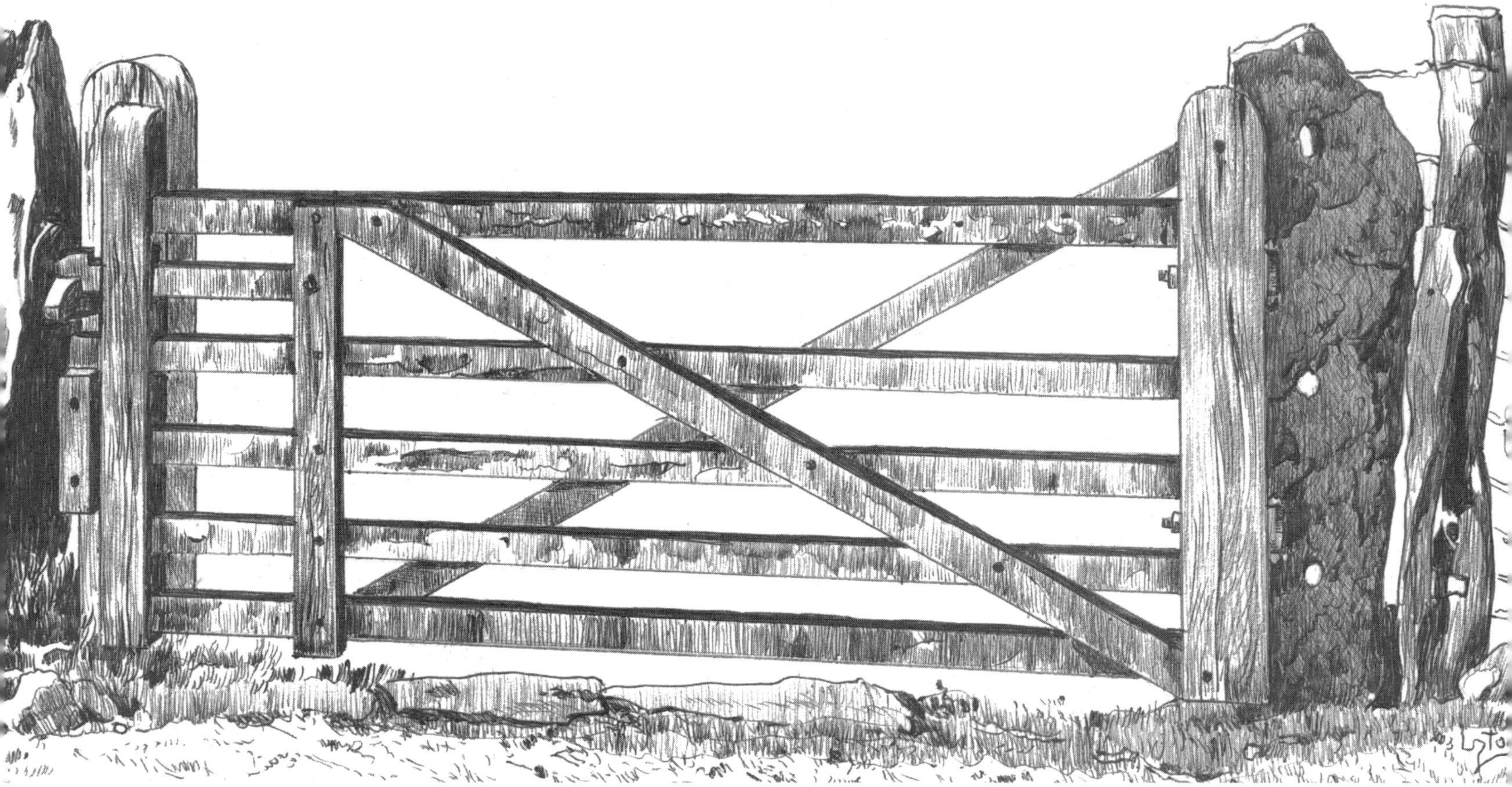

A Devon gate

Below, left to right:
A wooden step tile, a stone step stile and a squeeze-belly stile

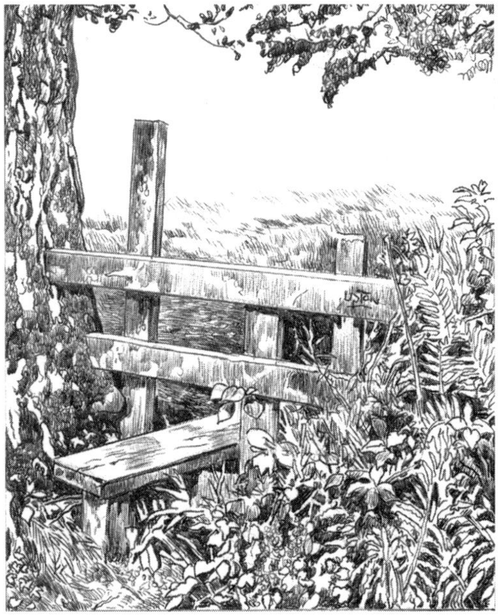

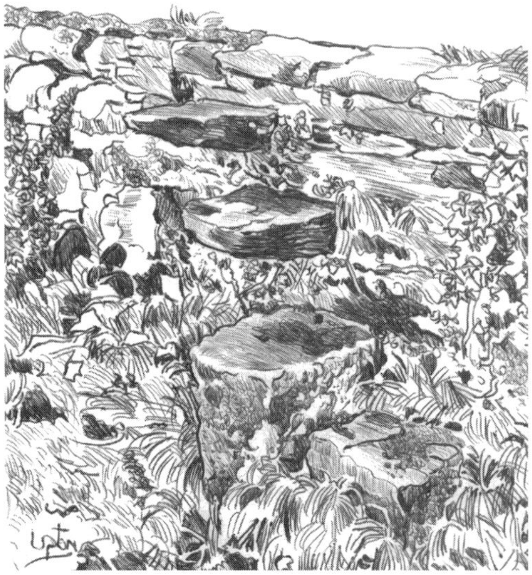

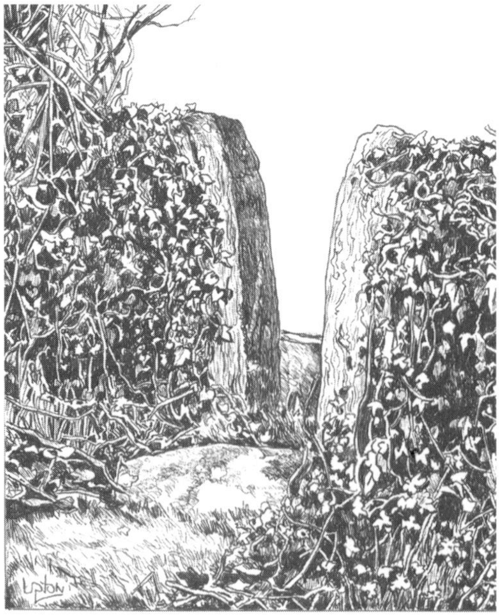

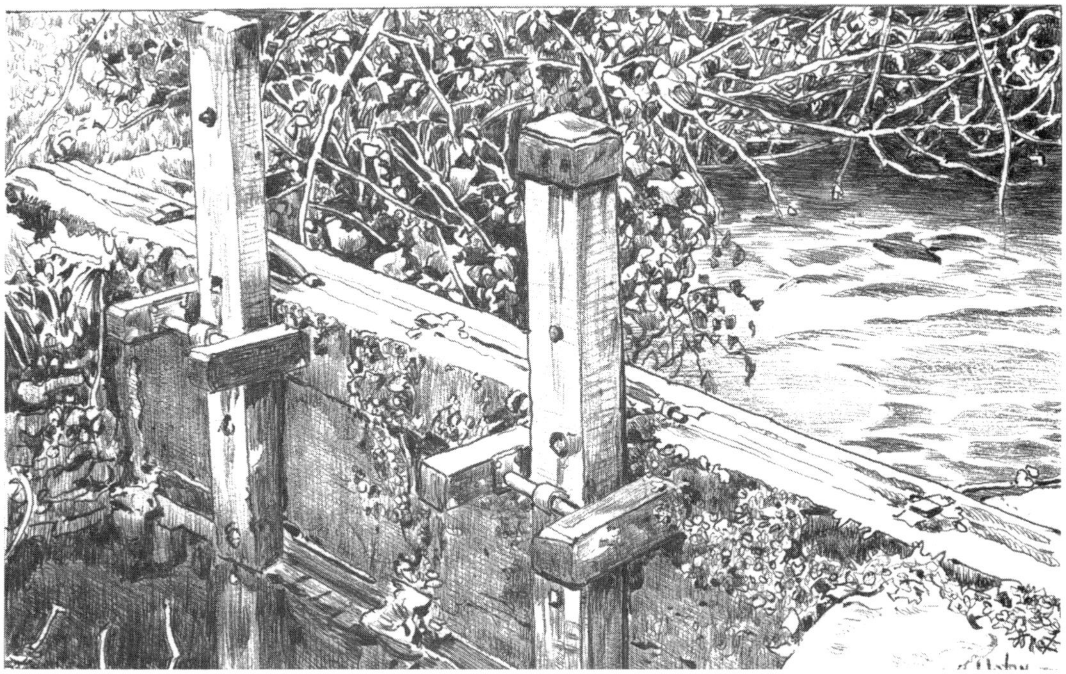

A water-meadow sluice

Yet another rural craftsman was the drowner. He looked after the water-meadows which he flooded normally in October from the nearby chalk-water stream. A sluice on the stream when shut down caused a build-up of water upstream, so that it flowed down carriers and into smaller channels. The water was kept off and on for the winter, so irrigating the land and providing early bite for the cattle in spring.

Today, most of these lovely meadows now lie neglected, the sluices broken and the channels overgrown. Yet another skill lost to the countryside.

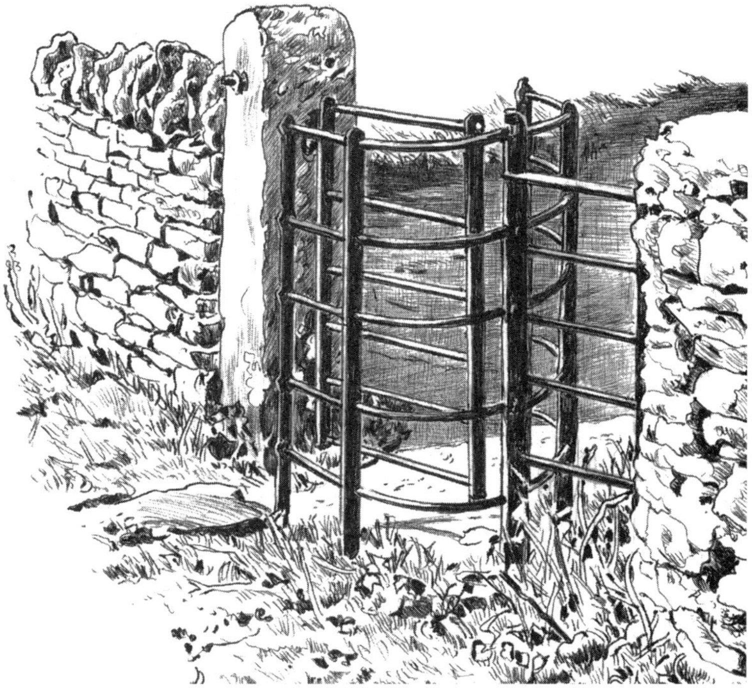

An iron swing-swong stile

Harvest in the Woods

Climb up the lane—No Through Road—take a left turn where the gate lies open and go down the muddied track into the wood. To the left beyond the larch plantations lies the valley, while to the right is a steep bank of coppiced chestnut butts. The poles are neatly stacked at the edge of the ride. Below, there is a small quarry where a thin line of smoke drifts upwards through the trees. Tarpaulins like open tents are propped up to make a shelter and here the woodman and his son are at work. They take up the chestnut poles and with draw-knives strip the bark. The fresh white poles are then held in a 'brake' so that they can be cleft. The froe, a wedge-shaped tool used for cleaving and riving staves, is driven into the end with a wooden beetle and then given a sharp twist, pushed down and twisted again, and so on until the pole splits clean in two. Later, the wood is used to make hurdles and paling fencing. The art of coppicing ensures that after a few years the same chestnut trees can be harvested again.

A Cotswold stone slab stile

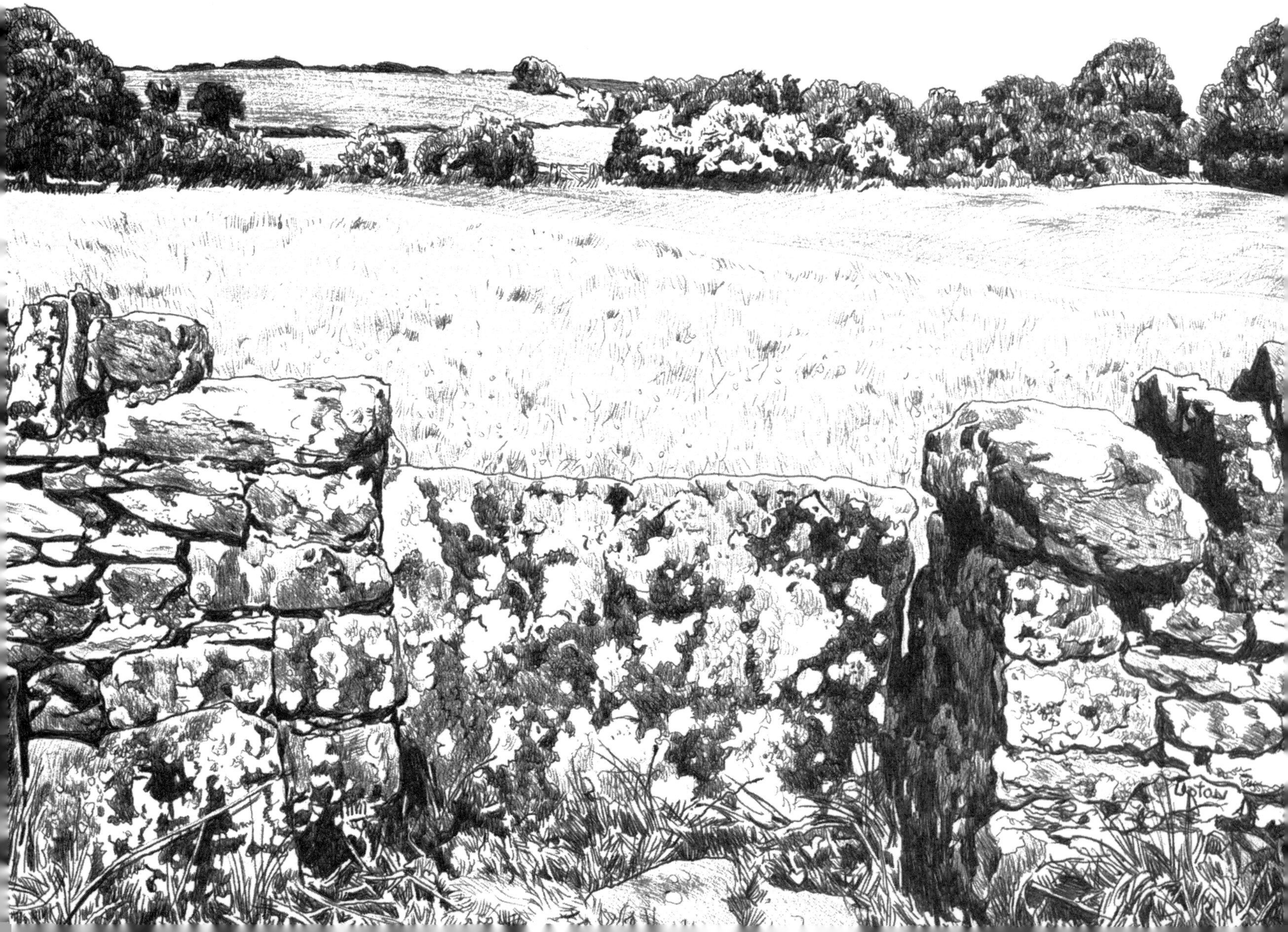

Farm Livestock

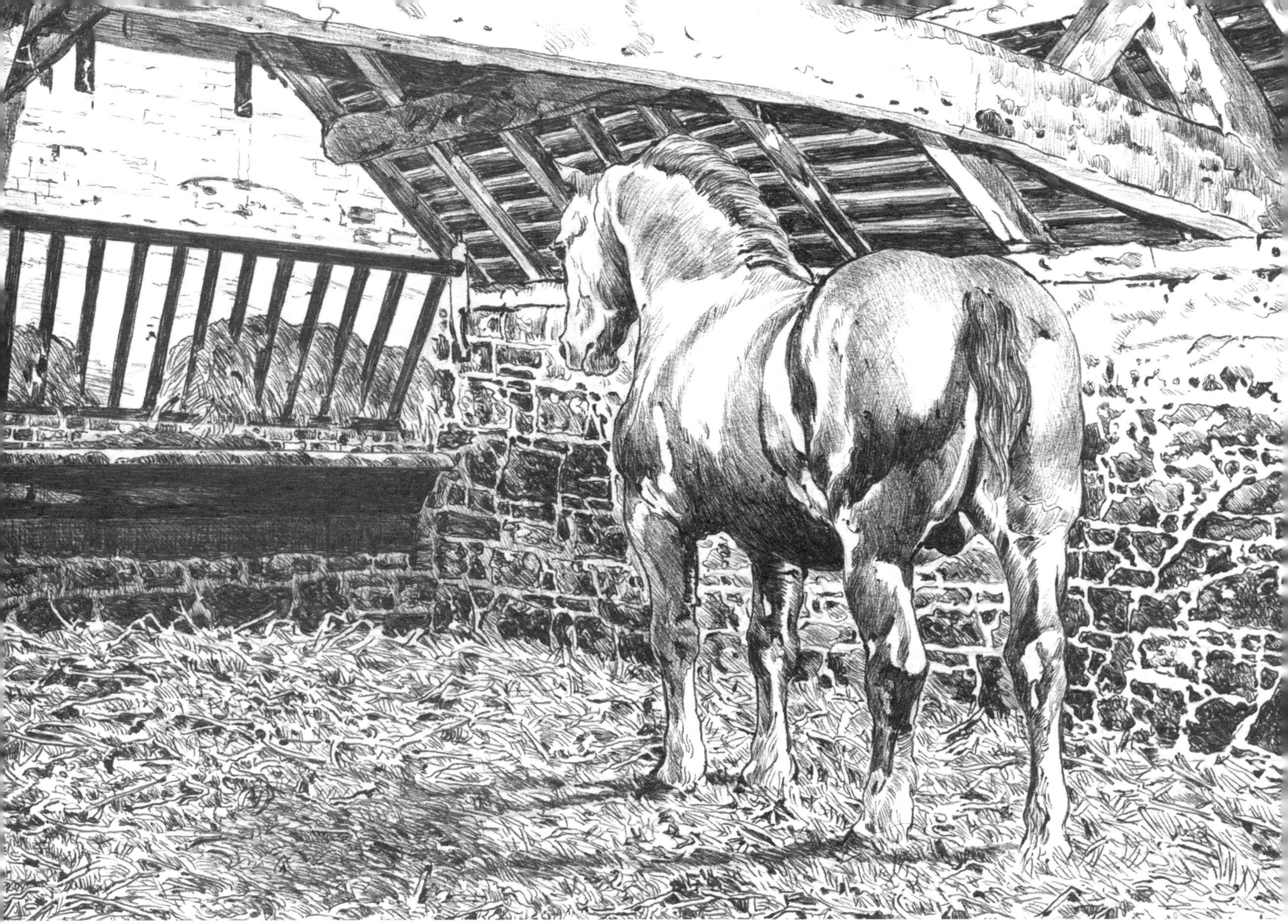

The Suffolk Punch Stallion

DEEP AMONG THE cobwebs of memory, mixed with briar roses and water meadows full of buttercups in the Kent countryside, I remember when I was seven years old the awe I felt as I stared at the stallion. From the confusion of smells and sights, I still see clearly his great quarters of a deep chestnut glowing and rich in the dark field barn. Leisurely he turned his head to regard us, yet with a kindly eye, and his shadow fled up the wall. Looking at him I saw power and strength, a great barrel of a body, broad chest and crested neck, dimpled and creased as he turned again. His legs were stocky with sparse curled feathers of a lighter hue.

The Suffolk Punch Stallion

I sensed primeval forces, his very maleness, deep in the shadows of that stable.

At last, we crept quietly away. Back in the sunshine of the afternoon we talked to the elderly father of a friend of the family who had taken us to see the horse, for he had been told of our fascination with horses. We walked back down a grassy path

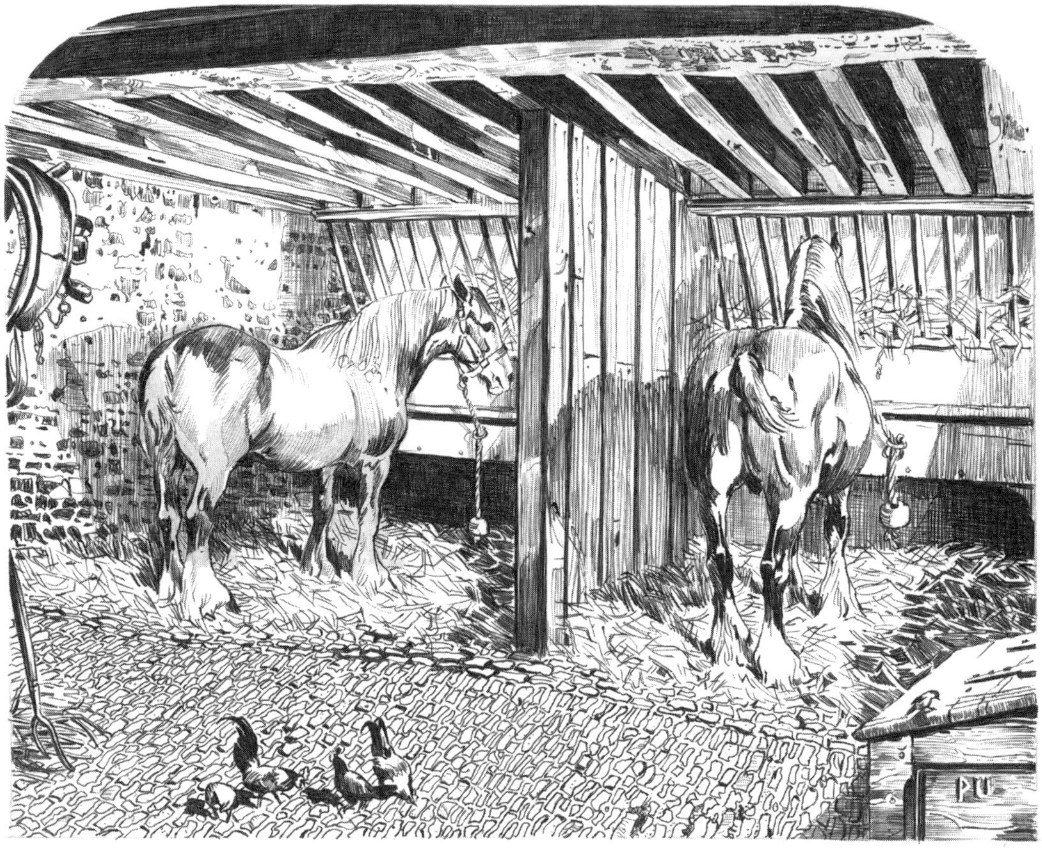

Farm horses in their stalls
Below: Two Percherons in plough harness

which led to his white weatherboard farmhouse, so typical of Kent. He was a true countryman immersed in the ways and habits of his countryside. He taught us much.

But I still clearly remember The Stallion.

The Suffolk breed possibly goes back to Saxon times in East Anglia. Certainly they are mentioned in 1506 and their history is known to trace to Crisp's Horse of Ufford, a chestnut coaching stallion. The Suffolk is a stocky, short-legged horse with very little feather about his heels. He is a fast walker, and is always chestnut in colour.

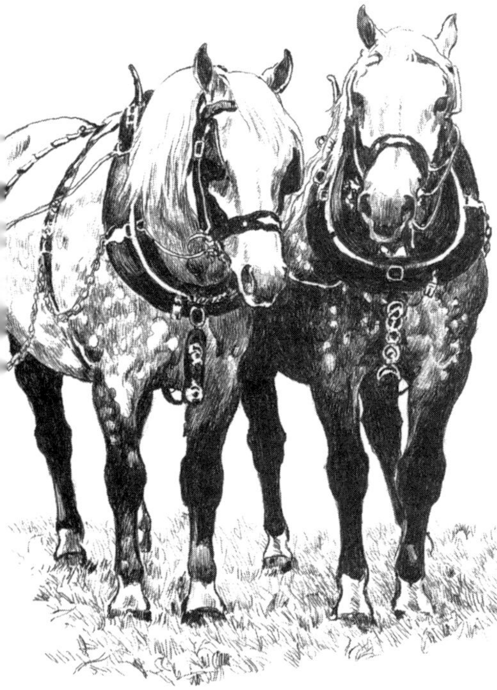

Percherons

Out in the paddock five Percheron horses rest beneath the avenue of trees, glad of their shade. They stand in the dust of summer, head to tail, resting a hind foot now and then, or stamping which stirs fine particles that drift and settle. Their short tails of curly white hairs continually swish back and fore. Old Gilbert, quite white now, puts his head close to Dora's flank so that her tail may brush the crawling flies from his face. All the mares are dappled grey, the younger ones still quite dark, though the sun through the trees complements the pattern of their shiny coats. Their manes hang in coils, their backs dip low and the quarters rise massive and fat: baroque master-pieces in the flesh.

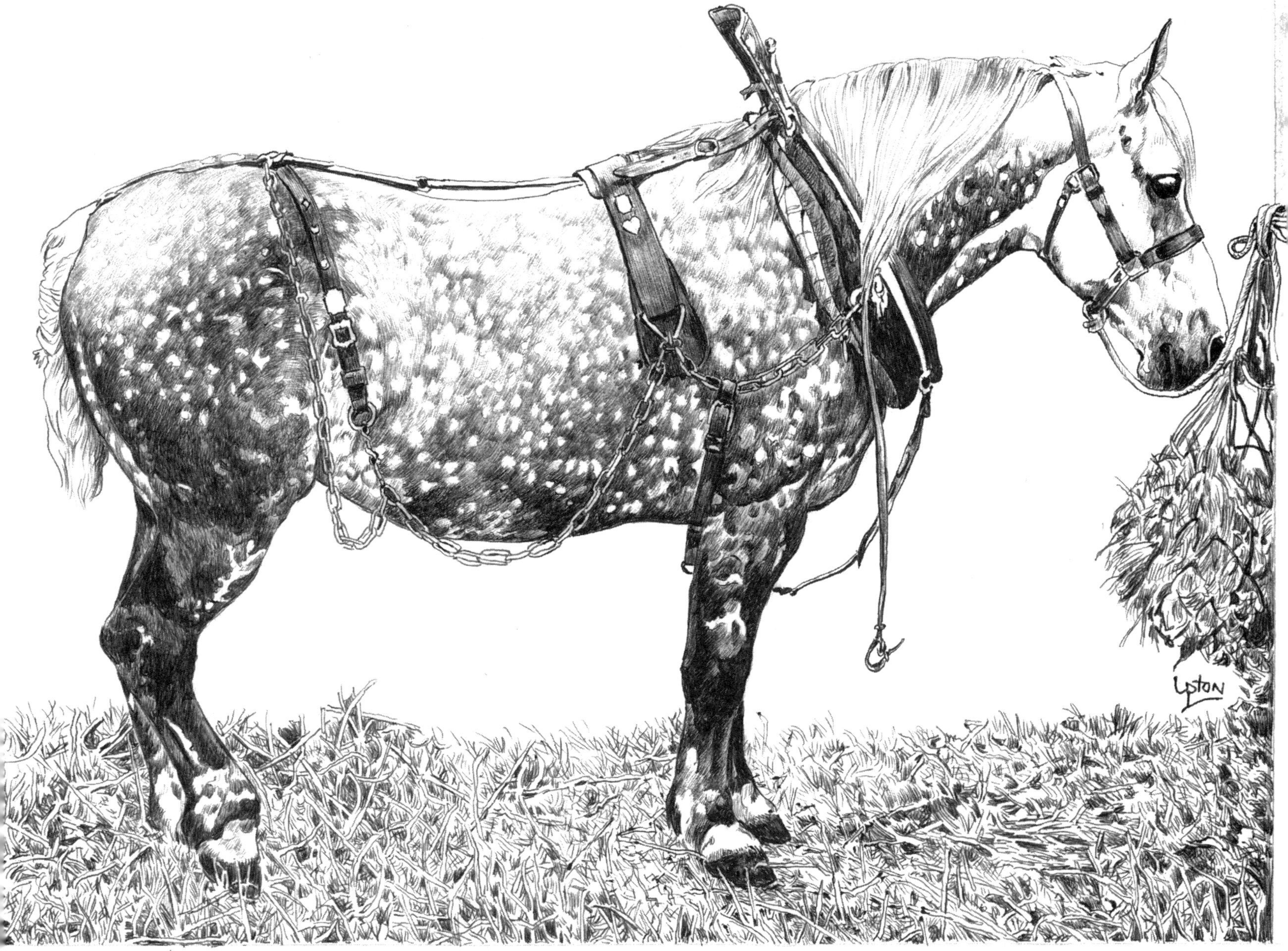

Old Gilbert

There are still sixteen Percherons in work on the farm and one hauling fallen trees in the woods at the top of the park. But that was in the 1940's.

Old Gilbert was quite a character and many were the tales told about his escapades for, as Walter explained, "E wus a clever ol' bugger".

One day Gilbert was taken up to Clay Piece to hoe between the rows of turnips. The weather had turned hot, so in no time both Gilbert and Walter were sweating. They had been up and down for some time and, as the old horse knew the job, Walter was quietly dozing, what with the heat and the flies. Gilbert was finding the 'Old Maids' (horse flies) really troublesome. Then all of a sudden Gilbert stopped. "I s'pose it was the jolt as woke me', explained Walter later, 'but I knew the 'ol horse 'ad bin round four times, 'cos all the corners 'ad bin cut short by the cunnin' ol' dapper".

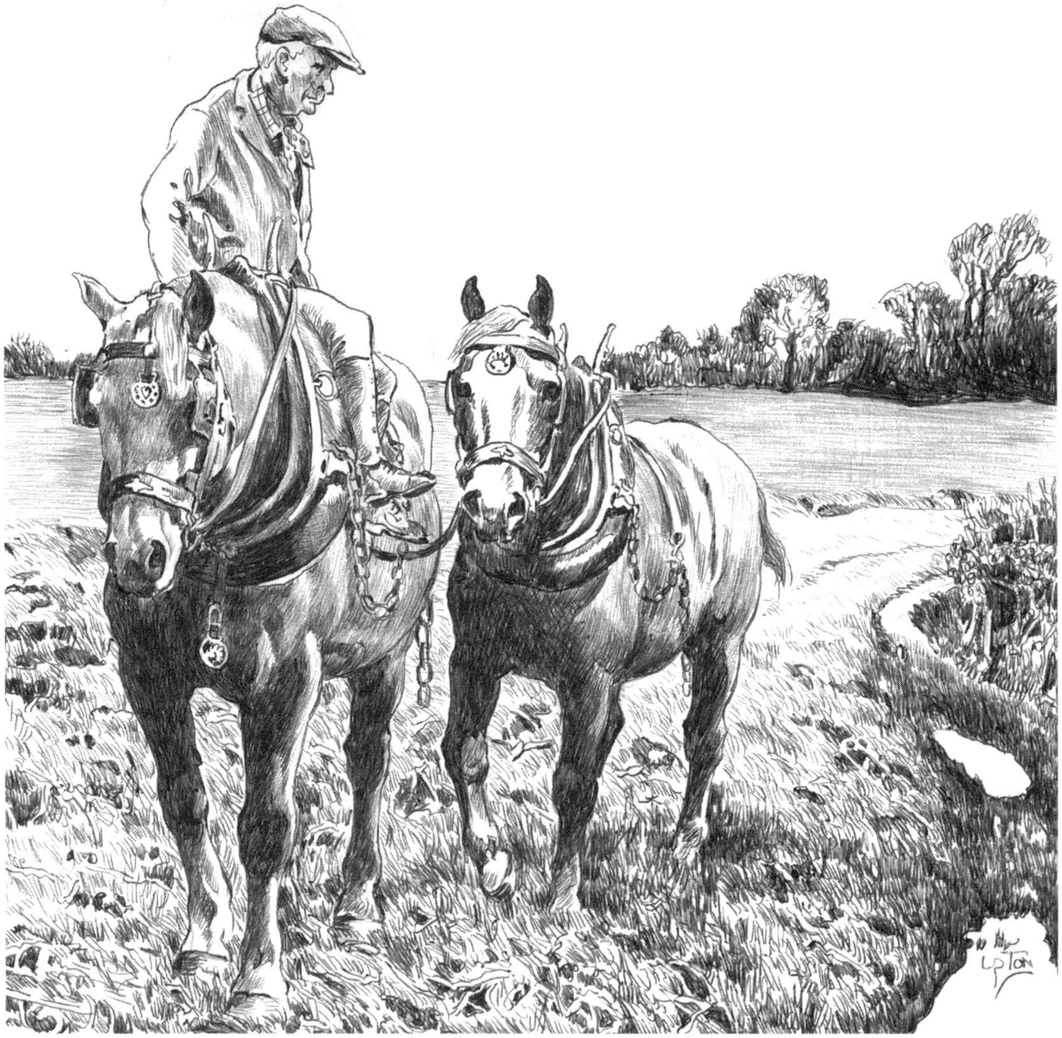

After a day's work

The Horse

The age of the horse was on its last legs, but the war saw the horse back at work, for farmers needed them to get through the hard times.

The old Fordson tractor, faded green, still coughed its way about the farm and alongside it worked the horses, while sons fought in a foreign land.

One farm managed with its Fordson and two horses, Bluff Red and Old Blackie. Rarely groomed, their harness tied in places with binder-twine, they still worked their best at haysel and knew their jobs. Bluff Red still had youth on his side, but that old philosopher Blackie had known better times. He slowly did his duty but was not to be hurried and took every opportunity to take a rest. So loose was his whiskered mouth that when he drank at the trough half of each intake he lost again, a matter he accepted with his stoic calm, as he did everything.

There was a harmony in work when it was man and horse. Today the machine waits for no man.

No longer do we see teams of farm horses at work upon the land, yet in my youth it was still a common sight. So quickly have they gone from the scene that I fear their passing will go unnoticed by all but a few. I do not advocate their return, for I too must bow before the power of technology, but do ask us to remember them, not as a romantic notion of past summers but as a vital part of our agricultural history for so many centuries.

The horse had many advantages over the tractor in working the land. He could get on wet fields much sooner and use his strength and experience to shift a heavy load. He knew the working width of the implements he pulled and understood ploughing, hoeing, harrowing and mowing. His common-sense soon enabled him to know when to stop at the next cock of hay to be loaded or walk between the rows of crops without a man at his head. To the farmer he was cheap on fuel and did not depreciate like the tractor, and he also understood that the farm worker liked a rest now and then as he did; for he could not work all day like a cog in a machine.

I remember enjoying the hard hand work of old-style haymaking, yet I disliked having to keep up with the never-ending flow of bales being punched out by a pick-up baler, like a factory worker on an assembly-line. Undoubtedly the major disadvantage of the horse was the need to see to him seven days a week, a responsibility few men are prepared to accept today. However, he is gone from the fields and we are the poorer for his passing.

Judy

In the winter of 1947, one of the worst for many years, many of the by-roads were treacherous and on hills and bends ice added to the hazards. In the early morning, many of the drivers of lorries collecting milk from the dairy farms of the Vale, found their job well-nigh impossible without the help of farmers.

The Manor Farm stood on a rise overlooking the main road which made a sharp turn where the farm track met it. There stood the milk-stand laden with churns. The road also dropped steeply into the bend. One morning that winter the dairy lorry, failing to negotiate the bend, careered across the icy verge and slithered into the ditch up against a hawthorn hedge. Its churns were tipped against the chains, many on their sides. There was spilt milk everywhere. A worried driver walked up the track to the farm buildings and explained his plight to Mr. Collett. So, the tall Fordson Major was started and with a heavy chain on board was soon on its way down the home field, for the farm track was too slippery. The remaining churns were quickly cleared off the lorry, then the chain hooked around its front axle. But, try as they might, the lorry refused to shift for the tractor also had difficulty in getting any grip in the icy conditions.

Well, that was it! We had tried, but to no avail. Then somebody said, "What about old Judy?" and with a "Yes, we'll get Judy", back up to the farm we went. The old mare was brought in from the paddock, her bright bay winter coat furry and long and tiny icicles on her beard. Soon we were wending our way with the horse down to the road.

Judy stood patiently while we decided how best to give it a try. The chain was then attached to two more chains and a swingle-tree fixed to the traces. Slowly she walked down the verge and into the shallow ditch, then stopped as the traces went tight. She knew it was a mighty load. Yes, she knew, and paused a moment or two. Then, without a word from any of us, she gathered her great reserves of strength, leant into the collar, her quarters low, and dug in with her toes and pulled. Again she pulled head down. She relaxed for a moment as we watched and she looked to be thinking it out. Then the old mare launched forward into the collar and the chain snapped tight. Incredibly the lorry began to move, the mare staggered sideways as the chains gave. Again she stopped, the traces tightened once more and the mare had got it moving and she kept on dragging it forward, slowly step by step, until the lorry was on the verge and upright again.

So, Judy stood, the traces slack. Her legs trembled and her flanks heaved—she had done it! The men and we boys patted her on the neck and rubbed her ears, "Good old Judy". Back up to the building she went for some warm gruel. The old retired Shire mare, kept out of sentiment, had done it! We were down at the farm and so had witnessed this amazing feat of equine strength. I fancy I saw a smile upon her whiskery face.

Cows

Flank deep among the buttercups in the water-meadows by Thunderbrook, the herd rests chewing the cud: roans, reds and whites dappled in the sunlight. The Dutch artist Cuyp who painted cows would have loved the scene. The cows rest, soporific, and so the forenoon passes. At four o'clock the cattle stir, and slowly, daintily wend their way along worn tracks between the grasses. No haste, rough tongues curl round tall stems to snatch in passing.

From the gate, the cowman calls, "coup, coup". The cows now walk with more purpose, their firm udders swing from side to side. The old lead cow turns down the lane, the herd following close. Feet patter and round the laggards the dog runs to keep them on the move. Each cow walks to her place in the long milking shippen, and chains are put around their necks. In pairs they stand, and soon the sound of milk filling metal buckets is heard. Three people, the cowman, his wife and an assistant sit on low three-legged stools, their heads against the cows flank, their rough hands gently and rhythmically squeeze the teats in pairs and the cows let their milk down in warm jets. They finish each cow by stripping out the last drops between finger and thumb. Each full bucket is weighed, then the foaming milk is emptied into a cooler and strained into a churn.

So the work goes on until finally all the cows are done until the next milking. For twice a day and on every day of the year the cows come to their stalls to be

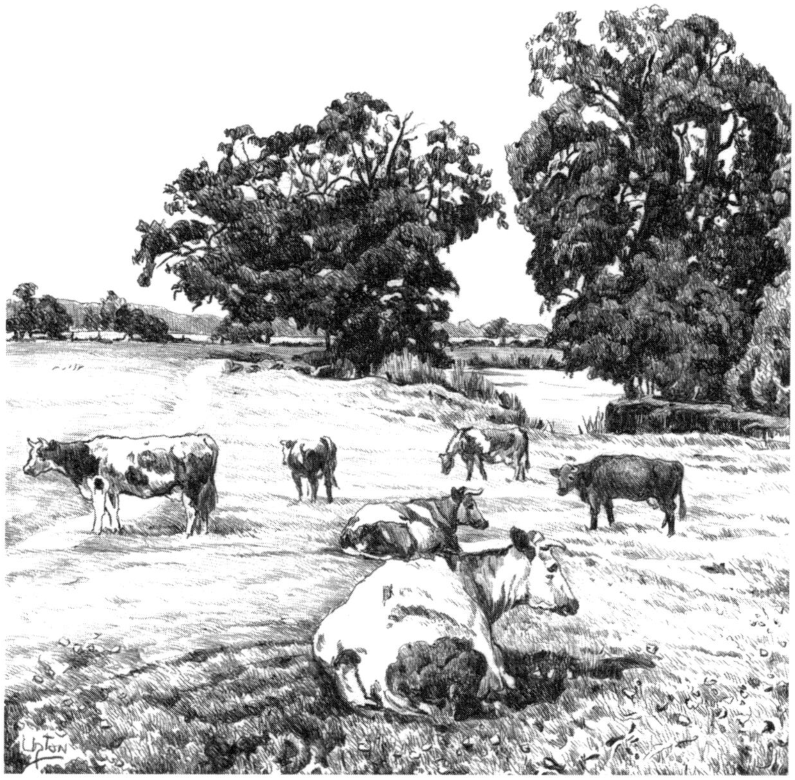

Short horn cows in the water meadow

milked. Rose, Queenie, Strawberry and Fillpail: each cow is known by its name, each is an individual and the cowman knows them all. Cows are inquisitive creatures and tend to come up to see what is going on. They are also herd animals, so generally easy to fetch in for the twice-daily milking.

When we were young, the majority of dairy farmers in the Vale were still milking the cows by hand, and the herd would probably number no more than forty or so. Shorthorns were the most common breed in those days, later to be replaced by the black and white Friesians.

At Spratt's Barn Farm, they had machine milking: the make was, I believe, Gascoigne. This made it possible for the milking to be done by fewer workers. Not all cows took to the cluster of four cups on their udder and would try to kick it off. After the machine was taken off, the cows were usually stripped of the last drops of milk. It was considered an aid against mastitis.

If you took a mug of that fresh milk straight from the cow, it tasted like nirvana.

After milking was over the cowman would turn them out into the meadow. He, on his way back to his cottage, always took with him a can of fresh milk. In the springtime he would sometimes pick up a couple of pheasant eggs from a nest and tip their contents into the can. By the time he got home, what with the shaking of the milk and eggs, he had custard for dinner.

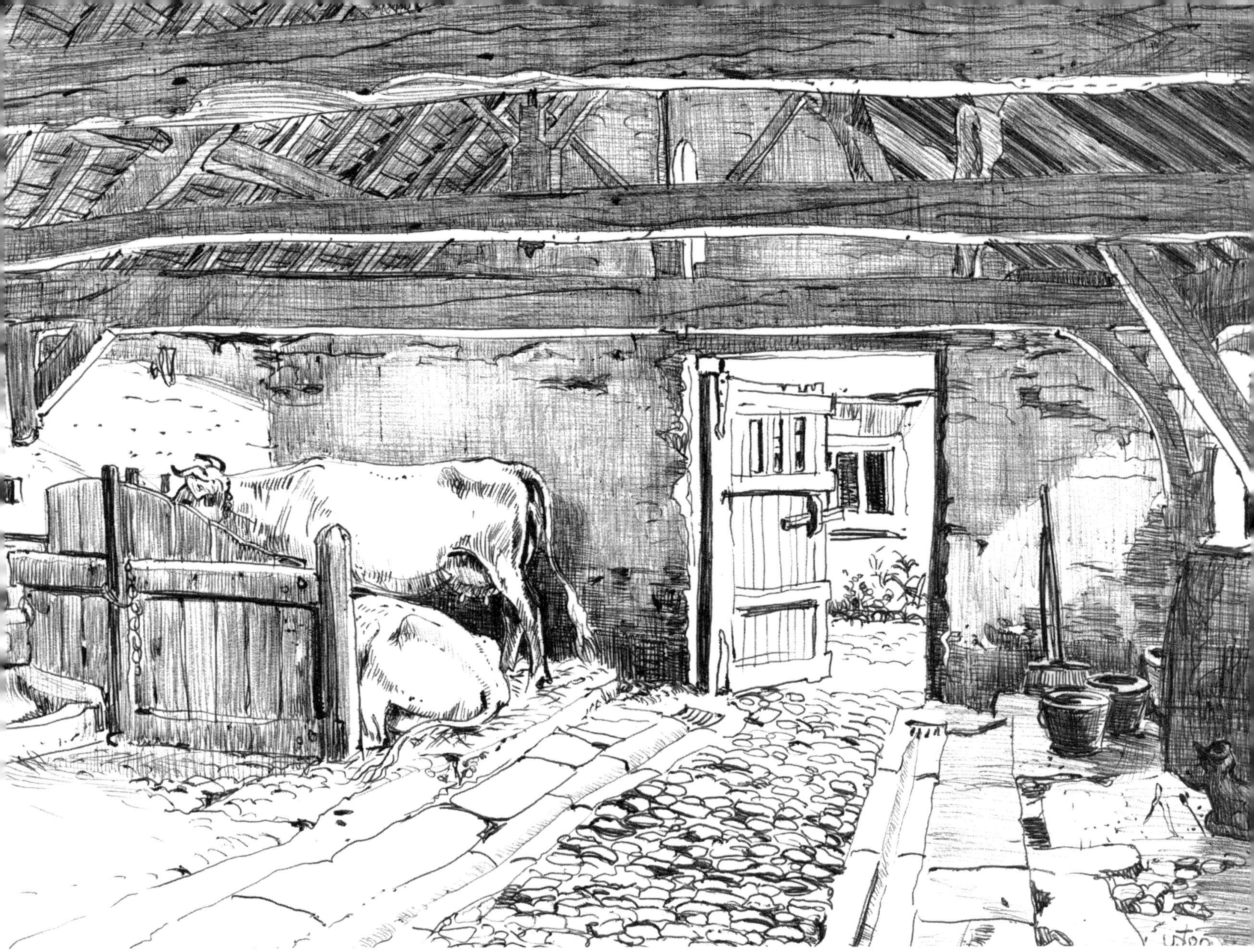

The Shippon

Plaister's Bull

I still see the bulky, muscular form and hear his deep moaning as he is led out to pasture. Sleek black and white coat, masive head with tightly curled hair between his short, thick horns. He curls up his lip as the ring pulls on his nose. He turns his head sideways to ease the pain and drool flecks from his jaw to splash his thick brisket.

He holds a certain fascination. Such power, such fertility: no wonder the bull was worshipped by early man!

A local estate had a pedigree herd of Aberdeen Angus, one of the best quality beef beeeds. One year they sold a pedigree bull at the Perth sale for £17,000, an astonishing price for those days.

It was a summer's day and the great house was open to the public. Just as a group of ladies was coming up the drive Fred the cowman, fetching in Gay Eric

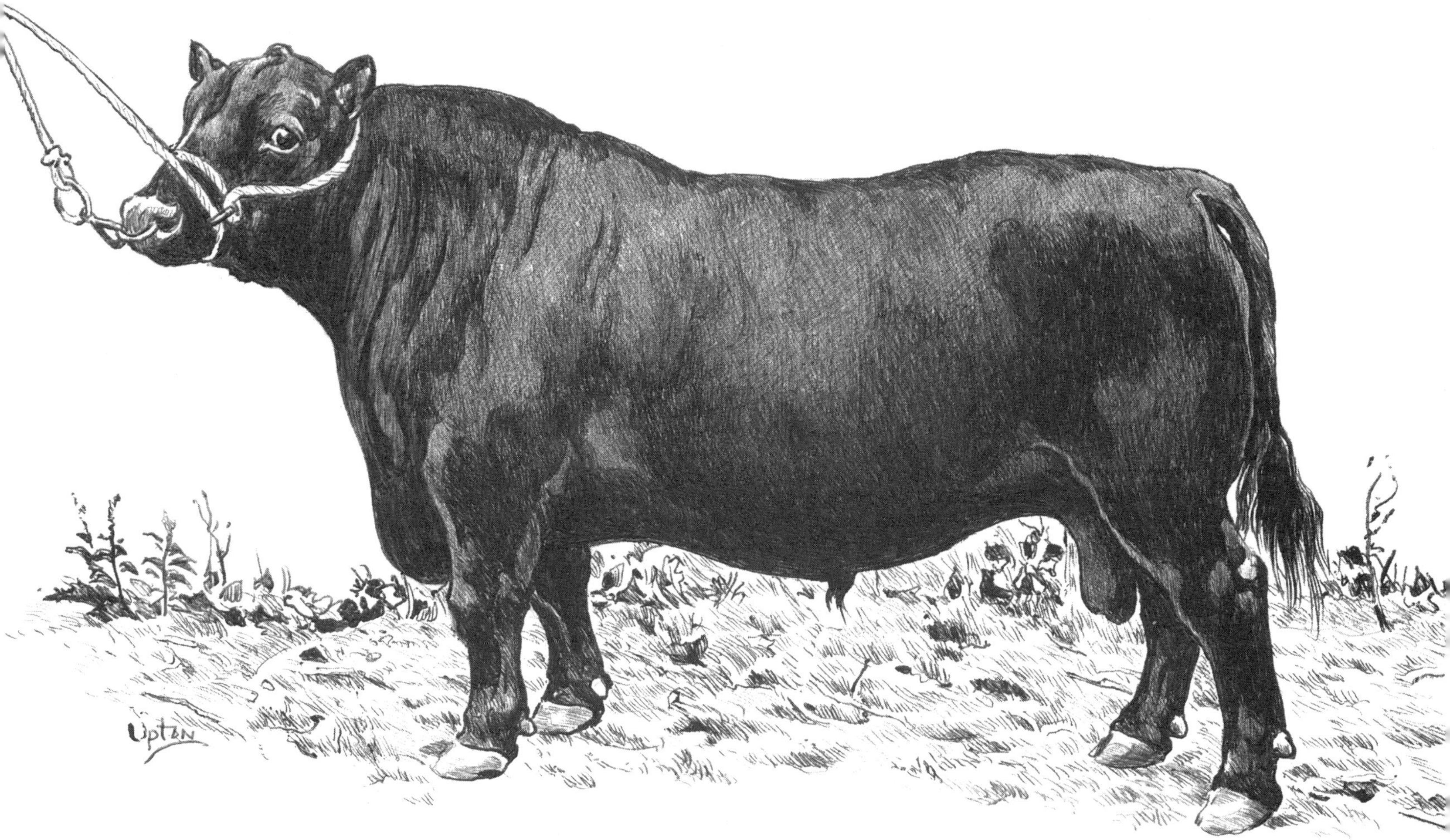

An Angus bull – Gay Eric

the bull, walked him right across their path. He stopped and, the bull being led by a wooden pole hooked onto the ring in his nose, opened his mouth to lick at the ring. "Cor blyme", said one of the ladies, "He's got no teeth!" "Well", said Fred, "He's got zum false teeth below, and I be takin' him to the dentist to get a new top set". "Do you know", said the same lady talking to the others, "I never knew that cows had false teeth, did you?"

Generally speaking, beef bulls are quieter than bulls of the milk breeds, but even so I remembered the shock in the village when we heard that the farmer who lived at Paradise Farm was killed by his bull. Some say that Jersey bulls are the most temperamental, which may come as a surprise, for Jersey cows are the sweetest and prettiest of all our breeds, almost doe-like in appearance.

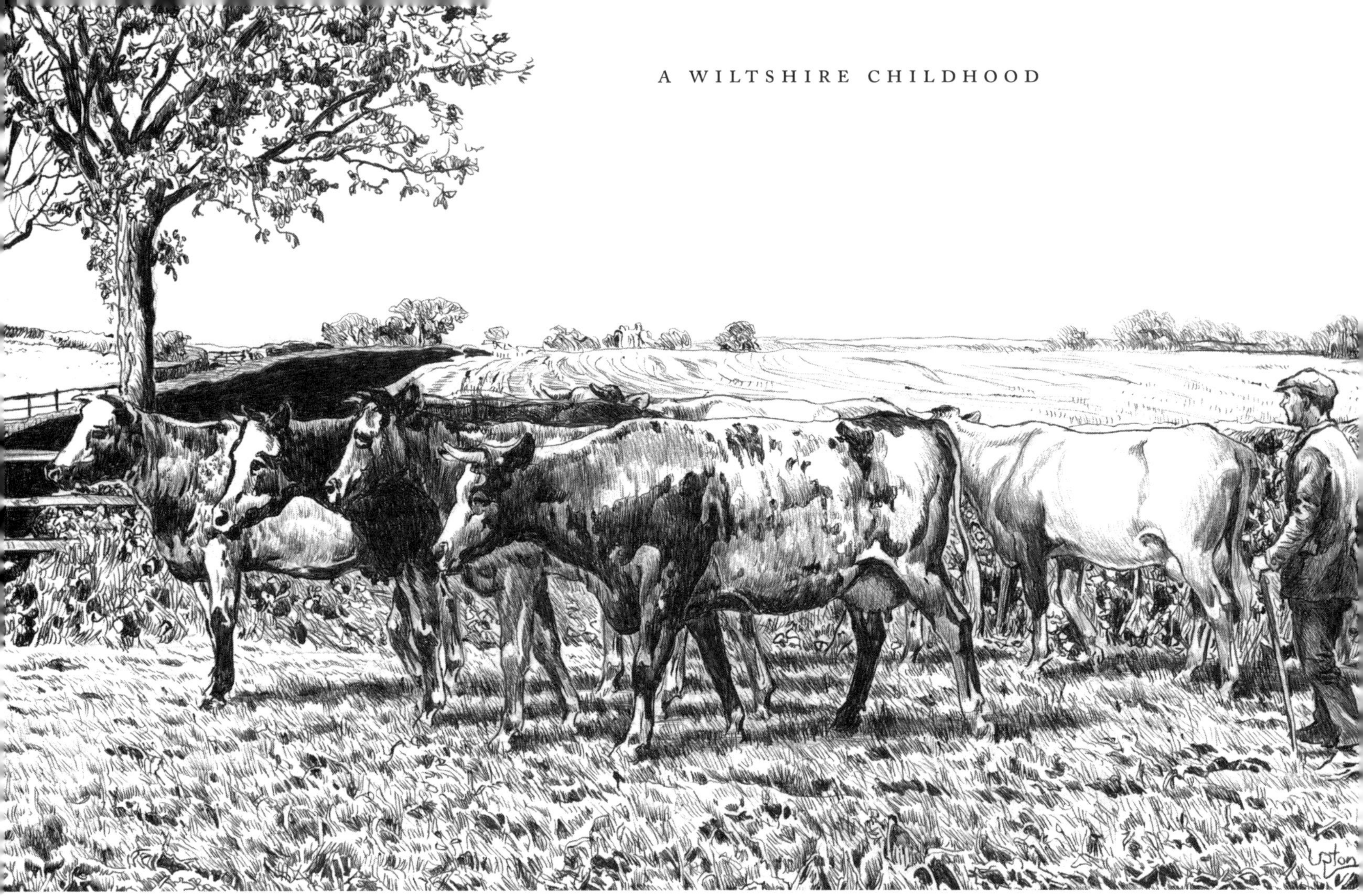
Upton

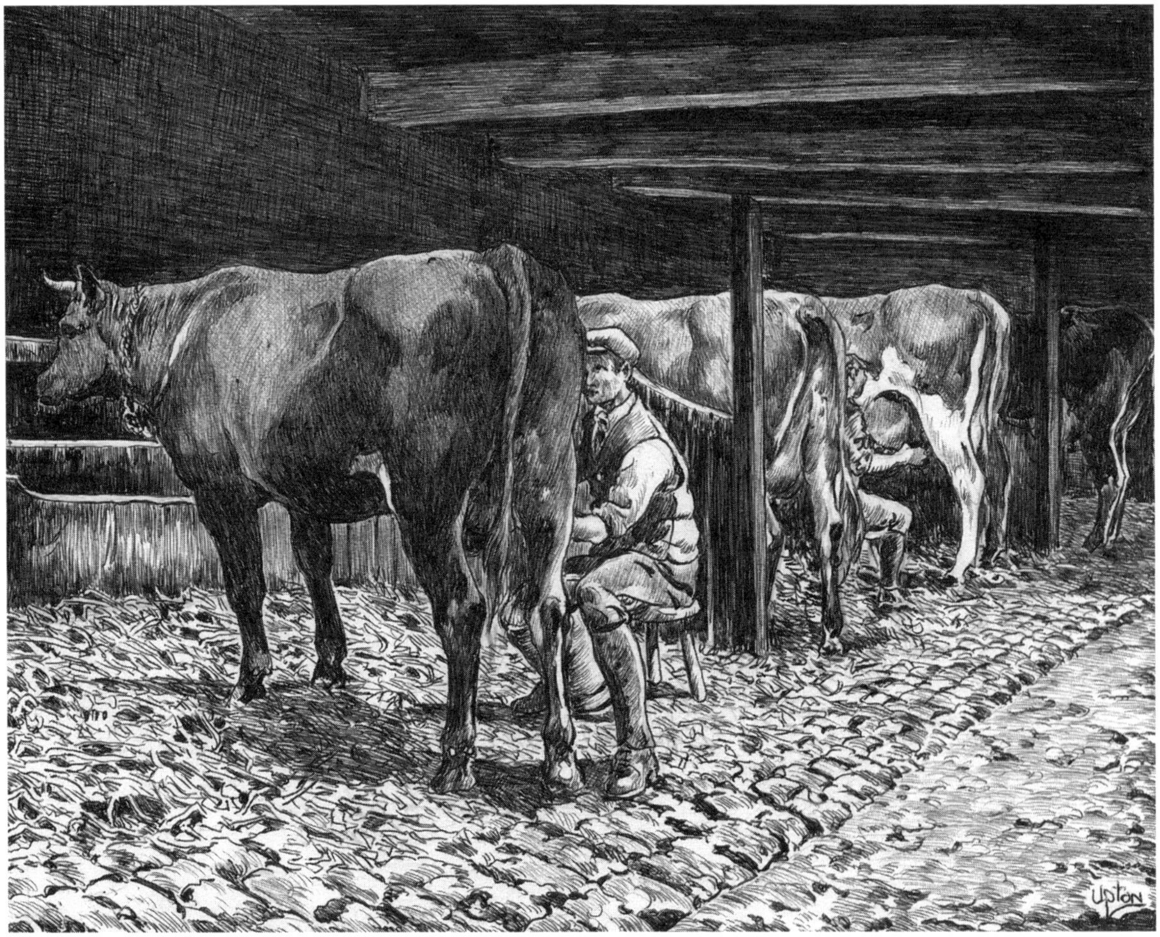
Upton

Dolly and the Market Cart

Every morning, Dolly the bay Welsh Cob would be harnessed to take the milk churns down to the road. Blinkered, she would stand, short black tail a-twitch, as the full churns were put into the open-backed cart. Then out through the yard from the dairy door we would go at a smart walk. A fat work-maid was Dolly. Once out of the gate, she would set off at a spanking trot, the churns a-rattle. Of her own Dolly would come back to a walk at the top of the hill, and her bay bottom would sit back into the leather breeching as her feet slid, then held on the stony incline.

At the main road, under a great leaved chestnut tree, was the milk stand. Here we would off-load the churns and exchange them for empty ones. A chain was then linked through the churn handles, across the back of the cart for the return jouney.

Now that we boys no longer had to worry about spilt milk, we could imagine ourselves as charioteers, the cart Boadicea's and Dolly a fiery stallion. Dolly joined in the fun as up the steep track she galloped, her broad back rising up and down. Sparks flew from her shoes and drunken churns clashed and slid against the restraining chain. Over the crest of the hill we would fly, our legs braced as the wheels bounced off stones, only to come back to a sedate walk as the farm buildings came into view, nestling in the tree-framed hollow. Dolly once more the market cart pony.

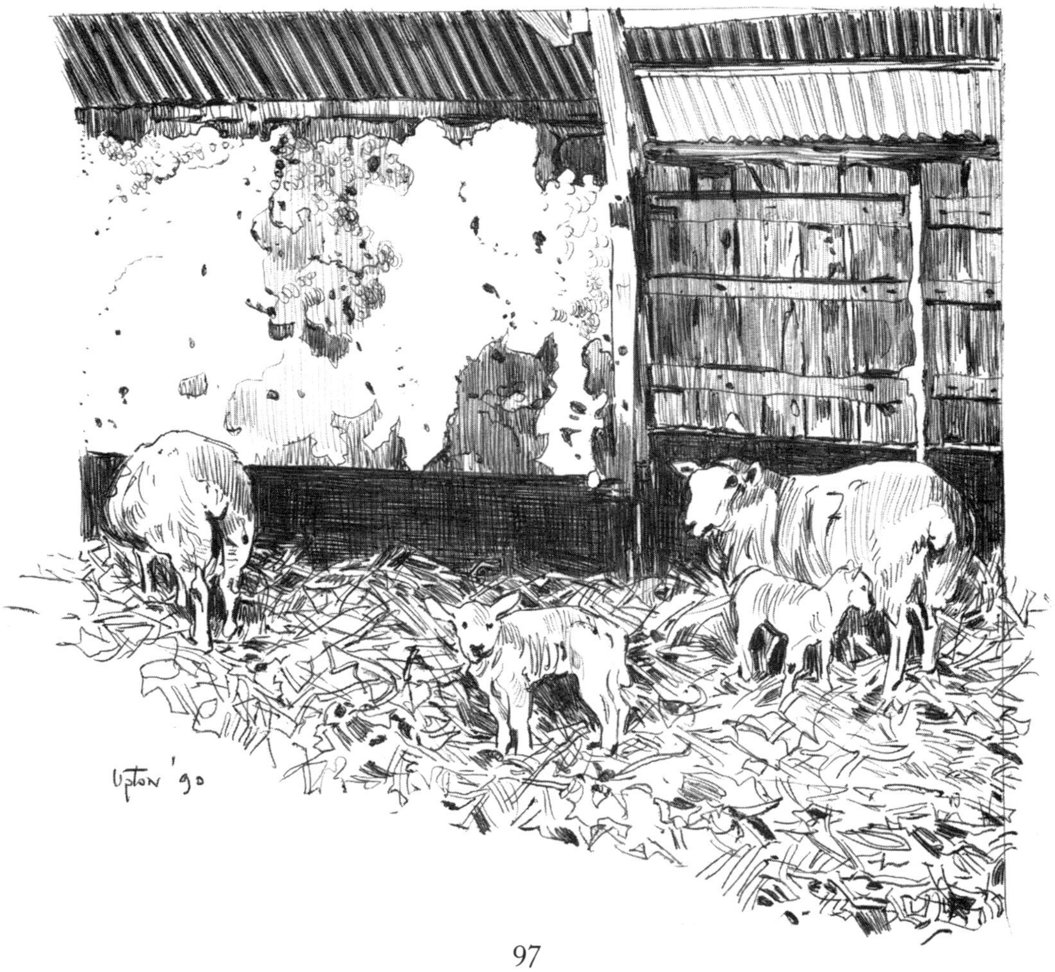

Opposite, top: Coming in for Milking.

Bottom: Milking.

Left: Ewes and lambs

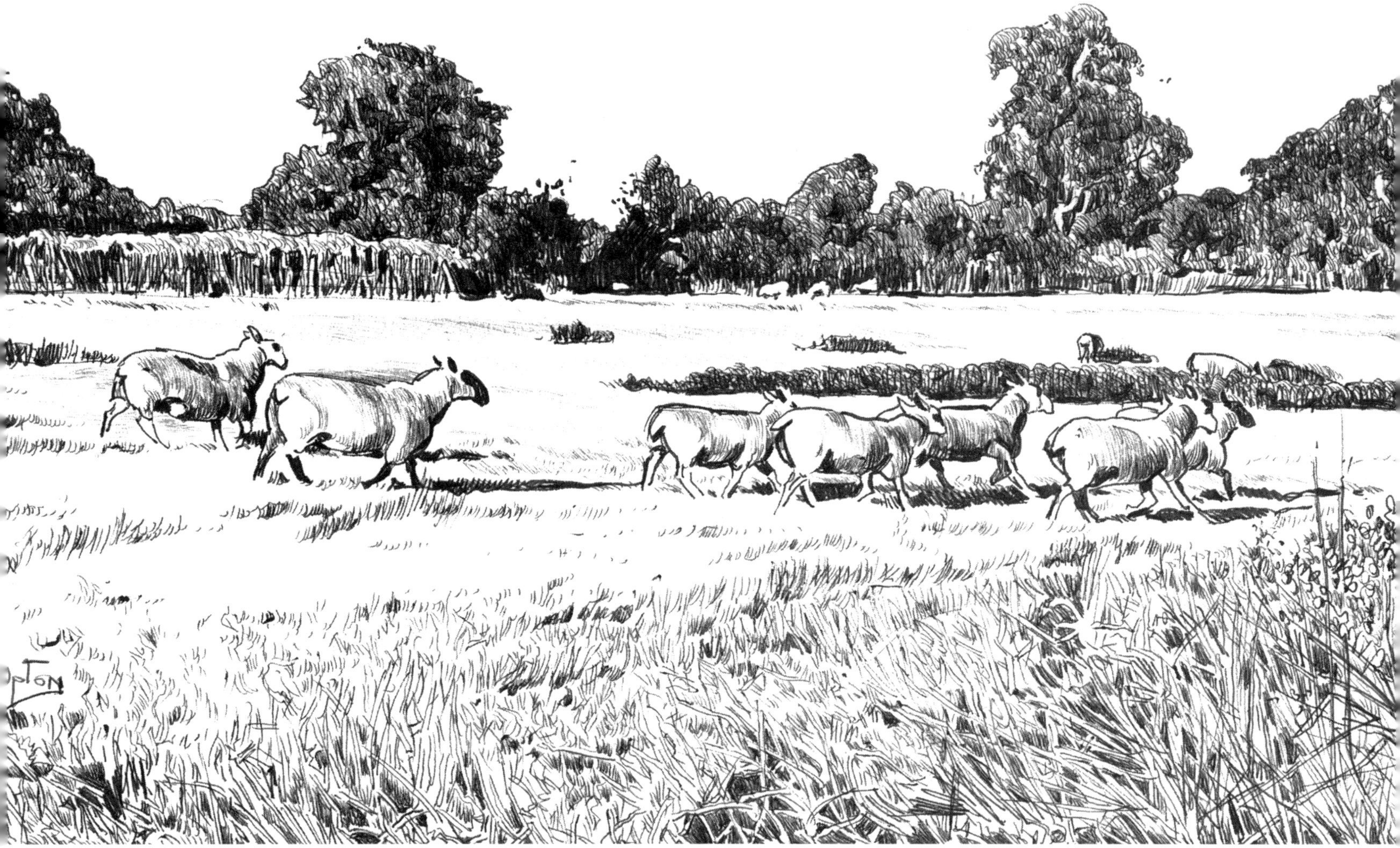

Sheep

Of all farm livestock sheep possibly had the greatest influence in earlier centuries, for England's wealth was in her flocks, and their wool was so important. Today, due to artificial fabrics, wool prices are no longer what they were, yet no cloth is better than that off the back of sheep.

In our Vale, there were few sheep, but up on the Downs large flocks of Dorset Horns, Cluns, Suffolks and other English breeds grazed the upland fields, almost every country having a breed of its own. However, it was not necessarily for their wool that they were farmed, but for their meat: mutton and lamb.

The busiest times of the shepherd's year were at lambing, dipping and shearing when he required extra help, for all three jobs were hard work. Lambing went on day and night: checking the ewes and assisting with a birth where necessary. It was considered bad luck to ask, 'How many lambs, Shepherd?'. It could go on for some weeks, but when all was done there was a deep satisfaction in seeing the ewes out on the hill, each with her offspring.

Why is it that lambs are so pretty and bright? They race around and play 'tag' together or 'I'm the king of the castle', while the ewes just get on with grazing or lying down, that is until the youngsters dash back for a feed. Yet adult sheep

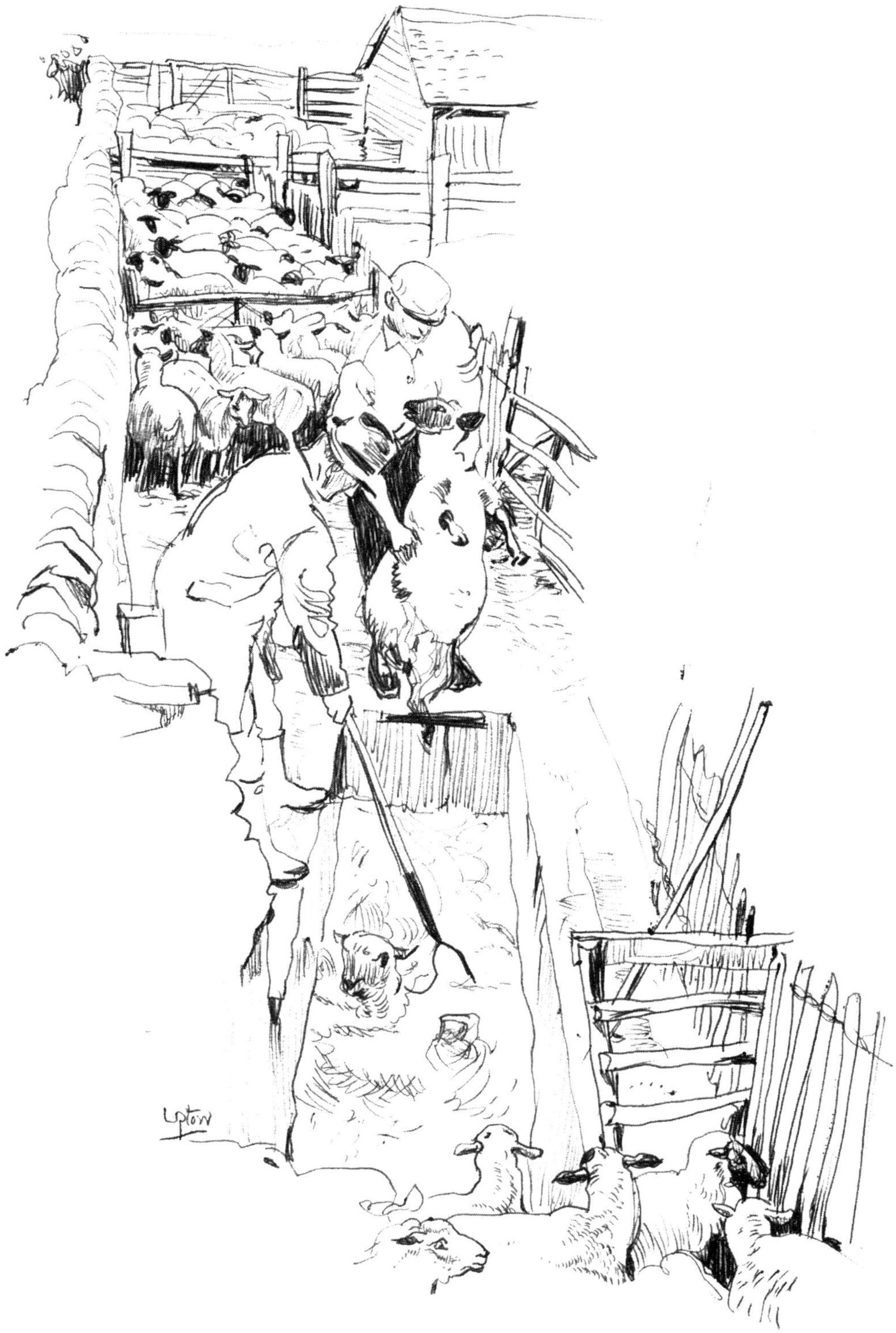

Sheep dipping

somehow lose that youthful liveliness, indeed nothing is more baleful than the look in their eyes. Is adulthood always like this?

When we were boys dipping the flock was a legal necessity and the local policeman PC MacDonald would be there to watch proceedings. Each sheep in turn was manhandled into a long trough of water into which was added an insecticide, then its head would be pushed under the water until finally it struggled out up a sloping exit into a concrete yard. Here it would shake itself vigorously before running off to join the rest of the flock which had already been through the ordeal.

Sheep are vulnerable to parasites, hence the necessity of dipping. Whilst writing about sheep, one naturally turns to the subject of the dedicated companion of the shepherd, his dog. Flora, a little black and white bitch with prick ears, a daughter of Wilson's Glen, was a natural worker with sheep. Her skills are in her blood, tracing back through Nell, Cap and so on to Tweed and Telfor's Old Hemp in the 1900's.

Flora 'eyes' the ewe who stamps her foot. She freezes low with shoulders hunched and , as in slow motion, slides forward a pace. The ewe breaks, the crouching bitch is at once slipping fast across the uneven ground at an angle to head off the recalcitrant sheep. Having passed it, Flora suddenly switches around, once more crouched in concentration, her eyes fixed on the ewe who backs off and turns to join the flock. The bitch relaxes and moves forward at a swinging trot; the sheep are penned.

Happy are the dogs who have a job to do, no boredom is their lot. They serve with joy and share their days with the shepherds who know and value their skills and companionship. Indeed, without the collie, how would the flocks, particularly on moor and mountain, be gathered?

On Totterdown the slopes are littered with boulders of Sarcen tone. In the lee of each rest Blackface ewes. Soon the slopes come alive as sheep bound up before the dogs. Today is the gathering. I remember that my mother, when passing a flock, would always say aloud, 'Good morning Mrs Sheep'.

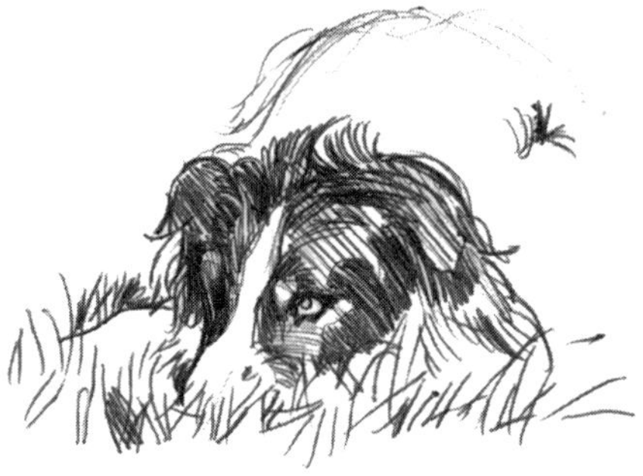

Sheepdog Trials at Ffair Rhos

Rain sodden, the long field by the lane lies high over th misting valley and among the rough grasses Swallows rise and dip in wind-blown freedom. Behind the pub at one end of the field men are gathered each with a sheepdog at heel or held by a rope. It is the day of the local sheepdog trials.

Suddenly the dogs cease eying one another suspiciously, and as one they turn, ears and eyes alert, to watch the far end of the field. Down in the dip five wild Welsh sheep come into view some two hundred yards away. The group of men

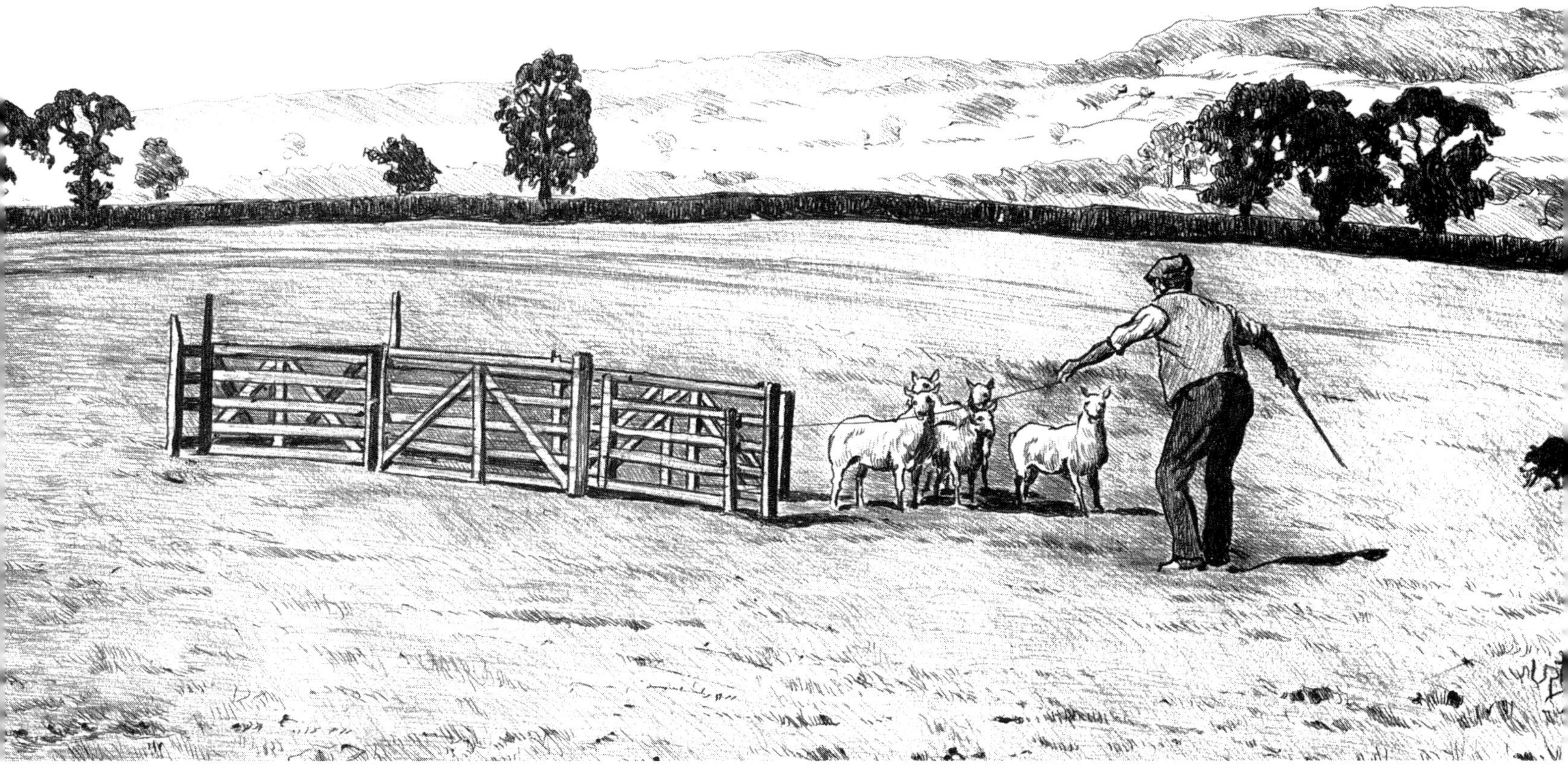

stop their gossip to watch the solitary man leaning on his crook by the pen made of hurdles. Beside him stands his dog, tense but motionless. A whistle and he is off, speeding low in an arc, a driving black and white bundle flowing over the undulating ground, casting wide to encircle the sheep who re-group in a rush. They move warily watching the dog crouched in the grasses, awaiting the next whistle. He creeps in 'eying' the sheep, freezes, then swings wide to the right, low-moving but surprisingly fast to intercept one sheep who tries to break back.

Sheepdog trials

Next they are driven between two stakes and on towards a gate around which they come, all close together and not too fast. Through another gap they go then up towards the shepherd who stands waiting. Here the sheep suddenly break away with heads stiffly held high and gallop off with tails-a-bob. A shrill whistle and the dog is casting round again to hold the sheep. They stop suddenly aware of the ever-present object holding their gaze and controlling them. They turn defeated towards the shepherd a second time. Tension mounts, then suddenly the sheep are in the shedding ring. Quickly one marked sheep is separated by the dog who then puts them together again and they move onto the final job of penning the five sheep. Successfully done, the shepherd calls out, 'that'll do', as the dog eyes the sheep through the rails. A fair trial.

Sheep-washing in the Brecon Beacons.

Six in the morning, couched under a rock on a cliff-face of the Brecons, we were checking on Peregrines nesting in the area. Beneath our rock is scree and small mountain ash; below again, the greener ground, rushy platts, a track and a white coiling stream. Sheep dot the valley and hillsides.

As we watch, movement begins, sheep bound and flow far below us then move on slowly to join the bunch. Two dogs, black and white, race around the sheep gathering. We then see five men, one mounted on a grey pony. The sheep are now all moving in the direction of a small stone bridge that bestrides the stream.

The noise of bleating reaches up to us as the flock pours down the valley. Dogs, their tongues lolling, move easier now. The track to one side of the bridge has been blocked with hurdles and here the sheep are held until one by one they are caught under the neck and by their wool to be pushed through a gap in the side of the bridge. They fall into turbulent water then swim strongly for the bank and scramble out. They call out in cracked voices and shake themselves and hurry away, fanning out to follow their tracks to the hill.

So, the morning wears on as we rest, watching through space until soft rain drifts, curling up the valley below. We, losing sight, stand in rock-strewn isolation girt round by soft vapours.

Goats

Goats are wayward creatures, each very much a character, inquisitive and mischievous.

The Brown family had an Old English nanny-goat of a roan colour who lived in their orchard, tethered by a chain attached to a leather collar. But 'Peggy', for that was her name, was always getting loose, usually to be found in the garden enjoying the last of the lettuces, or having pulled down the washing on the line.

A local farmer let the Boy Scouts camp in one of his fields. His daughter's goat chewed through the guy ropes of the Scout Master's tent. You can imagine the scene and the comments.

But to return to Peggy: one activity could never be completed without her 'putting her foot in it'- in the milk bucket! When she had decided that standing still was no longer necessary and milking over, the struggle started and somehow we always managed to get feet into the bucket of milk. While we carried the bucket into the house we tried, not always successfully, to remove the mud and straw floating on the milk.

The goat who remains my favourite was a billy, bearded and with large curved horns. My favourite because of his fantastic acrobatic ability and clowning—he should have joined a circus! He could also be a relentless pursuer of small children who ran in fear before his lowered head until the inevitable impact and lift-off was performed. Billy was often tethered by a chain fixed to an iron stake hammered

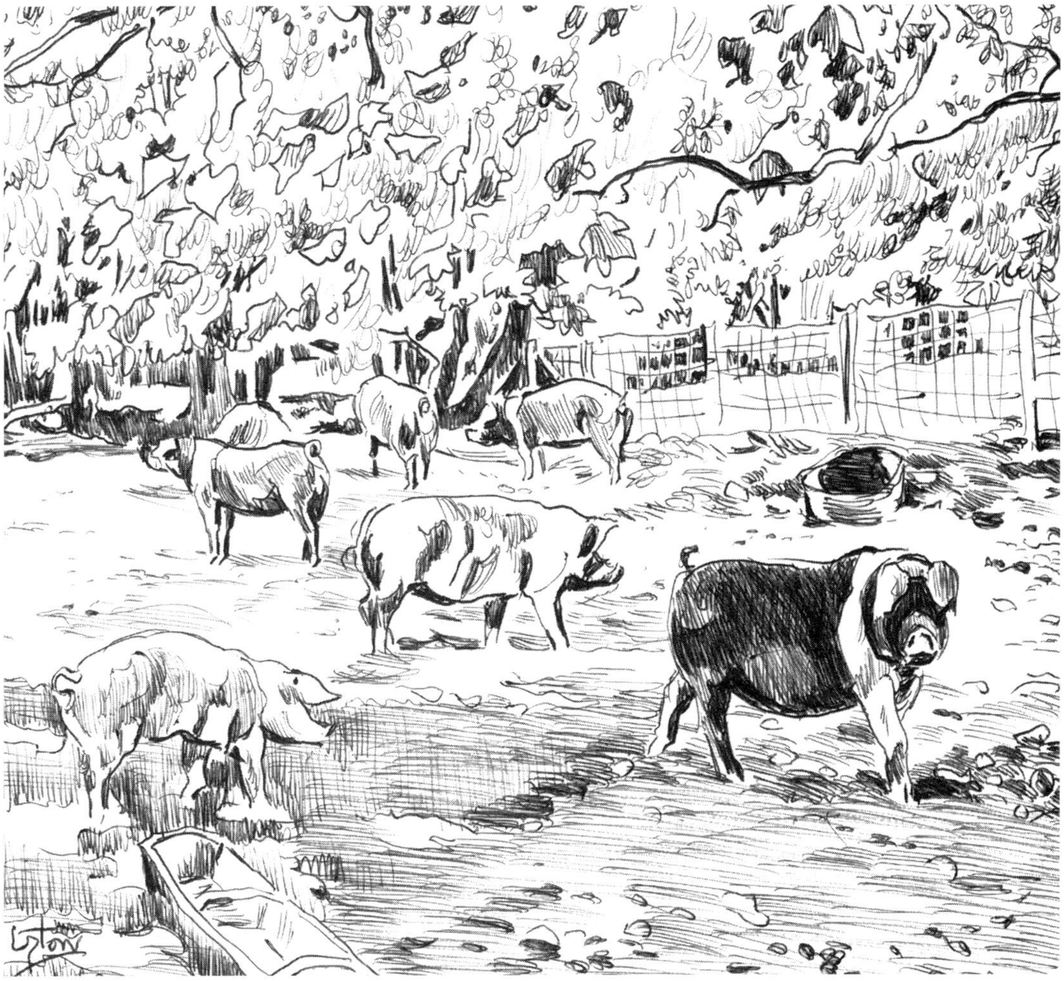

into the ground. Nothing was more amazing then to see him balancing, all four feet together, on top of the iron stake. His best act, however, was a puzzle which would have caused Pythagoras to scratch his head. In warm weather Billy liked to lie in an old chicken house, its door being open. Was it to enjoy the view? He would somehow get his head with the large curving horns through the small opening, where originally hens would have entered. It looked impossible and quite ridiculous.

Pigs

Today the pig is to be killed. The same pig whose back we have scratched and who has always greeted us with a friendly grunt. We have watched him grow up from a pink baby snuggling with his brothers and sisters in the litter. His bright intelligent eye will no longer reflect his humour. We hear, but cannot bear to watch, his death.

In the wash house, he is dismembered until nothing is recognisable as 'him'. Instead, it's fine hams which are hung above the range. Soon it is pork for dinner, ham for supper and bacon for breakfast. We don't even have butter on our bread, but fat from the pig.

The old Large White boar was lank-sided and scaly, his eyes bloodshot and

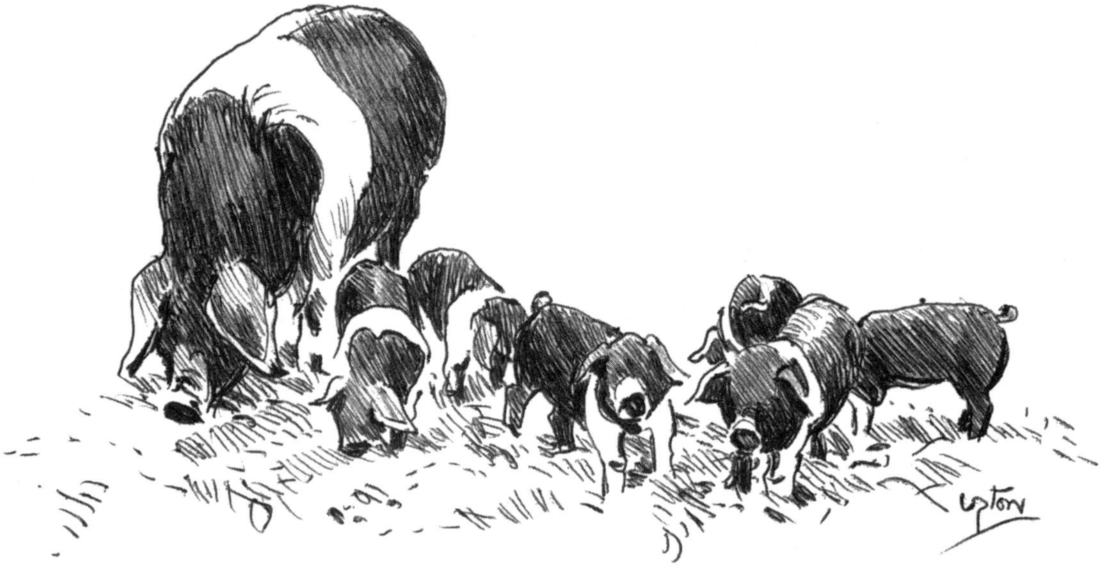

temper uncertain. His wives, both Wessex Saddlebacks and Whites, lived with him until their time was due. At the wood's edge, they rooted and excavated, or sunbathed flat out, occasionally to squeal in their dreams.

Later, as it neared farrowing time, the sows were brought into the pig sties in the yard. Once they began to pick up mouthfuls of straw to make a bed, their time was near. Soon there would be eight or more shocking-pink piglets scrabbling for their share of mother's milk. That is all but one little chap, pushed aside—the runt of the litter. Later he gets a chance and snuffs softly to himself as if realising his lot, while his avaricious brothers and sisters sleep in a higgledy-piggledy heap.

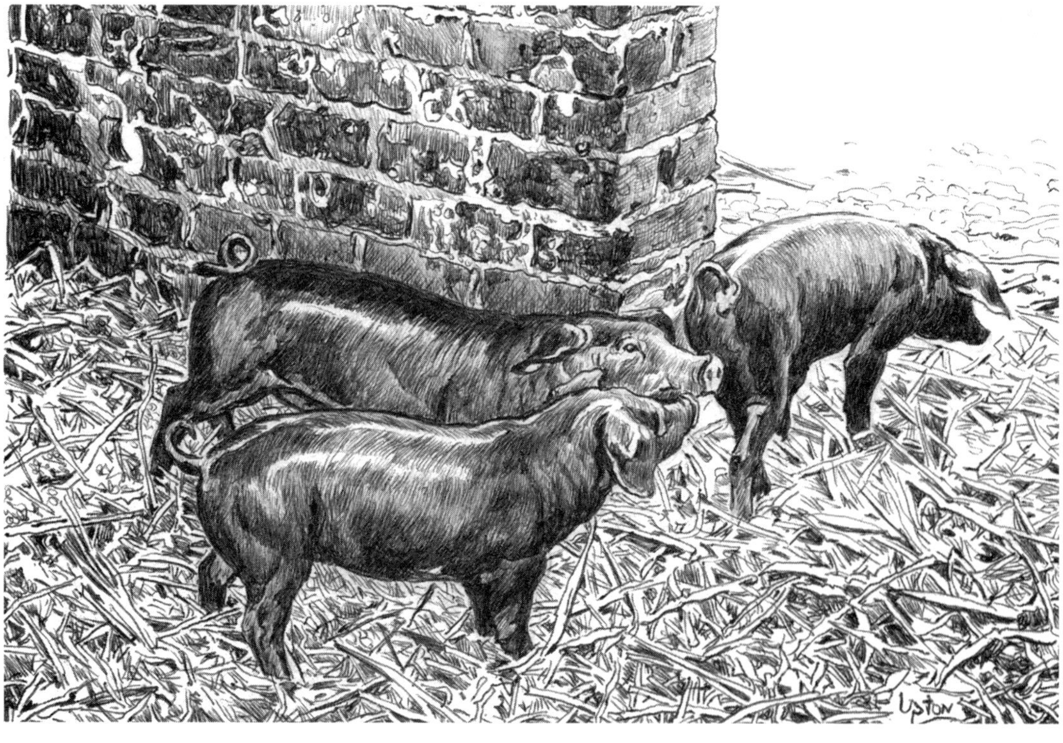

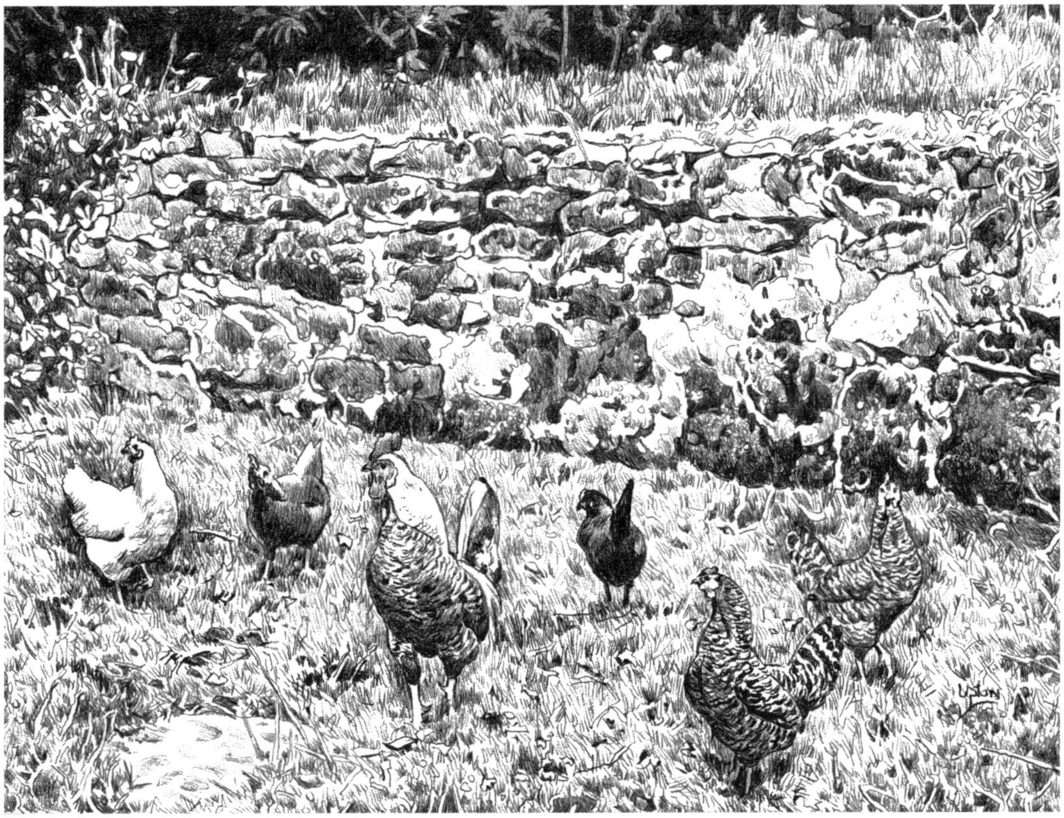

Marans, Leghorns and Rhode Island Reds...

Poultry

Beneath the ancient apple trees, the hens scratch and search for worms or grubs: a mixed flock of speckled Marans, racy Leghorns and Rhode Island Reds questing about in the sunlight. Around them overseeing his harem, struts the proud Maran cockerel. Occasionally he finds something of interest and calls to his ladies who come running to share in the find.

Their hen-house is built of wood and stands on four iron wheels with a ladder up to the birds' entrance. In one corner there is a cupboard, its three shelves serving as nesting boxes, lined in straw. In one a puffed-up broody sits tight, so we slip a

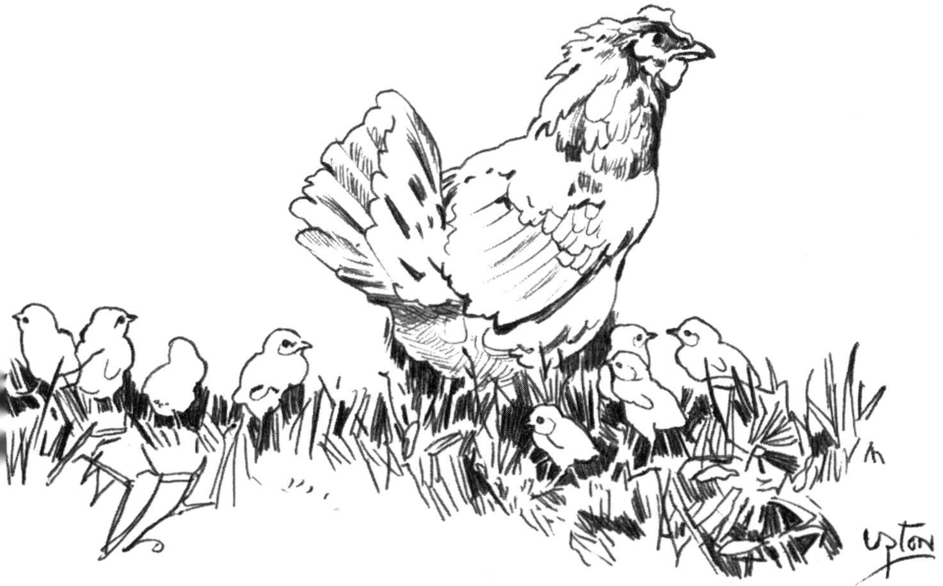

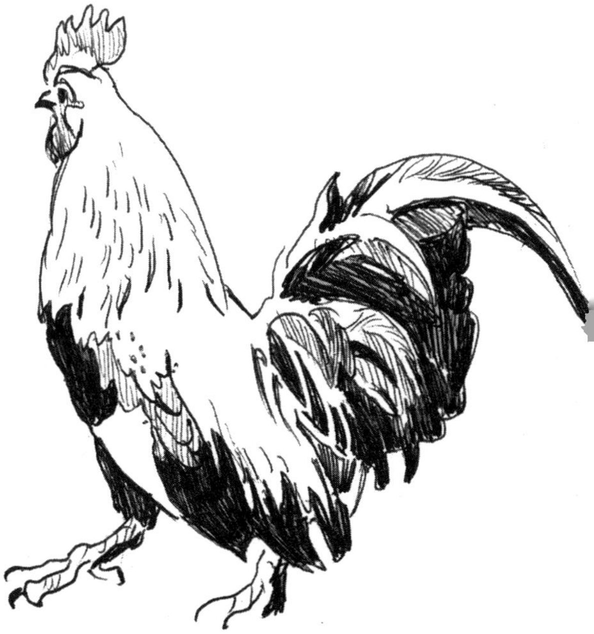

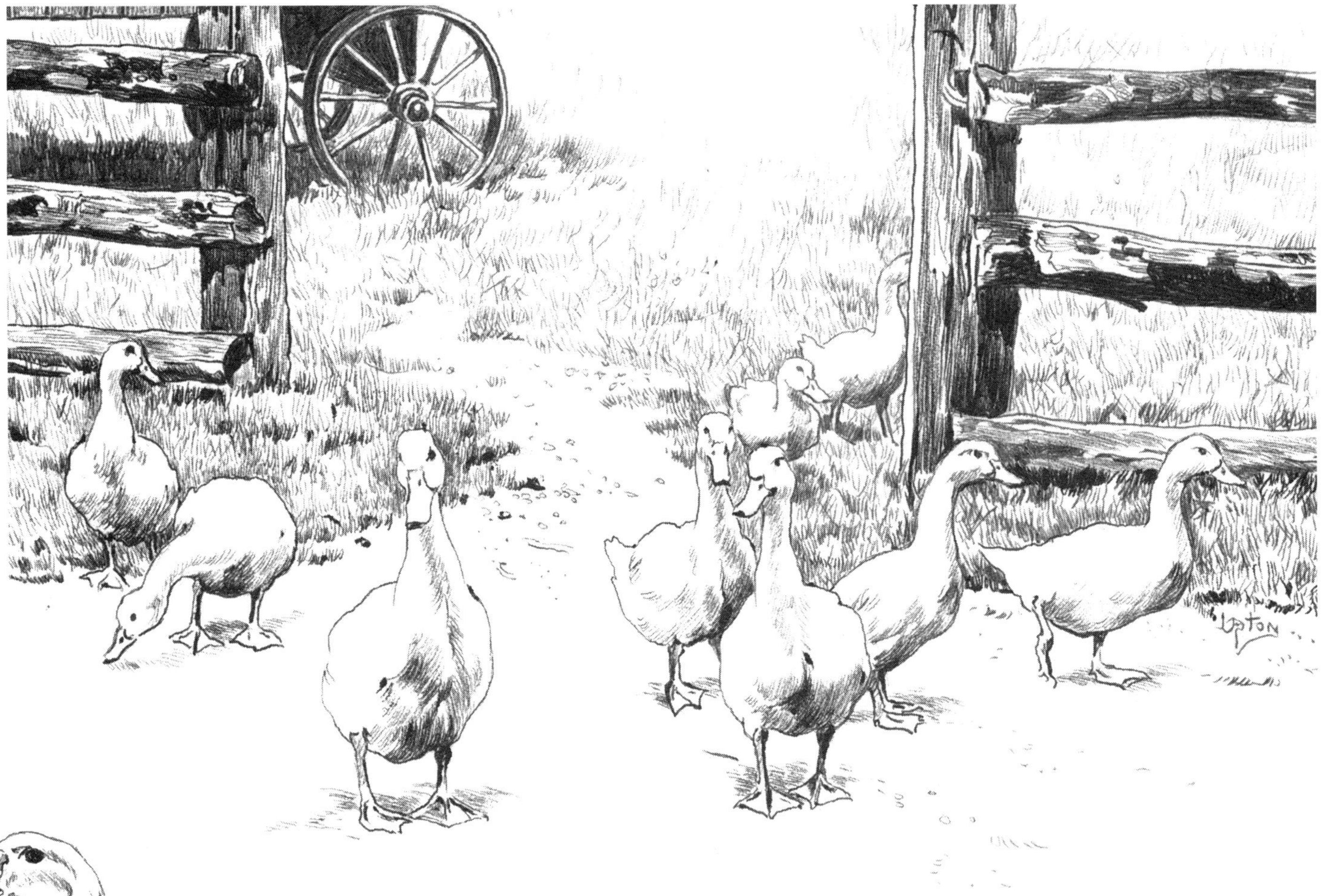

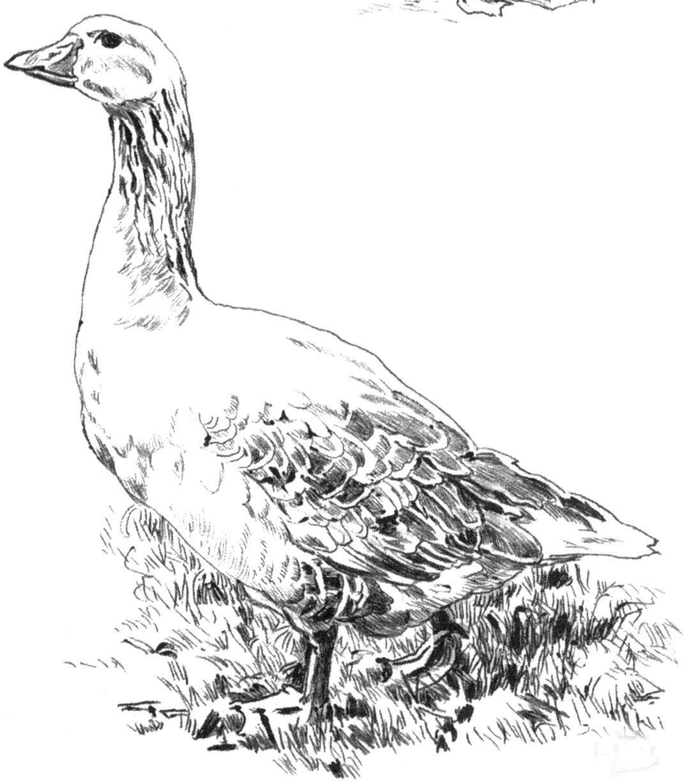

hand beneath her to take the warm brown eggs. These we put with the other eggs already found into a basket. Egg-collecting is rather like a game of hide-and-seek, for certain hens choose the oddest of places in which to lay their eggs. One had a nest among nettles close by the stone wall and there brought off a brood before she was discovered.

Down in the stable yard, bantams strolled around the horse boxes and the manure heap. A mixed lot of Seabrights and Old Dutch. And in a hen coop with a slatted front, an anxious mother jerks her head through the bars, clucking all the while to her striped babies who are darting about taking scant notice of maternal concerns as to their safety. But when evening comes, the

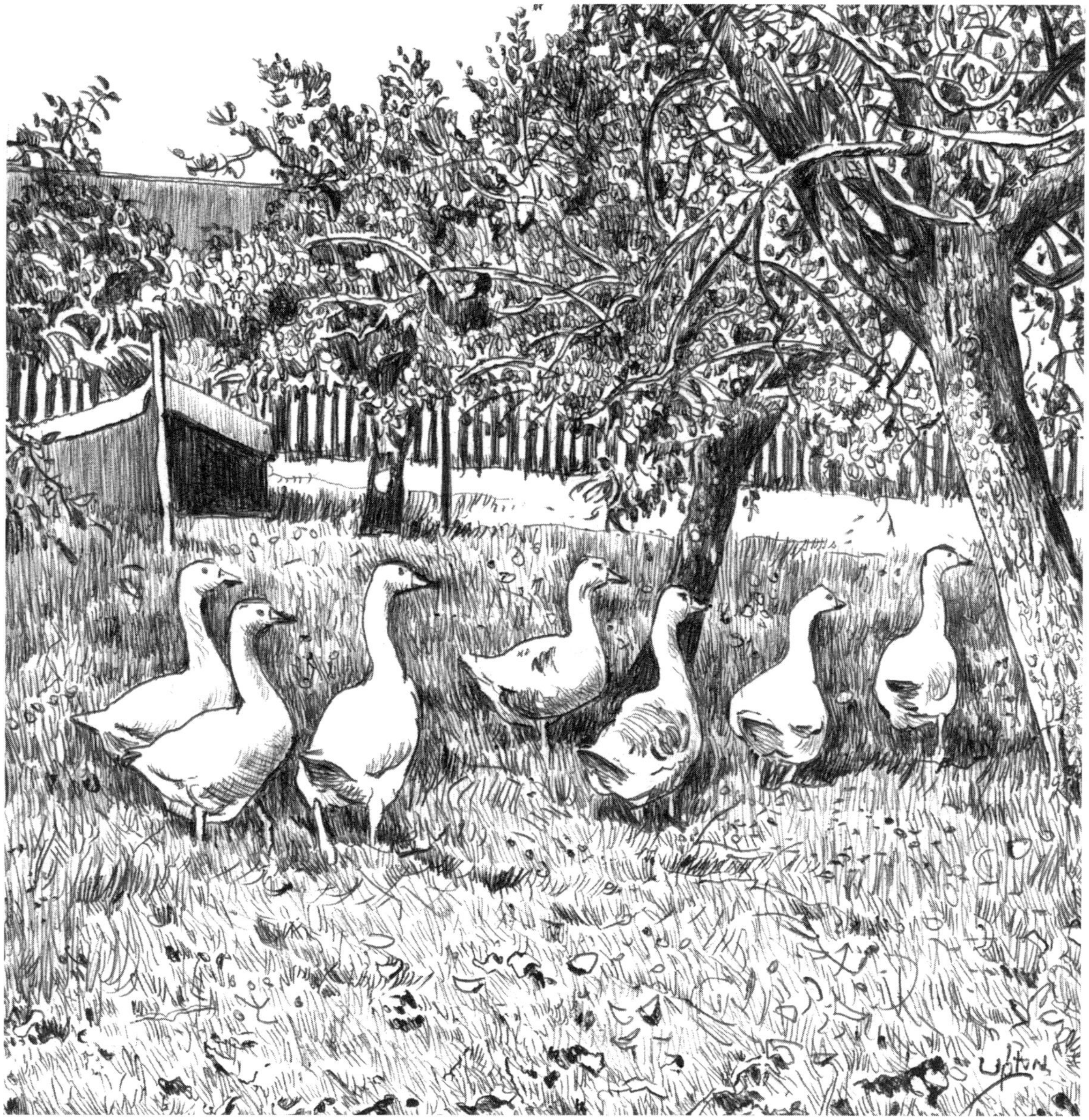

chicks snuggle up close beneath their mother's wings, as muffled chirps can be heard before they settle for the night. Once they are in, a board is placed infront of the slats to keep them safe until morning.

Why are ducks such comics? They march in line and seem to be always smiling. Ducklings, like naughty boys, are regularly up to mischief and worry the hen foster-mother out of her wits. On the pond, the white Aylesbury ducks sail along sedately, keeping company with their reflections, up-ending, paddles going like mad, with their tails in the air.

Geese on the other hand are the 'guard dogs' of the farm, alert and serious, ever ready to call out a warning at the approach of strangers. One grey and white Toulouse gander was to be avoided, for he stood no intrusion, and with neck outstretched and wings flapping he would drive off all but the bravest.

Opposite, top: ducks in the yard. Bottom: a goose.

Above: geese in the orchard.

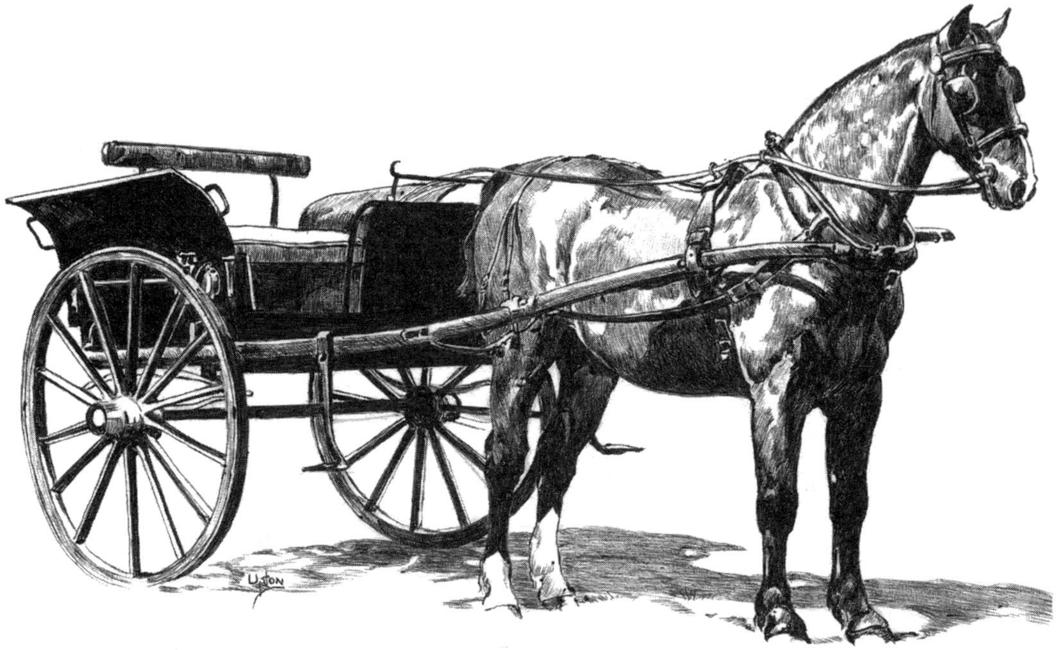

Travel by Ralli-car

What nicer way to travel the lanes than by pony and trap! Alas, today it would be a risky business indeed, but in our youth it was both possible and necessary as petrol was rationed.

Our ways were the quiet by-roads with hedges heavy with may blossom, and later in the season with dog-roses. These lanes wandering casually under a canopy of stately hedgerow elms, with dusty ribbons of sunlight and shadow. This was before the deadly elm disease turned our wooded vale into a version of Oppy Wood in World War II. Around each bend one would find something to note or wonder at and, sitting up high in a gig or governess cart, you could really enjoy the views.

These same hedgerows have mostly disappeared because of the widening of roads and the onward march of tarmac.

On Sundays Dolly the Welsh Cob would, after delivering the milk, receive a thorough grooming ready for an outing, perhaps a visit to friends for tea. This was always exciting for Dolly was a great trotter and went along like an express train. The best set of harness would be used for such occasions, made of shiny patent leather, black with brass buckles and terrets. The collar was slipped over her head and the harness with traces strapped in place. The back pad rested temporarily on her loins for her tail to be put through the crupper. This she always resisted by holding her tail down, but then the pad was buckled in place. Lastly, the bridle with its neat semi-circular blinkers and Liverpool bit was slipped on and the reins attached.

The ralli-car was a joy to ride in for it was light, superbly sprung and balanced, with glossy black paint-work picked out with yellow coach lines. Being so light, it could be held up by the elegantly curved shafts and drawn forward, slipped through the tugs and belly-band loosely buckled up.

Dolly was always eager to be off and you had to look smart once you let go of her head. So, first the passengers had to climb in, then with the reins and whip in your hands you mounted the step as Dolly fidgetted as if her feet were on hot bricks and the big wheels rocked back and forth. Once everyone was settled, a light click of the tongue and off she would go, the wheels spinning round, the car swaying rhythmically to the sounds of the trotting mare. My, she was a great trotter!

What a way to travel as Dolly settled to a steady pace which she would keep up for mile after mile. Sometimes we went to tea with friends living some ten miles away and thought nothing of such a journey.

In wartime Britain, relatives living in and near London would visit us for a break from the bombing. As they arrived by train at the town railway station we would be there to collect them with Dolly and the ralli-car. Even we as boys sensed their pleasure at seeing, at such a time in their lives, this reminder of a quieter, more graceful and happier way of life.

Our Ponies

While remembering the farm equines of my youth, I must not forget our ponies who played such an important role in our lives. Dolly, the Welsh Cob, is mentioned elsewhere, but the very first pony we got to know was a white part-Welsh mare named Misty. She actually belonged to a great friend of ours and taught us a lot about riding and driving. Her owner went to a girls' boarding school where pupils were able to take their ponies as well. Janette took two, Linette a bay mare of 14 hands and Misty. But Misty was expelled after just two weeks for naughty

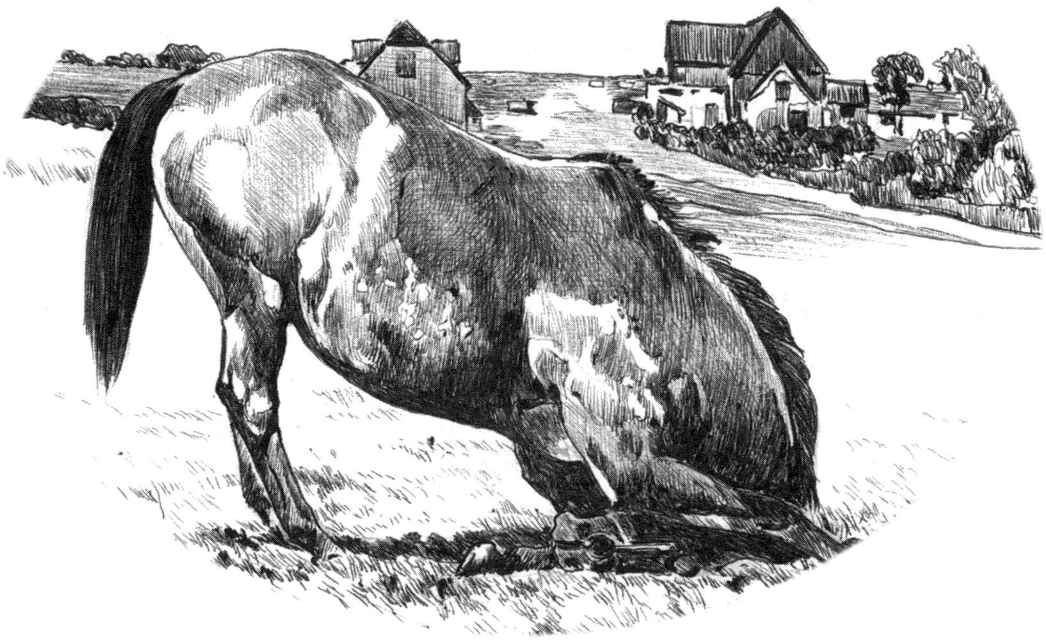

Tamarisk bowing

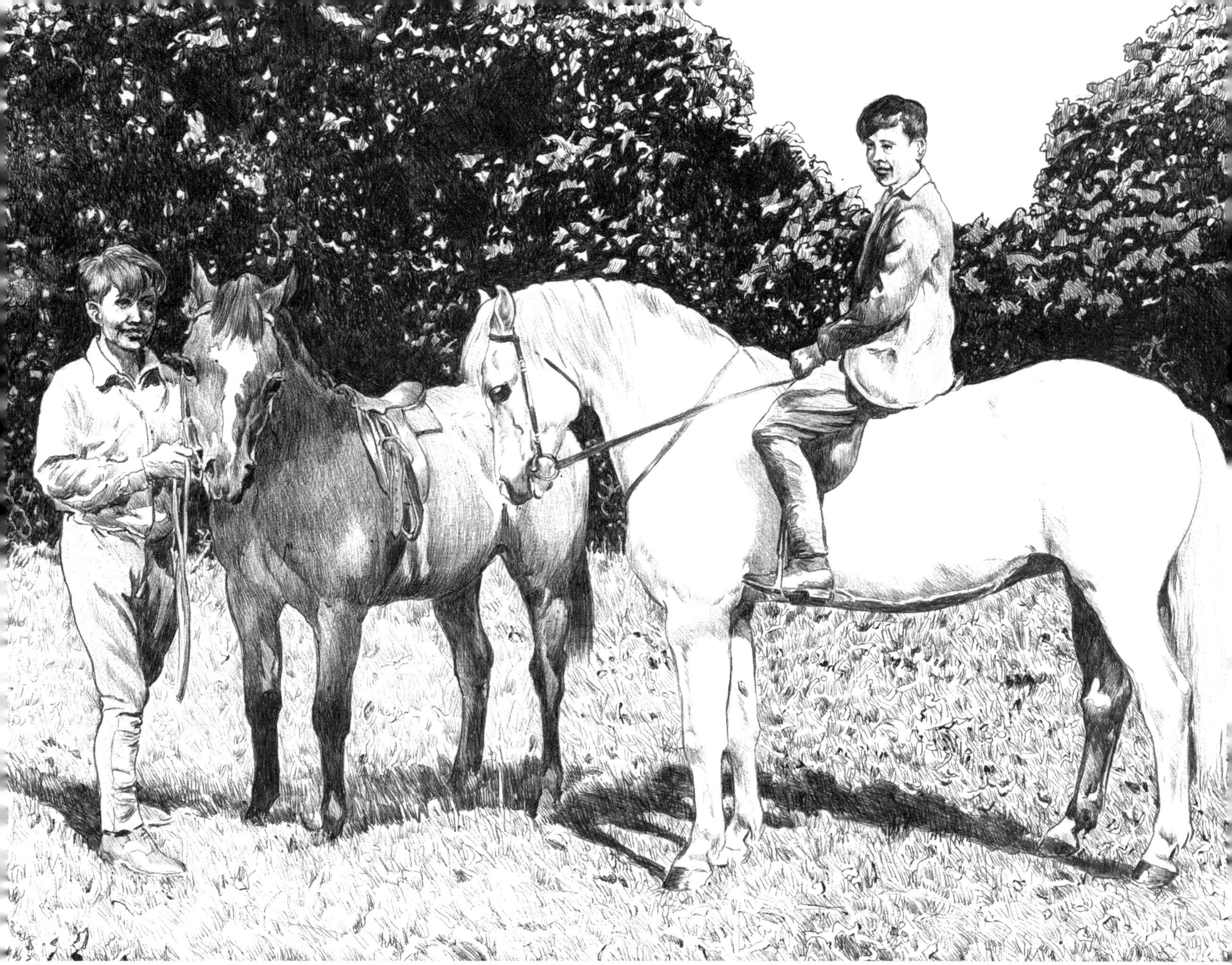

The Twins with Misty and Tamarisk

behaviour which included chasing the games mistress. We therefore had her to ride along with our own pony, a strawberry roan named Tamarisk, which our father purchased for us for £35. I still have the bill! She proved to be a hot little mare, always up with the front runners, but who took happily to being either a circus pony or a cowboy's mount according to our latest craze.

I won my first prize at a horse show on Linette who was by a small Thoroughbred from a New Forest mare, bought at the Beaulieu Sales. Miss Muffet, another bay, had some Hackney blood and a hard mouth, but she was fast and won many a flapping race. Later horses included Sir Ivor, a cob, Little Fellow who was big, and the list goes on.

We joined the local hunt Pony Club, for we lived in VWH Cricklade country. A red-faced Major was the MFH and Raglan the kennel huntsman, who was a good man with hounds.

Rallies were held in the holidays which were always great fun and we would hack up to twelve miles to join in. Most of the other members of the Club were farmers' sons and daughters whom we got to know. Then there were horse shows and gymkhanas which we travelled to with a horsey friend, in an old cattle truck, and usually came back with a rosette or two to show our mother.

Often we would take the long road up onto the open downs—no fences then, but rabbits everywhere—and we jumped our ponies over the brush fences on the racehorse gallops! Always wary of being caught red-handed, we would pop over a fence or two and then scarper.

We also went for picnics, driving Misty to a governess cart in which the food and drinks were transported, while others of us rode our ponies, often going up the steep bank to Binknoll where we would stop on the downland and laze the afternoon away before taking the long hack home.

One other pony not to be forgotten was 'Bimbo', a skewbald Shetland, who belonged to a farmer friend. Bimbo had at one time been in a circus and could perform numerous tricks, such as lying down to order, shaking hands and bowing, and we taught him one more trick. We knew that our baby sister would just love to sit on a pony, so we thought it a good idea to take Bimbo the three miles from the farm to our home. But how best to do it? We had regularly driven the cob Dolly to our parents' house, and she would trot like a train all the way. So, we taught Bimbo to jump up into the cart and stand between us for the journey. It worked perfectly, though some passers-by looked askance at what they thought they saw: a pony driving a pony!

Horses and ponies became an integral part of our lives, and remained so. Horse, hawk and hound—what more could one wish for?

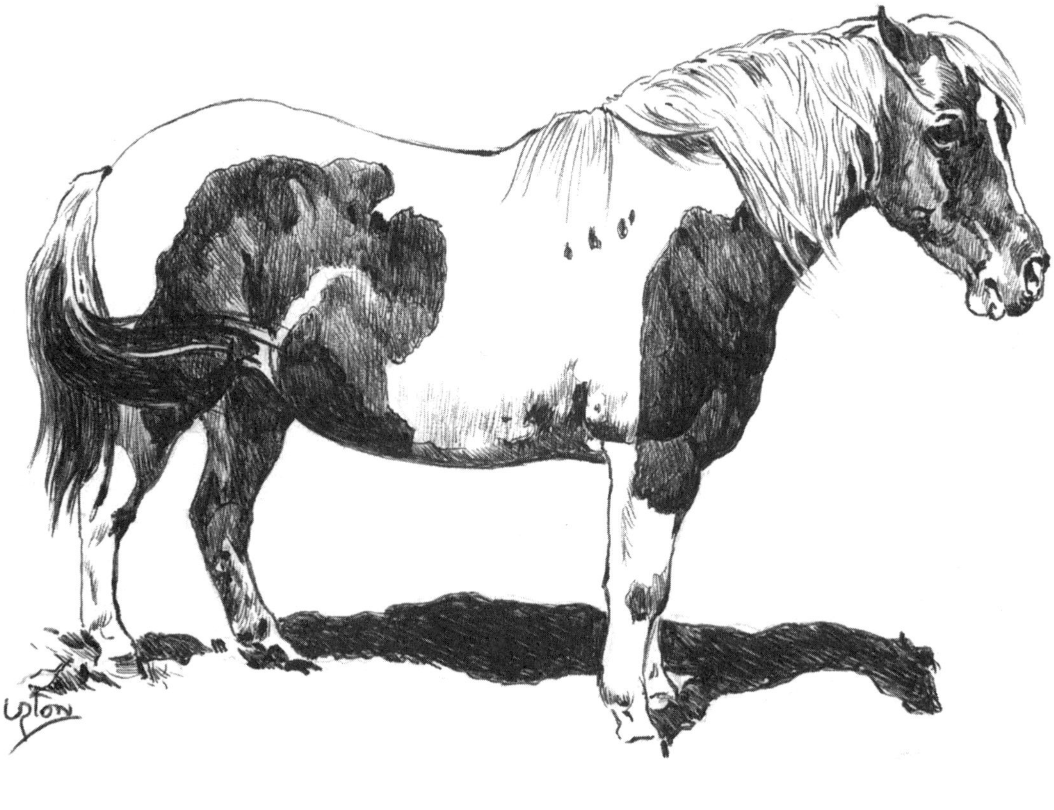

Bimbo

Countryways

From the Land

ALL ABOUT THERE were the rich harvests of Nature. Everything in its season was garnered and stored, just like squirrels with their nuts. Harvest Festival had a meaning for all of us in the country, unlike today.

What variety and richness was ours for the seeking! On dewy mornings we could collect mushrooms in the horse fields, which we would carry home in triumph in our caps. As a family, we children would go blackberrying along the hedgerows. Our baskets filled slowly as our fingers and mouths became red with the juice. The thought of our mother's blackberry and apple tarts gave an added impetus to our picking. Other wild fruits and flowers, like Elderberry and Cowslip, were collected in their season for home-made wine.

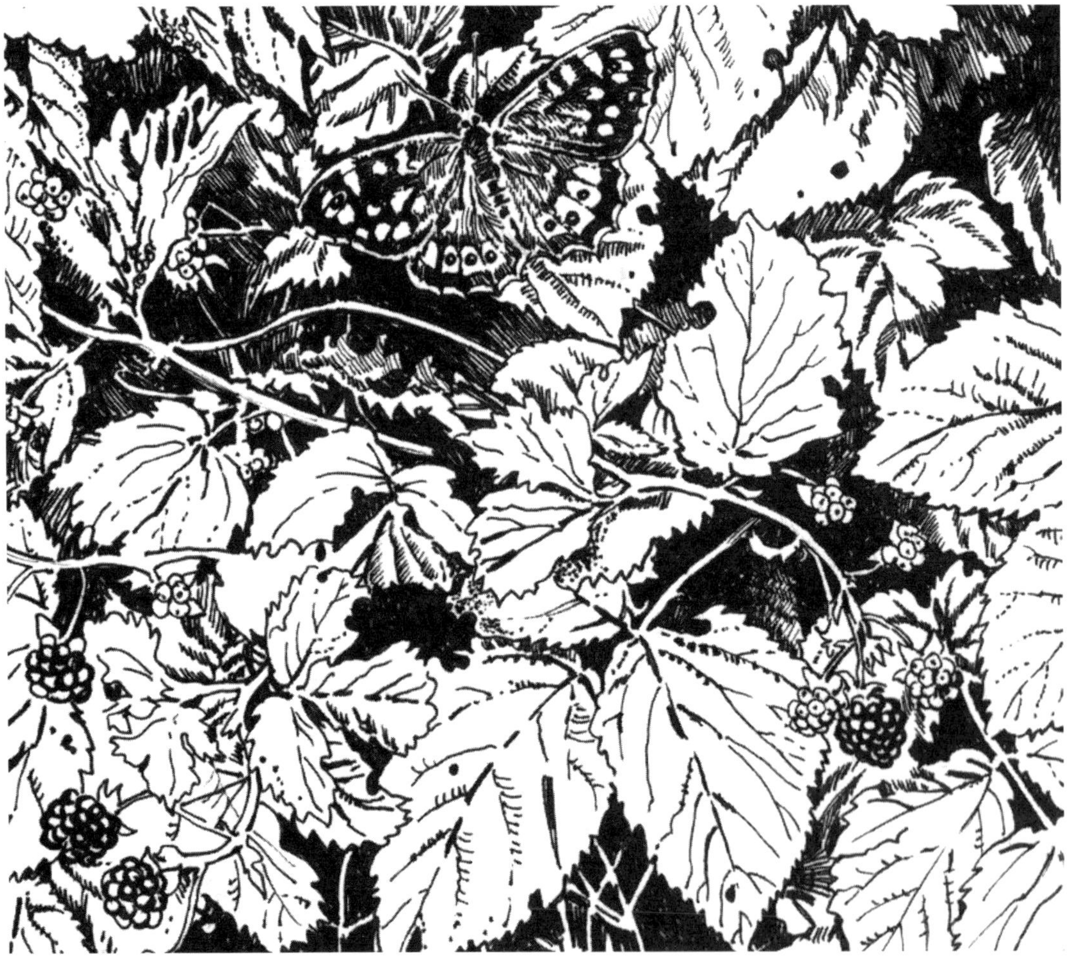

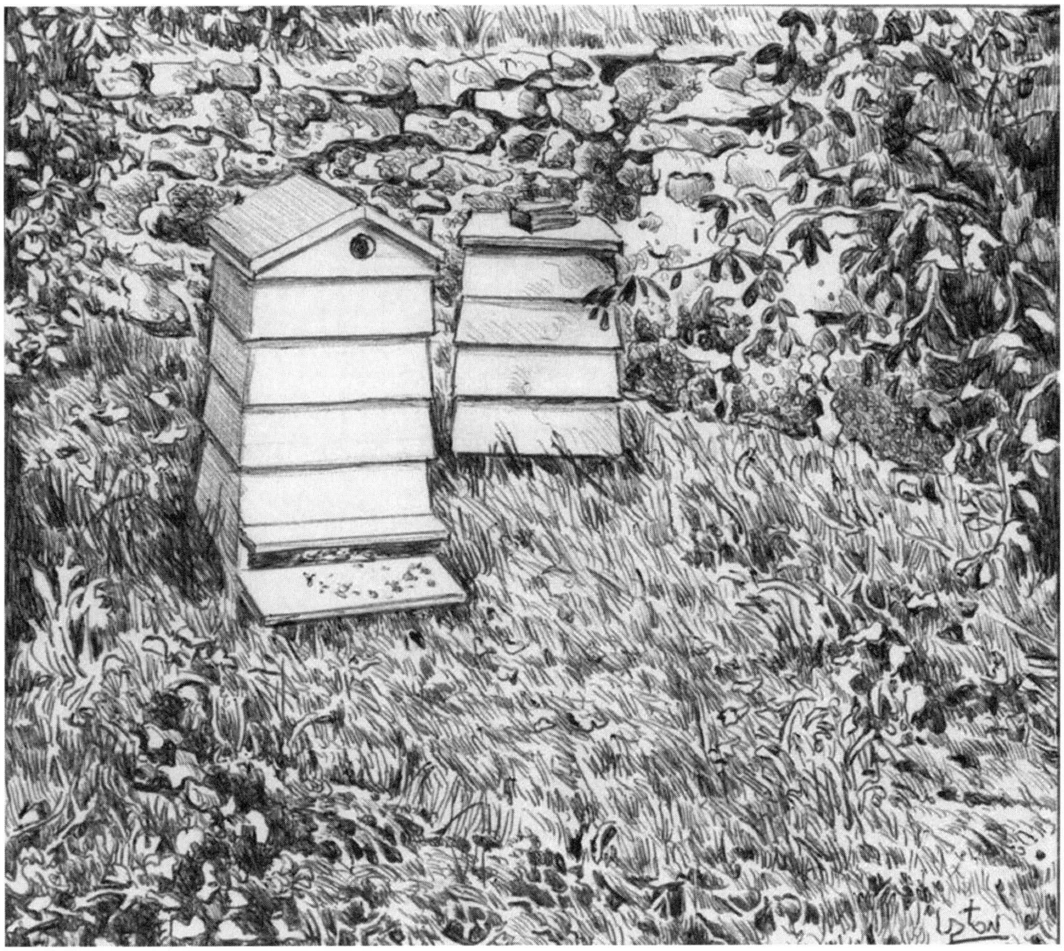

Left: bee hives
Below: the water pump

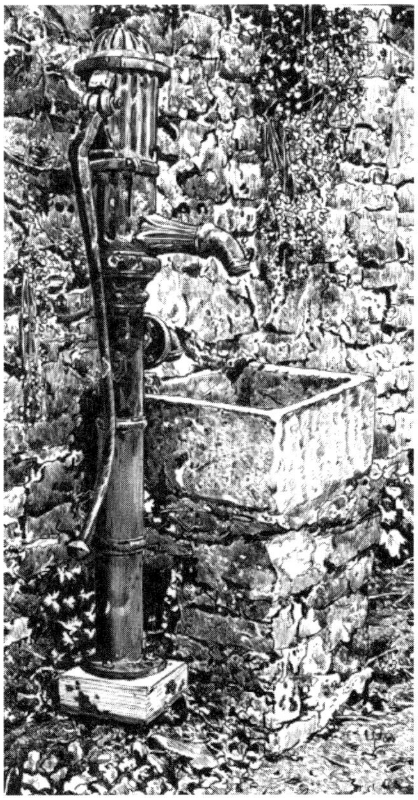

Mention of wine reminds me of honey! We were always ready to help friends whose family kept bees. It was fascinating to collect the combs from the hives and spin them to extract the honey. Then our big brother thought it would be great fun to produce the honey drink, Mead. However we were in too much of a hurry to sample the results of our experiment. Before it had any chance of fermenting properly we had drunk the lot!

At the edge of the wood the hazel bushes provided us with nuts, and the pigs were turned out to feast on the harvest of acorns and beech-mast. In the autumn the rusting bracken was gathered and used for bedding for the livestock. Young rooks, at the brancher stage, would be shot and the breasts made into pies. One farmer's wife made the most delicious rook pies.

Enough old and dead wood could be gathered from the woods and hedgerows to provide fuel. A great log pile was stacked up in a lean-to shed near the orchard. Fir cones made excellent kindling for starting the kitchen range or the weekly fire under the copper wash-tub. New besoms for sweeping the yard were made from birch twigs bound to an ash handle, cut from the spinney.

We were mindful of nature's wayward moods and grateful for her gifts so freely given. They were not to be wasted. Every drop of water had to be got by hard work at the pump, or hauled up in a bucket from the well. In hot dry summers the old folk would remember when water was so scarce that cattle and sheep died for the

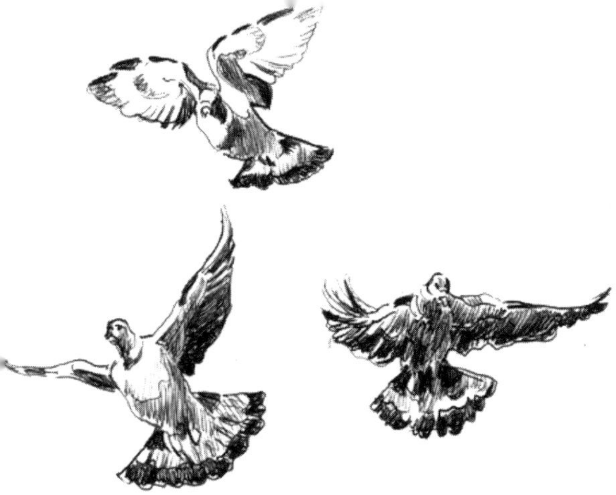

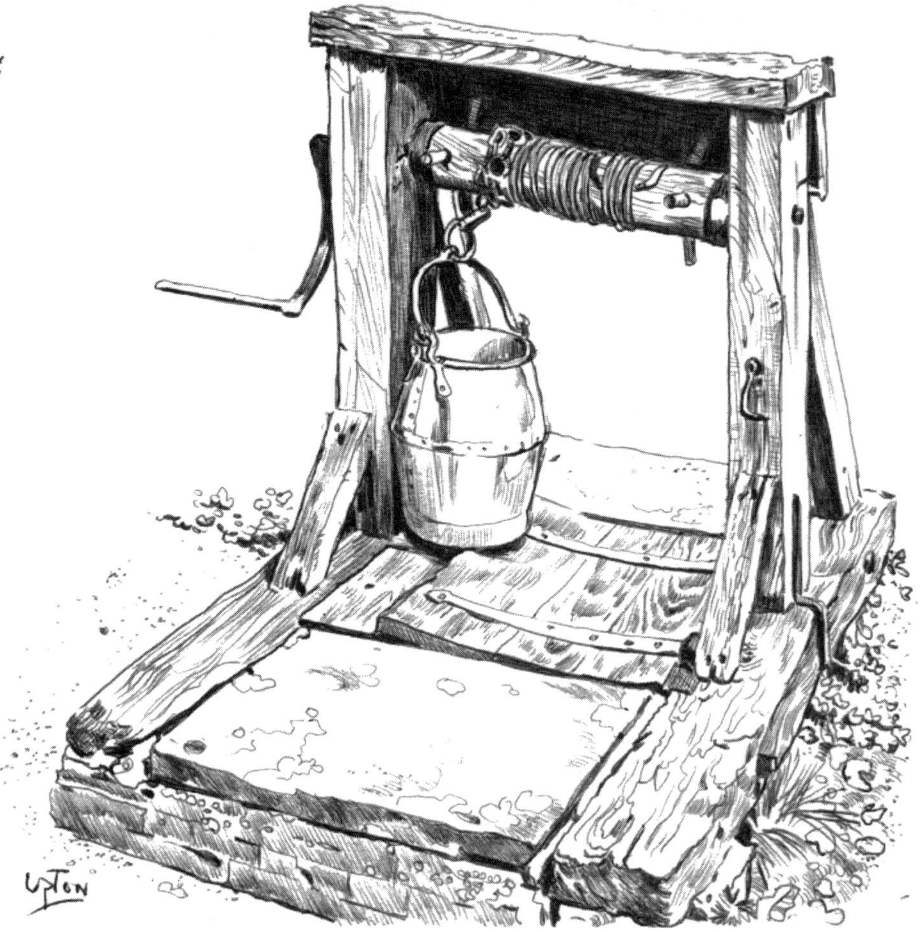

want of it. Some dairy farmers would boost their supplies of water by arranging for the United Dairy, when returning the churns emptied of their milk, to fill them with water. Yes, we all knew that water was not to be wasted, and how sweet, cool and pure it came from the well.

With all the fruits of summer and autumn stored for winter use, the country wife reckoned that she really only had to buy such essentials as salt, flour, sugar and tea, and a few other items that were not provided for by their own picking and preserving. Realising the value of things, people were not wasteful of nature's resources. Such items as string and paper would be kept and safely stored for future use.

Cottagers and labourers grew vegetables in their gardens and many also kept chickens or a pig. It was said of pigs that, 'the only part not used was its grunt'.

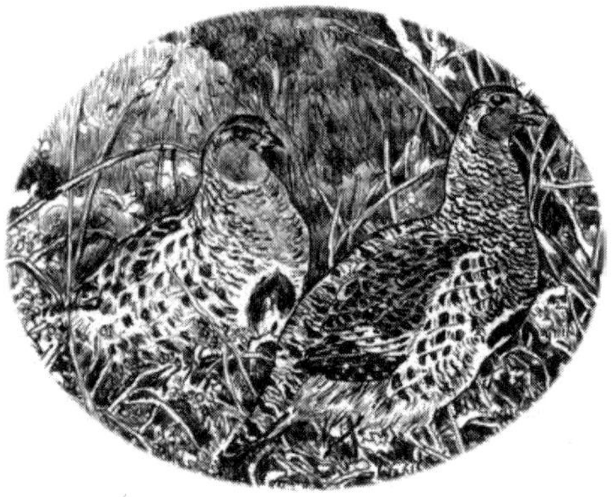

Rabbits were everywhere in our youth; too many of them. And on the Downs the big brown hares were plentiful. The Grey Partridge is a true countryman's delight and a well-hung pheasant or two didn't come amiss.

Especially for us children there was a profusion of interests: birds' nests to discover and trees to climb, camps to be made and the stream to dam. There is something compulsive for boys about stopping water flowing. Trout we tried to tickle, but not always with much success. There was also 'bread-and-cheese', the new leaves of a thorn hedge, and the vinegary taste of sorrel to sample. Sweetheart was our name for the Goose Grass that clings to you and Buttercups were held under the chin of a friend who should answer the question 'Do you like butter?'. Dock leaves eased the sting of nettles and Rosehips split open were dropped down an unsuspecting person's neck which soon confirmed its nickname of 'Itchy-Coo'. Blades of grass held between the thumbs made a good whistle sound when blown. Gix had a number of uses: a section of the hollow stem made an excellent pea-shooter, or even a drinking straw to sip from the stream if one was thirsty.

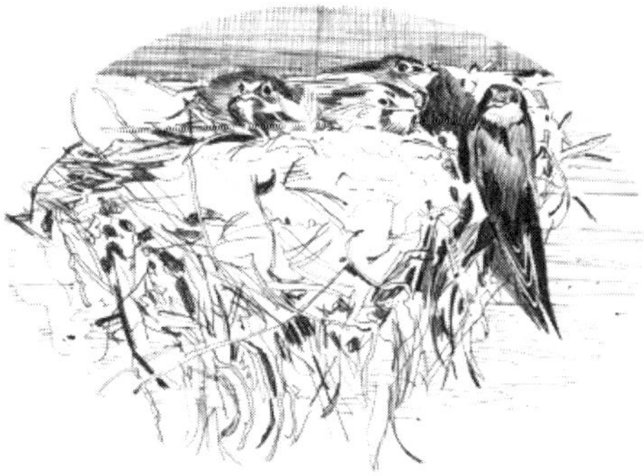

Conkers had their season and, in the winter, come the snow, there was tobogganing and skating.

My brother and I would love to visit the gypsies when they camped for a few days on a wide grass verge near Hooker's Gate before moving on. The women would make artificial flowers while the men carved clothes pegs to sell in the neighbourhood. The flowers were made from soft rushes gathered from the waterside. Firstly the rushes were split open with the thumb nail, which was then used to run up the inside of the stem until the pith came coiling out. This, dipped in a coloured dye

Above: Swallows' nest
Below: The Gypsies

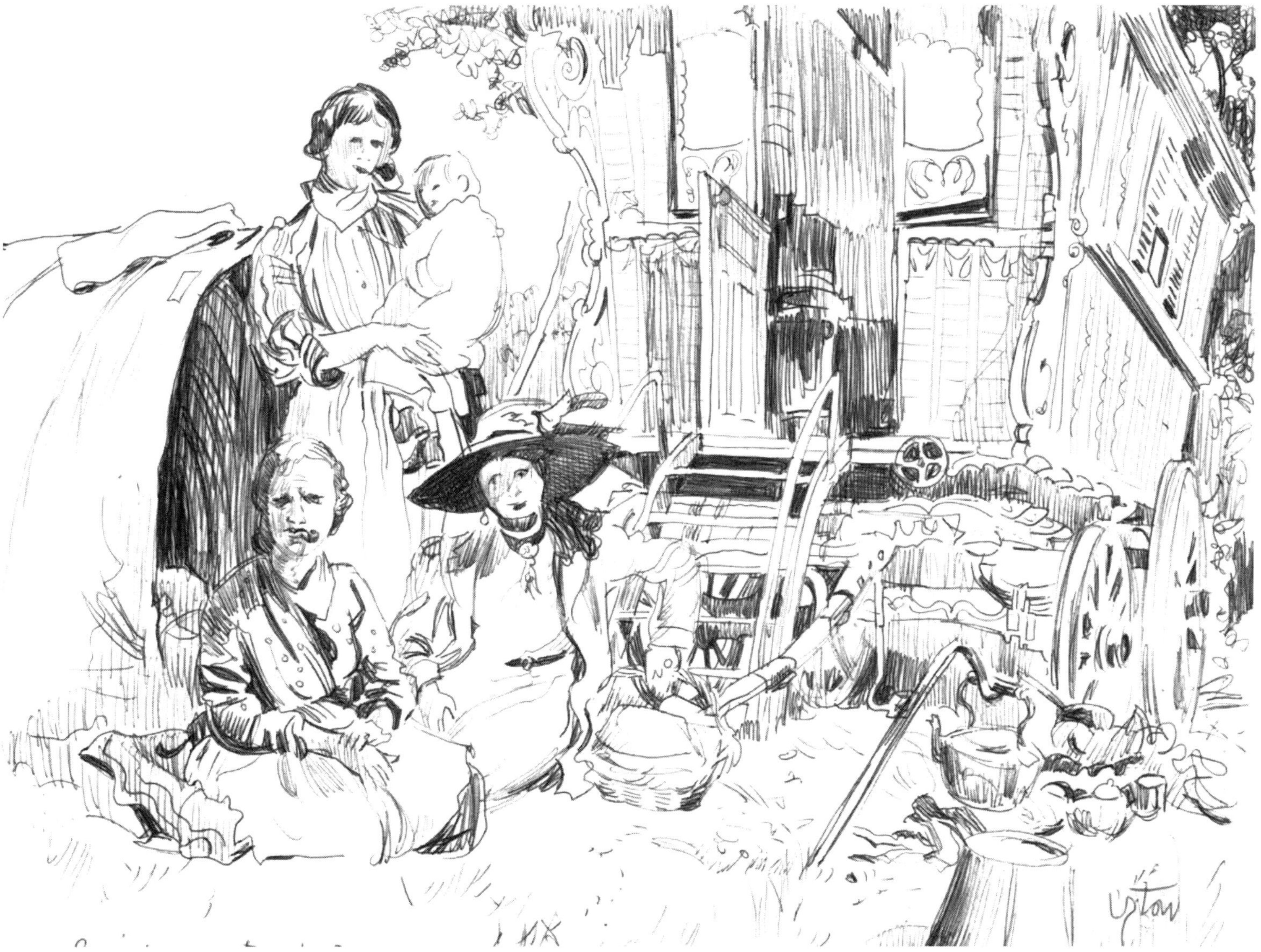

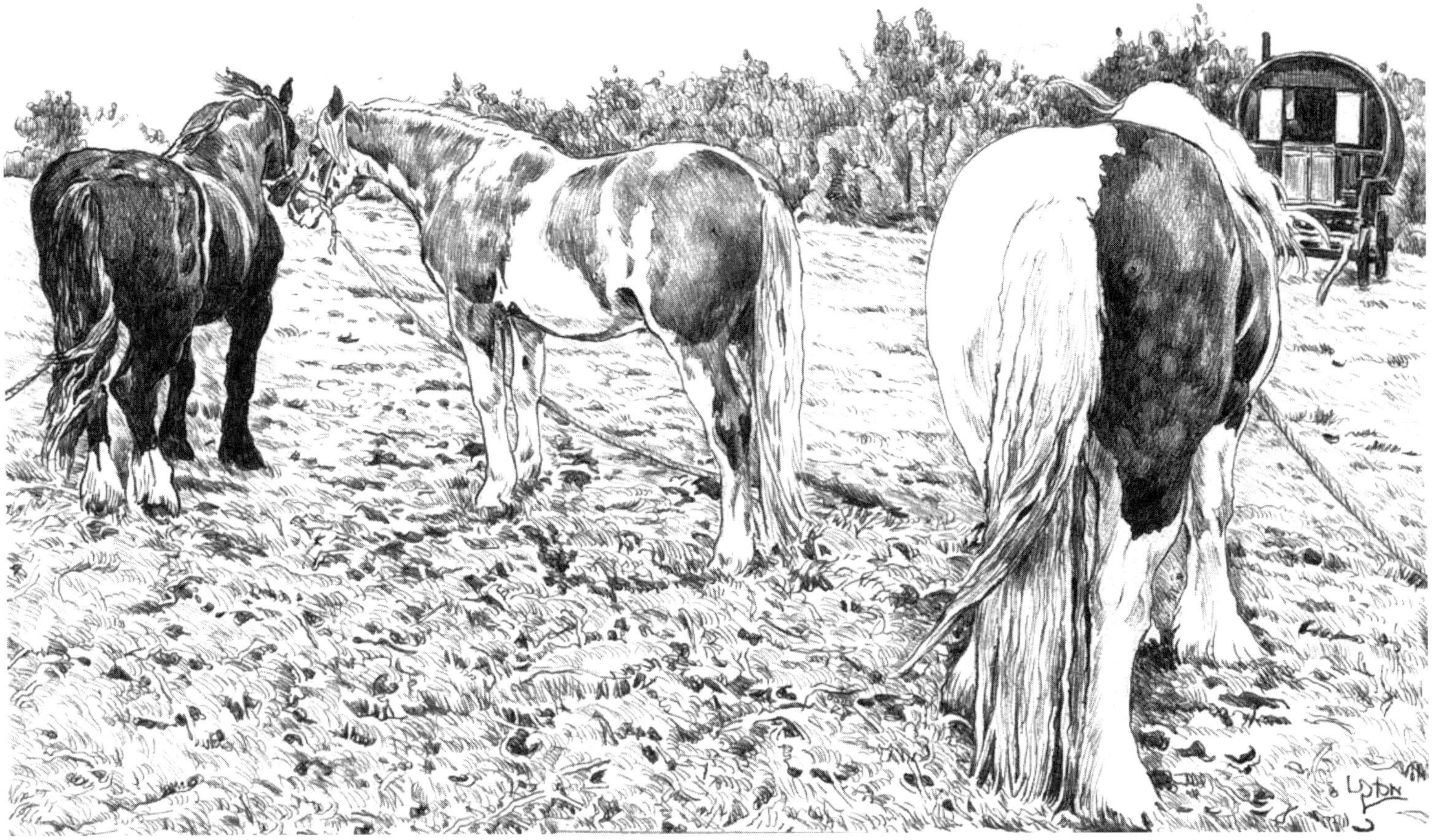

Gipsy ponies

and fixed to a twig, gave the illusion of a flower. More artificial flowers were also made of wood, partly cut with a knife, so that the slips curled back like the petals of a chrysanthemum. In the past rushes had been used for making 'rush lights'. We were fascinated too by the Vardos, their caravans. Some were very ornate Reading vans, others simpler Bow Tops, drawn up around the fire and nearby there would be tethered horses, often piebald or skewbald.

Childhood seemed one long timeless idyll in our youth. Each day and season brought the thrill of new discoveries, whether it was the first swallow heralding the summer, a new-born lamb or our bantam chicks bringing new life, and, of course, the arrival of our very first pony and our dog, Laddie. To bury our noses in wild flowers and smell the earthly sweetness of creation: we were surrounded by simple and natural beauty and our reward bubbled over with a love we would never lose.

Field Names

Field names on the farm often give us a key to their past use and history. Dayhouse Meade was the Dairyhouse Meadow. Oxpiece was where the oxen were turned out to graze, while Minchery once belonged to a nunnery. For Minchin was an old word for that saintly abode.

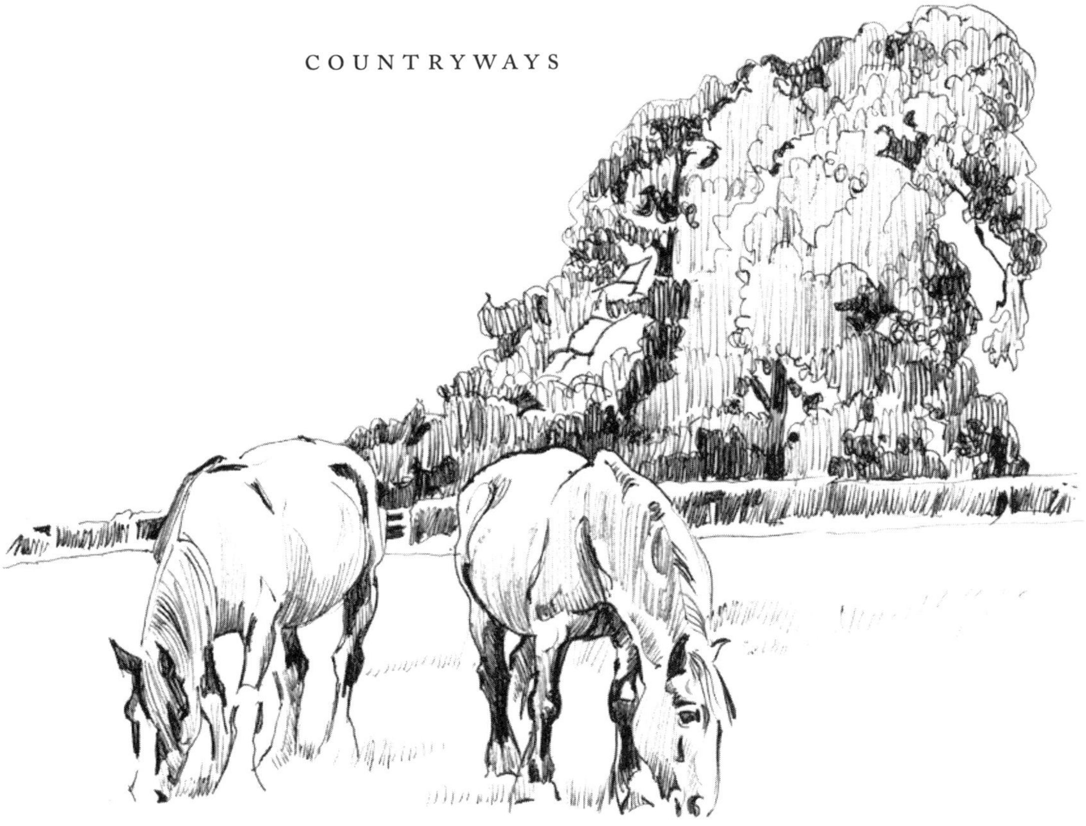

Starvealls is still a poor field on which the grass is thin. Sharpridge runs along the edge of steep banks of downland, while Hackpen could possibly have been where falcons were hacked, meaning allowed to fly free, but later taken for the sport of falconry.

Other field names may not be so easily understood, like Gorsey Leaze, Peckingell Meade, Cottrills, Pygle Dene, Bolehide and Glory Ann Bottom!

Many names have come about through the field's situation, such as Home Meadow or Thomas Close; others through their setting or soil, Clatford Bottom, Knaphill, Totterdown, Westfields, Clay Piece or Rowemarsh, Larkum, Fortnight Down and Chapel Haye.

I also like the sound of Bowman's Corner, Pound Close, Totterdale, Rookery Orchards – the rooks are still there – and Hole Bottom. These are all fields situated around one small village. What about Slait or Tags and Coniger, a rabbit-warren?

Before drainage, the clay fields of our valley had been very marshy and many small streams and field ponds added to the Valley's beauty. Bittern Pond at Little Park Farm is a reminder of the days when Bitterns were familiar in Wiltshire.

Measures

Fields were very often just known by their acreage, Eighteen Acres or Six Acres Piece. In the past not all acres were the same size! A Dorset acre used to be much smaller, a Cheshire acre was more than double the size of a present acre.

The acre was a day's ploughing on most soils and measured originally forty rods by four rods. A rod – or lug- was the length of an ox-boy's goad, just over sixteen feet long.

The chain, introduced nearly four hundred years ago, measured four rods in length, so ten square chains equalled one acre. Much farm work was calculated by the chain. A hedger's pay was based on "Chain of 'Adge".

Many farm measurements originated from the length of barley grains and the weight of wheat. In the reign of Edward III, measurement of volume was ordered to be eight lbs. of wheat makes one gallon, and eight gallons measured a bushel. When filling a bushel measure, a piece of wood, known as a strike, was used to level the top.

In the North, grain used to be measured by the "bol", which seemed to vary considerably from district to district. In East Anglia the "comb", which equalled four bushels, is still in use, I believe.

With the sale of wool we get the "sack", equalling three hundred and sixty-four lbs, or twenty-six stone, while the "tod" is worth two stone.

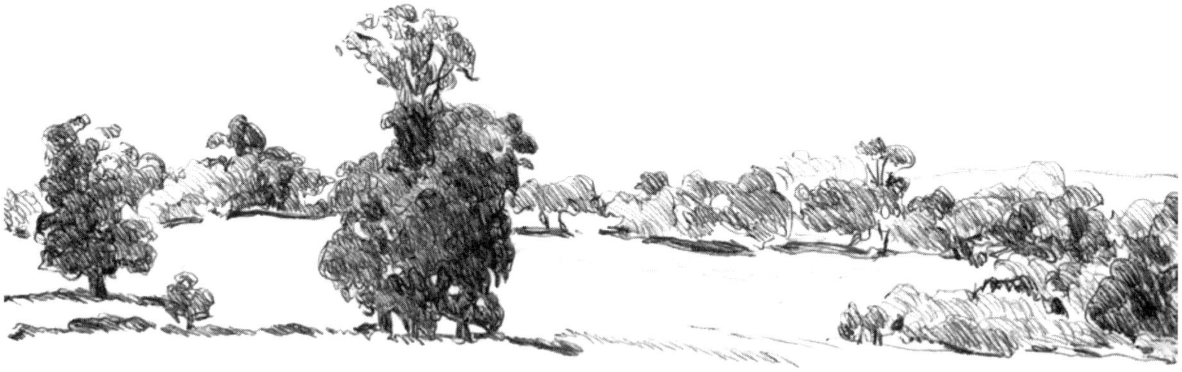

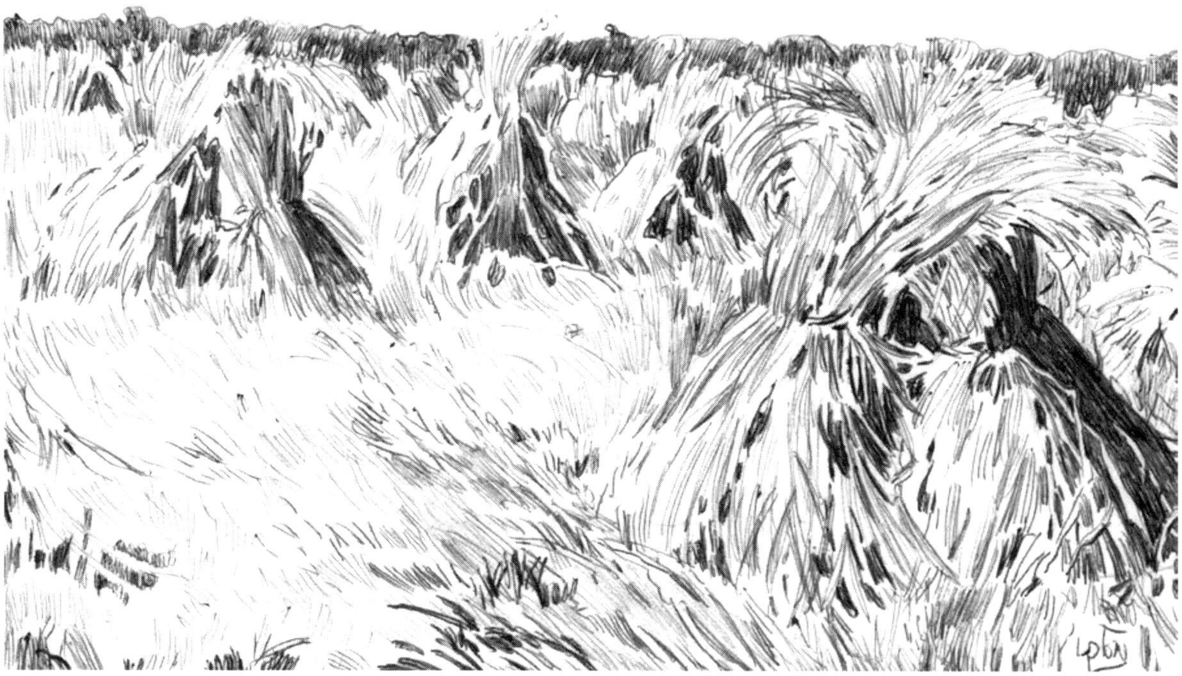

A stone was originally sixteen lbs, not fourteen lbs, as it is today. An earlier measure was the "wey" which equalled half a sack of wool. In some parishes in the C17, people were "buried in wool" and an old custom was to put a tuft of wool in the hand of a dead shepherd at his burial. It was said that this act would explain his job and any absence from regular worship when he met his maker.

Butter and cheese, made by many a farmer's wife, were sold by the stone and the firkin, and eggs were occasionally sold by "the long-hundred" which was one hundred and twenty eggs.

Many and varied were the names and ways of measuring farm crops. Hops were sold by the "pocket" which weighed one-and-a-half hundredweight; teazles to hat-makers by the "staff" consisting of fifty bunches; wool by "poke" one ton in weight and ozier, sold for peg-making, by the "bolt".

A load of hay was thirty-six trusses and a truss weighed fifty-six pounds of old hay and sixty pounds of new. This meant a load would weigh just under a ton. Flax was sold by the reel, which measured two yards round, and corn in stooks. A stook was once evaluated as a thrave of twenty-four sheaves.

Dialects and Tales

The countrymen in the Wiltshire Vale of my youth had a gentle manner of speaking, broad as the acres over which the plovers flew and soft as the dimit light, yet cast in a poetic mould of ancient words.

I spoke their way myself, and only when I left the Vale and heard the hard voices of townspeople did I realise the richness of rural speech. Their manner of speaking was further enriched by simple phrases and words not to be found in books, although they were better suited, for their intent was clear if you knew the countryside ways and skills.

A boy from Cumberland came to work as a hunt groom in West Wiltshire. His lodgings were to be in the village, some little way from the stables, so he enquired of Jim the gardener the way he should take. This octogenarian Wiltshire man hobbled slowly past his walled kitchen garden to a wicket gate from where the tall church tower and roofs of the village could be seen.

"Do a moind thiccy futpath. Well, vollowun drew thic field ov ol' ssos. Go drew yon swing-swong. Do a zee un znow? Up along churchyard, then yow do cum up tew a lil ol' drang a'tween Mrs Whitchard's and ol' Joe's. He do av wants terrible bad along of 'is tetties – leastways 'e did. Then you'm rite by the Rattlebone. Howsumdever, you best cross thic road smartish loike, for they cars an' charrybanks dew go in a terrible 'urry. Thy housen be the vust on the roite jus' avor Whoam Varm. Missus 'ull feed thee up a bit bwoy, fur thee be loike a mawkin, an' vair shrammed in this yer wind - Oi dew reckon."

To the lad from Cumberland, it was like coming to "furrin-parts", and what with the broad speech and strange words, the old man's directions were not of much use. Now ssos are thistles, and the meadow behind the stables was full of them. A stile, or kissing gate, in the stone wall led to the churchyard, and beyond a narrow passage – a drang – gave a right of way between the cottages belonging to Mrs Whitchard and Old Joe, whose potatoes were being disturbed by the activities of moles. Jim had noticed that the new boy was thin, like a scarecrow, and looked as if he would freeze to death in the cold wind.

Local names for birds and flowers were often the result of a knowledge of the habits and aspects of wildlife. In Wiltshire, the Whitethroat was the Nettlecreeper, in Devon, the Wagtail a Mazed-Vinch. Little Grebes were known as Dive-n-Dops in Norfolk and Chaffinches were called Twinks in Gloucestershire. In our valley, Cow Parsley was called Gix and Hedge Parsley Dry Gix, Lesser Bindweed was known as Hug-me-Tight and the beautiful blue harebells of the chalk downland were called Our Lady's Thimble. We knew Goose Grass as Sweetheart in Wiltshire, for it clung to you; yet a few miles to the West it was known as Clite.

Many local names differed widely from county to county. We used the word Stouts for Horse-flies, yet in Gloucestershire they were known as Old Maids, while the Yorkshire name was Clegs. Other words appear the same in many parts of the country, such as Dores meaning bees or beetles in East Anglia, Devon and Wiltshire. Fitchews, the word for ferrets in Wiltshire, appears in Devon as Fitchey for the weasel and stoat.

On the farm many words were particular to the seasonal tasks like ploughing and haysel. In much of Wessex a ploughman would halt his team with a quiet, "Wey", and when he wanted them to turn to the near side (left) he would call "Toerd". So coming about at the Vor'adge, or Headland, to start in again, he would cry "Cum, Di'mond, Captun, Toerd, gee Toerd". To turn to the off-side (right), his call was "Fromerd".

Ploughing cries differed in many counties: in the South East it was common for the ox-boys to keep up a rhythmic chant. The Shropshire ploughman called "Haw-woop" to start his team and "Jiggin" to stop them at the end of the furrow.

Even the different parts of the plough had their own local names. The share was called the shear or the mouldboard. The turn-farrow and the wipple trees were known as bodkins which were attached to the head of the beam by a hook called the drail.

When the farm workers went out into the fields they took their lunch with them in a basket known as a frail. Today, the usual drink is cold tea, but it used to be cider or ale. In the South West, cider was most commonly drunk and the workers carried it in a gallypot, a stone jar with a handle. In the summer time it would be put in the shade or under a hay cock while they worked in the meadows. The mown grass lay in swaths after being cut by a team of men swinging their scythes in unison, each man an acre a day. Later the horse-drawn mowing machine replaced the mowers, usually pulled by a pair of horses. After the swaths had dried in the sun, the farmer would tell the men to "bray thic hay up in rollers" or turn the hay, then to be side-raked or "windrowed".

Once dry, the hay was loaded onto the wains by men with long-handled pikes or pitchforks. Rakes made of wood with split-ended or hoop-braced handles were still used for turning the crop.

We called dung forks "cromes" and the drowner spoke of his "nuncheon", meaning the narrow bladed spade he used for cutting channels in the water-meadows.

Wiltshire shepherds called their she-lambs "tooties", and in the country around Tetbury they were given the name "chilvers".

The runt of a litter of piglets received a variety of names: in East Anglia "cadman" or "cad", a "wreckling" in the North, and a "nestle-draft" in Devon.

Stooks were called "Hyles" in South Wiltshire. A cold or sharp wind would elicit the comment "Tis pert".

The quiet humour of countrymen was often based on the personal characteristics of friends or fellow workers. Much farm work entails long hours spent alone or, in some jobs, in the company of a team of horses or the shepherd's dog. Therefore on those rare occasions when the men were working together, many were the ribald remarks between them and the tales told.

"Do you remember ol' Ewart and 'er Ladyship? Well, one haysel the weather was that hot an' close, so ol' Ewart threw down 'is pike, and sed, 'cum along wi' I, bwoys', and off we did troop to the park where thic river do widen out into a fair zized pool. In no toim we was all stripped naked an' splash into water us dived. Oh, it were cool an' good! Now Ewart 'e wus the far side o' sixty an' in all those years he ud never bin zeen wi'out 'is ol flat cap on 'is head, but there 'e wur splashin' about wi' a poor crop o' white hair, all wet. We wus enjoying ourselves, sportin' about in the water, when 'oo shud we zee cuming along but 'er Ladyship. 'Oi be undressed, undressed', muttered Ewart, so in desperation he jumps out o' the water an' grabs 'is flat cap, an' slips back into the pool. When 'er Ladyship cum past ther wus ol' Ewart treading water an' touchin' 'is cap an' sayin', 'Afternoon, yer Ladyship, afternoon', ver now 'e 'ad 'is cap on 'e felt dressed. Oi duno what 'er Ladyship thought o' the goings on."

In the barn on an old farm, just over the borders of West Wiltshire, I remember listening to many a tale, about friends and their ways. One tale would lead to another as the older men remembered, and a wet afternoon doing indoor jobs would soon pass in their company. One character they all enjoyed telling tales about was ol' Webby who had been Head Carter on the farm.

"When I wur ony fifteen, an jus startin wi horses, I ad to goo up to help Webby do some turnip hoein wi ol Gilbert. We adna bin thur long when it cum on tew rain wi splutting girt drops. So we un'itches in a terrible 'urry, get ups on ol'Gilbert an away we go droo the gate, an down the Park at a rare ol' gallop. Then oo do we see but the Dook riding by wi 'is coat collar turned up, so old Webby, bein' in a bit of a fix, claps 'is heels in an' hollars, 'Av e seen 'ounds, yer Grace?'

Obviously, ol'Gilbert, a Percheron gelding, was also quite a character because he appears in a number of other stories. Bill, one of the men, then remembered ol'Art, Art Viner, "Art he was carter vor Farmer Scammel, an' altho' they only 'ad an hour vor dinner, a wood allus go to'sleep for a whiles, even when out in the fields a ploughin' or a mowin'. Anyhows, wun day a wur snorrin' under the hedge while 'is tew horses wus stood-by 'itched to the plough. So up cropped young Garge Salt, quiet like, an a slipped the bodkins off the whipletree, so they horses weren't no longer hitched up. When that wur done, up 'e jumps an' shouts 'Yer cooms the gaffer'. So up gets ol' Art in a scartin 'urry. Now Art did allus keep is lines (reins) ower is wrists. He then claps is horses a smart wack an' off they goes wi Art stutterin' and cussin'behind 'em, and 'e falls ower is plough, on the ends o' they plough lines, affor he could stop 'em."

Bill, once he got going liked to tell a tale or two. "Well, ol'Varmer Scammel, 'e wuz all push an' urry. A never did up is boot laces, an one day e shuts one in the door of 'is Land Rover, and up e rushes to zee how the hay wuz lookin' for it wuz a Sunday, an 'e was hoping it wud be ready for cartin' the next day. As 'e arrives at the field e goes tew brake, but he casn't move is foot so e hits the gate 'ard. There is a terrible splinterin of wood and vor shure some terrible words too.

Still it bain't right to work on a Sunday, be yew push-an-urry or no".

"No, oi d'never work on a Zunday, 'taint natural, noo. Oi allus moind when ol' Watts up Hawkes way wur wantin' to cut 'is barley an it happen that next day wur a Zunday. Anyhows 'is bwoy comed along wi' is binder, set 'im out an' started cuttin' and the ol' man wur watchin'. Then all of a sudden-loike the barley cotched fire an' they flames went scortin' across thic field. It were bootiful jagged barley an' all. 'Es bwoy were a smart lad an' as soon as 'e seed what wur on, 'e druv like mad across thic field cuttin' a swath to stop the fire, an' he were only just in toime. Over vowr acres wus burnt, and the ol' man swore e wud ne'er again work on a Zunday, an' nor 'e did neither."

Bill liked to tell a tale or two about himself. One evening when it was raining hard and growing dark he was reminded of a time when the weather had been much the same.

"It wus a day jus' loike theesun, wi' rain vlingin' down, when oi 'ad tew go an dig a grave. Now oi warn't sexton, but oi''elped 'im out at noights if e wur hard put. Our churchyard wur a bit full, zo I 'ad tew dig this yur grave up 'neath the ol' yew trees, wir it wus zaid some ol' graves wus.

Ol' sexton, he wouldna dig 'em thur as'e wus aveard. So oi sets up me lantern as it wus commin dimsey, an' oi starts a diggin'. Oi toils away vur some toime an' ad got down a main vew feet when as oi sticks in me spade, oi hears a low hissin' zound. No oi ain't sceart o' reshits, but oi broke out a sweatin', an' me whiskers did prickle. So oi jumps out, narry stoppin' vor me coat an' lantern, an' oi flashes roun' the church porch roight into parson. He cotched oi by the arm, "What's wrong with you, Bill", he did zay. "Danged if oi knows", I sez, "But will 'ee come an' zee if thic grave be aroit, Parson, plaize zur", fer oi wanted tew get me jacket and tackle. An' do 'ee know, we got there and 'oi zees that rain drops wus droppin' on me lantern, which made an hissin' zound. Oi felt a bit of an ol' vool."

It was while I was listening to the stories in the old barn, with the rain lashing down outside, that to my surprise Bill recited the story of Old Nick—the devil—in poetic verse!

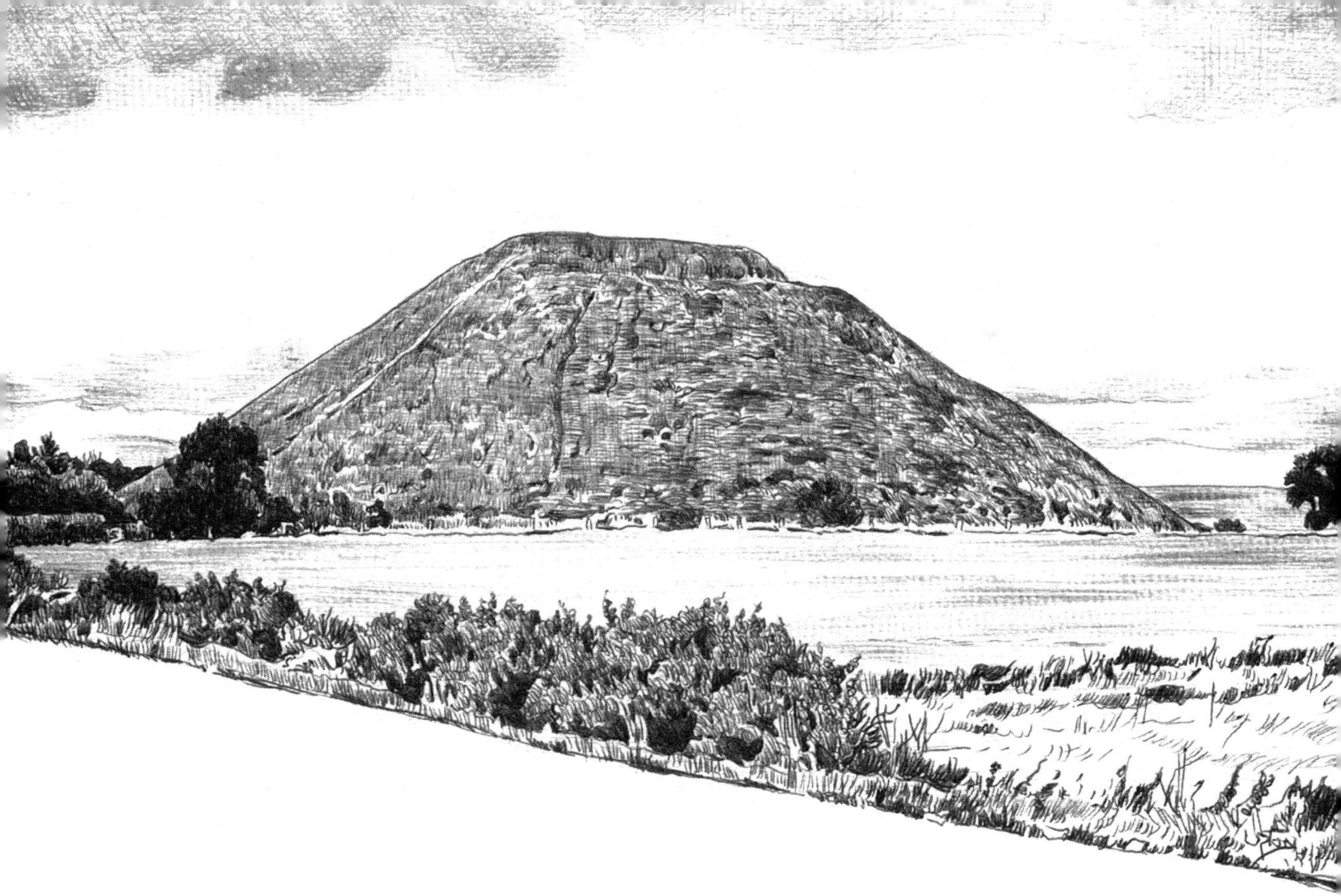

Silbury Hill

Ole Nick, one fine mornin did set out to pay
A visit to Marlborough, or so I've heard zay.
When he gets to thic spot where Zilbury be.
A shepherd, a dog and zum sheep 'e did zee.
So, Master Nick says to him, "How do 'e do?"
Shepherd says, "Tarblish, I 'ope you be too—
An where be 'e bound vor at thic time of day?"
"To Marlborough," says Nick, "but I can't find my way."
But lucky-like, shepherd did zee Ole Nick's tail,
An knowin' who twer, put 'im on the wrong trail.
Then when 'e were gone, away 'e did pelt
To tell Marlborough volk what he'd heard, seen an' smelt.
They were nigh scared to death, until a wise man
Said he'd stop Nick a'comin, he'd got a good plan.
"What plan 'as they got," they aksed, he said, "marry,
Bring I all the old boots an' shoes I can carry."

They brung 'im a nation girt lot in a zack.
He says, "Heft the lot of 'em up on me back."
Off 'e goes, an' did meet Nick, who did say,
"How far off be Marlborough, do zeem a main way?"
"Well," said thic wise man, vlingin' down 'is girt zack,
I can't say 'ow far 'tis, but be miles an' miles back.
When I come from Marlborough they boots an' shoes were all new,
An' I wore 'em all out travellin' this far, znow you."
"Lord," said Ole Nick, "If it's far off as that,
Then Marlborough's a place, I shall never be at."
Off 'e goes. This wise man ud done Nick by 'is craft,
And 'e near splut 'is zides by the manner 'e laughed.
While them boots and them shoes which he'd tipped from 'is zack,
He looked over and around, they weren't worth takin' back.
So 'e left 'em there, an'you med know,
How in 2,000 years or zo, tackle do grow,
An' them boots an' them shoes be a-layin there still
Which wi' dirt and wi' gravel made Zilbury Hill.

Then and Now

I HAVE ENDEAVOURED to let my writing dwell on happy days, but I find all too often that I cannot help thinking back to those early times comparing then and now, and a certain bitterness creeps in.

What have we done? What are we doing to this land of ours? The very fields we walked, whose names we knew are lost, as hedges are uprooted and wild flowers grow rare. The meadows where grass-hoppers and butterflies were common, have lost their green mantle, as developers build houses where once the badger made his nightly round. Yet village and town, where life should be, have grown derelict, lost to concrete, car parks and roads, for cars not people.

Travel to any town and pass through subtopia, be it Victorian or modern and take a moment to close your eyes, and try to imagine how it once was, a green land of living trees and grasses. Then look again at what stands there now: no wonder we grow disheartened and turn to unnatural ways to lose ourselves.

But, you will say, we must live. Yet do we really live? No, we exist only to serve technology, perpetually craving a higher standard of living and mindlessly using up all natural resources in the rat-race, always dissatisfied.

I do remember my youth with happiness, for I was indeed happy. Could we all but recapture that simplicity of life when each new day is sown with spring sunlight.

Peter Upton

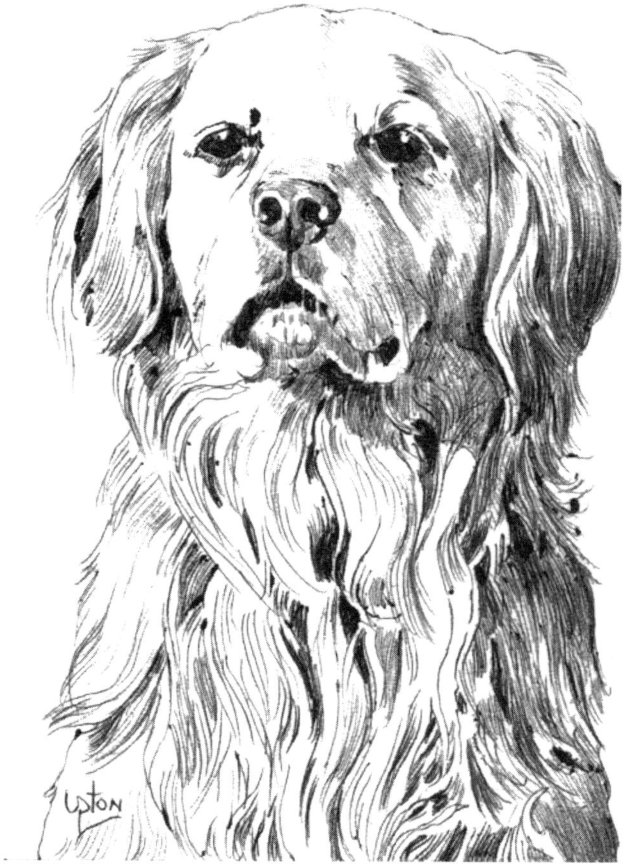

Boy, our dog.

Glossary

A

Allus	*always*

B

Bist	*be*
Bitel	*wooden mallet*
Bodkins	*iron/wooden bars to part traces on plough harness (see Whipple Trees)*
Bolt	*bundle of osiers*
Bond	*iron ring around the stock of a wheel*
Bout	*once up and down when ploughing*
Butty	*a friend*

C

Can'st	*can't*
Cleaving	*separating by splitting a length of wood*
Costrel	*a farm labourer's drinking vessel*
Coulter	*plough blade*
Crome	*a four-tined, hooked fork*

D

Dive-n-dops	*Little Grebe*
Dors	*bees and beetles*
Dumbledores	*(see Dors)*
Drail	*the hook to which the swingle chain is fixed to the plough*
Drang	*a narrow passage between cottages*
Drashel	*(see Flail)*
Dree	*three*
Droo	*through*
Drowel	*tool used for making straw ropes*
Dwun	*Don't*

E

Eave-Swallow	*House Martin*
Emmets	*Ants*

F

Felloes	*the rim of a wooden wheel*
Fitchew	*ferret*
Flail	*a hand-tool for threshing corn*
Fogger	*a farm labourer who fed fodder to cattle*
Froe	*a wedge-shaped tool used for cleaving*
Fromerd	*turn right (an instruction to a working farm-horse)*
Fuller	*a tool for making grooves in horseshoes*
Furrin	*foreign*

G

Gallypot	*a stone jar*
Gee	*walk on (instruction to a horse)*
Gentils	*maggots*
Gilt	*a young, female pig*

Gix	*a hollow stemmed umbelliferae*
Gurt	*great*

H

Harling	*gutting a rabbit*
Har	*the upright gate-post at the hinge end*
Hug-me-Tight	*bindweed*
Hummeler	*a tool for removing the 'awns from barley*
Hyles	*stooks*

J

Jagged	*headed, ripe (applied to barley)*

K

Kissing Gate	*(see Swing-swong)*

L

Lilly-bind	*convolvulus*

M

Mawkin	*a scarecrow*
Mazed-vinch	*a pied wagtail*
Med	*May*
Mixen	*manure or dung heap*
Mould-board	*also known as Turn-wrest (see Turn furrow)*
Mullin	*farm horse bridle*

N

Nation	*large/a lot*
Nave	*(see Stock)*
Nettle-Creeper	*Whitethroat*
Never 'ad no truck wi' it	*had nothing to do with it*
Nibs	*the handles attached to the snead of the scythe*
Nuncheon	*a narrow-bladed spade*

O

Odd-me-dod	*a scarecrow*
Old Maids	*horseflies (see Stouts)*
'ood	*wood*
Our Lady's Thimble	*harebells*
Owl-catchers	*heavy gloves used when hedging*
Owld	*old*

P

Pike	*a pitchfork*
Pile	*a large wooden stake*
Pritchell	*a tool used for making nail holes in horseshoes*
Purty	*pretty*

Q

Queues – oxen shoes

R

Rave – sideboards, or ladeboards, to a bow waggon
Reshit – a ghost
Riving – splitting apart a piece of wood

S

Scortin	*scrambling or hurrying*
Seed	*saw/noticed*
Shackel	*a twisted wood or plaited string loop*
Shippon	*cowshed*
Shore	*a small stake for sheep fencing*
Shrammed	*cold or freezing*
Sloppetting	*the movement of a rabbit when feeding*
Snead	*a scythe handle (also called a snaithe)*
Spik	*a thatching spar of wood (like a large staple)*
Splut	*split*
Squeeze-belly	*a narrow stile*
Ssos	*thistles*
Stavel	*a mushroom-shaped staddle stone*
Staves	*narrow pieces of wood*
Stilts	*plough handles*
Stooks	*a tent-like group of sheaves*
Stouts	*horseflies (see* Old Maids*)*
Stowel	*the butt of a felled tree*
Strake	*the hub of a wooden wheel/a section of the rim of a wheel (see knave/stock)*
Summat	*something*
Swath	*a line of hay or straw as it falls when mown or reaped*
Sweet-heart	*goose-grass (also known as Clite)*
Swingle	*the shorter part of flail*
Swingle-tree	*(see Whipple-tree)*
Swing-swong	*stile with gate which swings as one passes through (see Kissing Gate)*

T

Tackle	*stuff or rubbish*
Tangli-legs	*cider*
Tarblish	*fairish*
Teart	*a sour, sharp taste*
Temser	*a sieve to sift or bolt flour*
Thic	*this*
Thiccy	*this one*
Thiller	*a shaft-horse*
Tourd	*turn left (instruction to a working farm horse)*

Tooties	*female lambs*
Tumbril	*two-wheeled farm cart*
Turmuts	*turnips*
Turn-furrow	*a mould-board on a plough*
Twink	*a chaffinch*

V

Vool	*fool*
Vossel	*a wooden stake*

W

Wakes	*lines of hay (see Windrow)*
Want	*mole (see Yunt)*
Wain	*a four-wheeled waggon*
Wey	*an instruction to stop a horse (see Whoe)*
Whipple-trees	*(see Bodkins)*
Whoe	*(see Wey)*
Windrow	*a line of hay*
Wrest	*(see Turn-furrow)*
Wrexs	*hay-wain ladders*
Wunt let 'ee	*won't let you*

Y

Yelms	*bundles of straw or reeds used in thatching*
Yer	*here*

Z

Znow you	*you know*

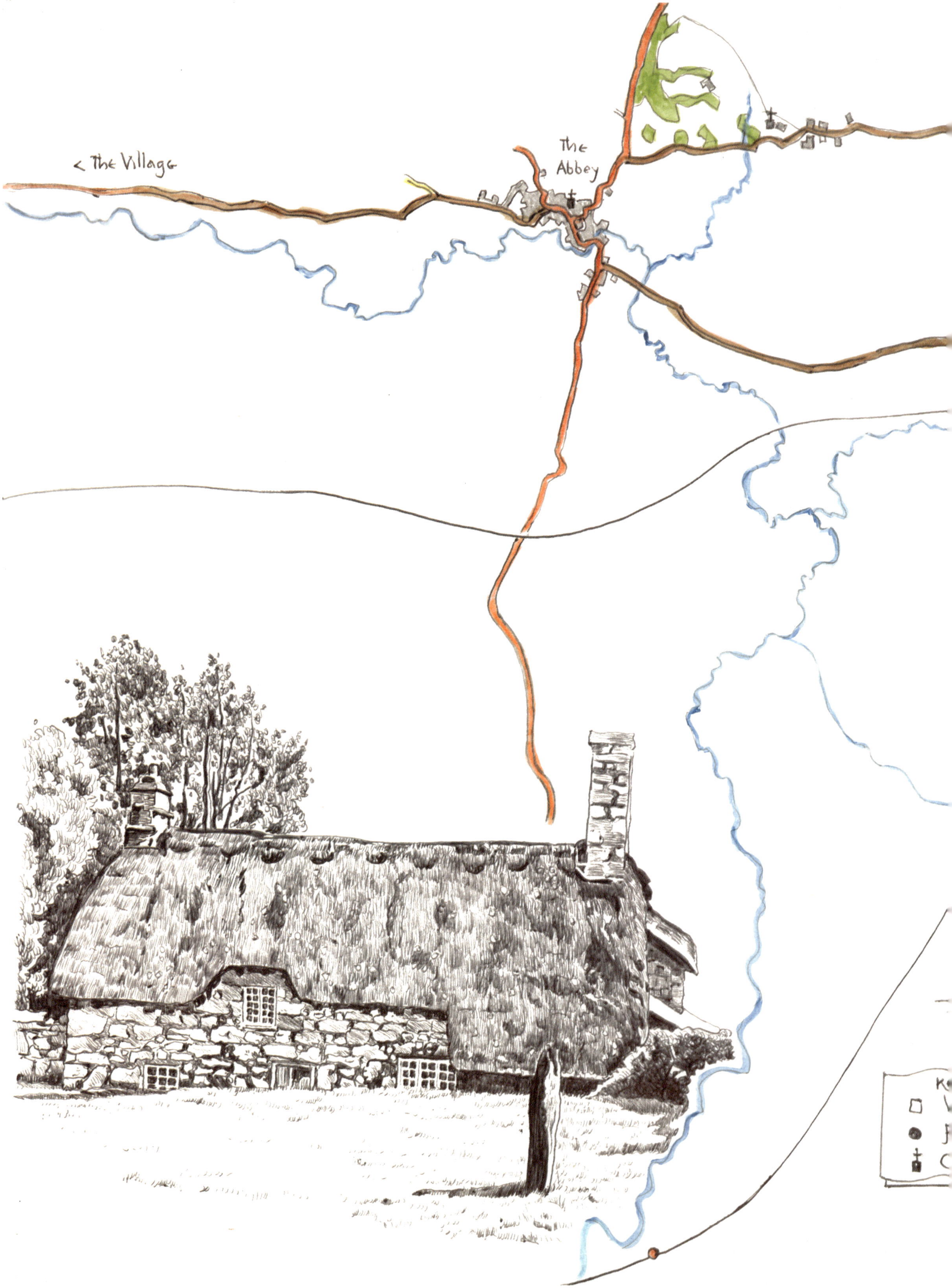
< The Village
The Abbey